PRAISE FOR *PRISON BREAK*

I really enjoyed Arthur's book. It is an intelligently written memoir written by a highly talented author, remarkable for its honesty, candour, and Arthur's obvious passion for natural justice. It is a fast and racy read, the pace of which never flags throughout.

The reader's attention is grabbed from the start, with detailed and exciting narratives based on Arthur's obvious capacity for recall and the detail he includes to colour his stories. He comments with complete candour on the characters and personalities of many of the high-profile criminals with whom he has associated over the past 65 years, as well as many of the justice officials and judges he has encountered.

He also provides interesting and detailed explanations of some of the many legal battles he has been involved with against the Department of Corrections and some of its officials. Over the years I have read many memoirs of criminals and inmates, published in New Zealand and internationally. With the high quality of its writing, the intelligence of its analysis and the excitement of the subject matter, this book certainly stands out as one of the best.

Greg Newbold
Professor Emeritus
University of Canterbury

PRISON BREAK

ARTHUR TAYLOR

WITH KELLY DENNETT

ALLEN&UNWIN
SYDNEY·MELBOURNE·AUCKLAND·LONDON

Allen & Unwin
Level 2, 10 College Hill
Auckland 1011, New Zealand
Phone: (64 9) 377 3800

Email: info@allenandunwin.com
Web: www.allenandunwin.co.nz

83 Alexander Street
Crows Nest NSW 2065, Australia
Phone: (61 2) 8425 0100

A catalogue record for this book is available
from the National Library of New Zealand

ISBN 978 1 988547 68 8

Internal design by Megan van Staden
Set in 10/15 pt Tiempos
Printed by McPherson's Printing Group

10 9 8 7 6 5 4 3 2 1

MIX
Paper from
responsible sources
FSC
www.fsc.org   FSC® C001695

The paper in this book is FSC® certified.
FSC® promotes environmentally responsible,
socially beneficial and economically viable
management of the world's forests.

To my brothers and sisters still in prison — whose lives and that of their whānau are being blighted by the failure to offer them meaningful assistance to rehabilitate themselves.

CONTENTS

Stone walls do not a prison make,
  Nor iron bars a cage:
Minds innocent and quiet take
  That for an hermitage.
If I have freedom in my love,
  And in my soul am free,
Angels alone, that soar above,
  Enjoy such liberty.
— 'To Althea, from Prison', Richard Lovelace, 1642

THE
BEGINNING

Goose Bay. Kaikōura. 1975

It all started with a Holden Torana and a caravan, both stolen. I had driven up to Kaikōura from Christchurch on a hunch that the cops, the fucking pricks, were after me. I'd been staying in a Christchurch motor camp for a few months, sleeping in the caravan, doing a bit of paid work, but the newspapers were panicking about a burglary at a sports store in Hokitika where all the guns and high-powered rifles had gone missing. A disquiet descended on the South Island. The police put an alert on my name, and had my parents up about me. My poor parents couldn't tell them where I was; they didn't know.

That's when I decided to moonwalk. I was nineteen, fresh off a jail stint in Australia. I packed up my caravan and drove north to the small settlement of Goose Bay, south of Kaikōura, where there was only a campground to speak of. For a few days I had a good time there, enjoying the sun, watching the seals, perusing the township. Then, one day, I decided to practise some target shooting. I was shooting at these rocks in Goose Bay, and some bastard thought I was shooting at the seals. They must have rung the cops, right? The cops must have put two and two together and thought 'Shit, that's that bloody Taylor', because there weren't so many people running around committing crime back in those days.

The local police called in the Armed Offenders Squad, which happened to be on an exercise at West Melton, near Christchurch. They knew I was armed, so they packed up their choppers and flew to Goose Bay. It was dark. A loud-hailer started kicking up and the power went off while I was watching TV in the caravan.

'Taylor, throw out your firearms and come out with your hands above your head.'

Christ, I thought, I won't give up without a fight.

DUNEDIN, 2020

I was born Arthur William Taylor in 1956. I have ten aliases. Terrence Brown. Herbert Chandley. Peter Dursley. Peter Greene. Peter Murphy. John Newman. Paul Richardson. Michael Smith. Alan Wilson. Mark Taylor. All names of real people who had a short start in life. It was easier to get a job if you didn't tell people who you really were, so I shopped around the sections of cemeteries reserved for newborns or stillborns, and registered a birth certificate in their name. Nobody checked. Nobody cared who you were. They just cared about whether you could do the job.

My criminal record, including traffic offences, runs to sixteen pages. From 1972 to 2012. Thirty-eight years in prison, or so the Parole Board tells me — I've lost track. And 155 convictions. I'm fighting a few more. I was released from prison on parole in 2019, after being jailed for seventeen years and six months for kidnapping, escaping, and possessing drugs and explosives. My sentence officially ends in 2022. On the page it sounds bad, but the record doesn't tell you the whole story.

Life's a bit different now. I live in Dunedin in a small tiny home, near Baldwin Street where the tourists come and take their photos. Right near student-town. It's semi-rural and you can't hear much except the lovely lambs and the birds and the occasional crunch of gravel when the police circle by. My cameras detect them crawling up and down the road, maybe once a day, sometimes once a week.

A security car swooped by at midnight the other day. Fuck knows what they're looking for. I'm inside, typing on my computer; preparing submissions, writing letters to Corrections and answering calls from prisoners. There are cherry tomato plants growing on my deck. They'll be beautiful in summer if the Dunedin snow doesn't get to them first. A family of ducklings walked past the other day.

When I look back, I think: Be careful. Slow down. Take things slowly. Think things through. When I was young, I was cocky and brash. We have choices in life and we are responsible for them, but sometimes our ability to lead a happy, productive life is taken away from us. It took me a long time to learn that there is always something you can do to change things if you have the right encouragement and support, and the will.

What I'm left with, though, if not memories of a life on the outside, is a world of adventure and a path that's led me to help others. My will is iron. A sniff of injustice gets my back up. Prisons are failing our inmates. This book is for them. The stories are for me.

CHAPTER ONE

EPUNI

Qualities that were considered good in my old
world, such as empathy, kind-heartedness, and
helping those in distress or need were seen as
signs of weakness, and had to be relegated far
into the background if one were to succeed in this
new world. This new world was ruled by violence,
constant fear and anxiety . . . Beatings, fear, tears,
and an aching void where your whanau used to be,
seemed the norm.
*Arthur Taylor writing to Dame Susan Devoy in
support of Royal Commission of Inquiry into state
care abuse*

APRIL, 1968

I think they must have told my parents they were coming to get me.
They must have just said, 'We're taking Arthur. It's a court order.'

They turned up at the dairy in Masterton this morning in April.
I was a little over eleven and a half years old. It was a weekday. I think
they had told Mum to keep me home, because I don't remember
being worried about not being at school. Dad was in the dairy that
day, too, which was unusual. They must have already had a warrant.

When the Gestapo arrived it was a hell of a screaming match.
I was helping Mum at the dairy when they walked in the front. I
took off in the other direction, only to run into two more advancing
through the back. It was a proper operation. I was trapped. And I
was terrified.

Mum was very upset; she and I were particularly close. There
was a fifteen-year age difference between my parents. Dad, being
a former army man, was made of sterner stuff. But they wouldn't
have known what me being carted off would have meant. They'd
never had any encounter with the state before.

I was screaming and resisting so much that they called a doctor to sedate me. Dad was saying, 'Get this over and done with, stop upsetting all the customers.' By that time the doctor had arrived and was planning to give me an injection. While they were holding me down on the floor, Mum was promising 'I'll get him a milkshake to calm him.'

They eventually got me in the car and held me down in the back seat, an upside-down sky guiding my way all through the precarious Remutakas, then diverting off the main route and winding around the suburb of Epuni, following a stream, until we reached a bleak set of buildings at 441 Riverside Drive, Lower Hutt, squashed in behind thick brush and state housing.

I had nothing with me. They took my clothes and gave me shorts and a singlet. Grey-on-grey and pull-up knee-high socks. They put me in a room, pulled the curtains shut, and said, 'You're off to sleep'.

I didn't know where I was.

> I was a Pakeha New Zealander that came from a
> very loving family. None of my family had ever been
> involved with the State child care system, criminal
> justice system or Police.
> *Arthur Taylor, writing to the Royal Commission of*
> *Inquiry into state care abuse*

I'd never not been tucked up at night by Mum. In the dark that night at Epuni Boys' Home I mentally traced the route that had led me to this separation.

I blamed the move. It had all started with the move. Three years before, in 1965, our family had moved to Masterton from small settlement near Rawene in the Hokianga, up the road from Opo the Dolphin's hometown, Ōpononi. Ngāpuhi heartland. Te Tai Tokerau country. The summer Opo became famous, I was six months old.

My parents owned a small, 100-hectare dairy farm in Waiotemarama. The Hokianga was virtually cut off from anywhere, linked only by gravel roads and a small lane through the Waipōua Forest. The community was mostly Māori, Rawene being one of the oldest Māori settlements. We were the rare Pākehā. There were five of us children. I was the eldest. My sister Sandra was born a year later, then my other sister Diane a year after that. Then came Shirley, followed by Jonathan in 1963. Jonathan was a twin, but his sister Gillian died of cot death not long after she was born. Later — after I'd been taken to Epuni — my parents had another baby, Joanne, who was born in 1969.

Life revolved around farming and hay-baling, building forts in the bush, and chopping trees and cutting scrub. I'd sit with Dad on his tractor while he slashed blackberry and taught me about surviving on bush food. He showed me how to find the base of the nīkau palm shoot, rip it out and eat the heart of it. The land was my playground.

Life was idyllic, but my parents wanted out of dairy farming. They longed for my siblings and me to have a good education, and they were hard workers, entrepreneurial types, so they bought a dairy some 900 kilometres away on Masterton's Queen Street. One day, we loaded everything onto the big farm truck and headed off. Dad and me in one truck, Mum and my siblings in the family car. We'd never really travelled out of the Hokianga before and just driving to Auckland was a big deal. I was in awe of the toll booths on the Auckland Harbour Bridge, where suited and tied men in peaked hats collected money.

The drive was long, and the only break on the way down was a night in Tokoroa. I was treated to an ice cream dipped in chocolate, and it all seemed like a bit of an adventure until we stopped as it became clear that something had happened to the truck. Dad put the thing in park on a steep hill. He was underneath, tinkering around while I sat in the front passenger seat, when I felt the truck start to roll downhill. Realising what was happening, I yanked the handbrake up. Dad's ashen face emerging from underneath the truck told me all I needed to know about *that* close shave.

And so began a life of suburban toil in Masterton. I put out newspaper signs, swept, ordered the storeroom, and carried in crates of bottles. I delivered *The Dominion* in the morning and *The Evening Post* at night, while Mum and Dad were tied to the dairy seven days a week. We lived in a flat above the shop, seven of us crammed into three bedrooms. Mum and Dad had one, the three girls shared another, and Jonathan and I had the other.

The move had been filled with promise but Mum and Dad quickly became bogged down, working every hour that God sent to compete with the Copper Kettle Dairy further down Queen Street. Dad also worked as a mechanic at Masterton Motors in the Hutt Valley, and took on various other part-time jobs to support the family. Labour was scarce, and so the companies like General Motors and Ford put buses on for their staff. Workers piled onto these buses at Masterton, lumbered all the way over the Remutakas, and the companies brought them back at night. As Dad left early in the morning each day, Mum ran the dairy and raised us kids. I look back now and think she must have had a hell of a job, but we never went without. She always had plenty of love to give.

Where once the bare land and bush of Waiotemarama had been the stage for my imaginary army, suburbia was something different: a maze with noxious characters on every street corner. A battleground. Authority was the enemy. It was a game of outwit and outsmart. Weekends and summers I played my game of survival, swimming in the Waipōua River and tramping through the bush. Friday nights were ripe for duelling it out with other kids, fighting in The Block, the rough part of town — usually over someone's nicked bike.

Looming in the background was a spiralling societal panic

about child delinquency. A couple of years before I was born, two teenage girls from Christchurch, Juliet Hulme and Pauline Parker, had knocked off Pauline's poor mum, and there was outcry about the behaviour of teens in general. Kids were having sex! They were committing crime! Snubbing school! While I was fighting in the streets of Masterton, The Rolling Stones and The Beatles were cadencing about drugs and rock 'n' roll.

Back in 1954, Oswald Mazengarb, a lawyer who had chaired a special committee on delinquency among New Zealand's youth, blamed society's lowest of the low: single mothers and working parents, who didn't keep a tight leash on their children. Mazengarb warned that families should return to their puritanical Christian, traditionalist values. How this manifested in what was to come for me was that parents were supposed to make sure their kids were at school — if they didn't, they were liable for prosecution. The kid would be taken into 'care' (for lack of a better word), and shipped off to a boys' or girls' home. Little did they know what a tragic path this would lead to for many. And that's what happened, you see? That's what happened to me.

At Lansdowne Primary School I elevated my job as the milk monitor to sell chocolate, Jaffa and strawberry milk flavourings that Dad landed at his part-time job at Hansells. My earnings bought me a tape recorder and popularity; I continued to work. I made milkshakes for customers at the dairy and watched as New Zealand changed to decimal currency, saw Mum and Dad swapping out the pounds for $2 notes, the biggest I'd ever seen. I loved the 50-cent coin for its milled edge.

My toil in the dairy shuddered to a stop, however, when the cops, who sometimes came in from the courthouse down the road, spotted me — this fair-haired sprog — behind the counter and had a word to Mum about it. Any interaction with authority was a big deal. Mum fretted. My only other dealing with the police had been finding a police helmet in an alleyway while delivering papers. I had taken it straight to the police station and carefully handed it to the officer on the desk, who said thanks. They'd been looking for it after one of them had had to wind down an all-out brawl the night before. That interaction, just that once, inspired in me a sense of awe about the men in blue. Looking back, I can see the emergence of a pattern throughout my life — police interfering in something that was supposed to be good. I was hardly a slave to the dairy.

School was tedious. The only thing I was fascinated by in the classroom was the swan plants and the monarchs, their metamorphosis from a stripy caterpillar to a fragile chrysalis to a remarkable butterfly, shedding its skin, turning into something else, something beautiful.

My school reports remark that eleven-year-old Arthur had the mental age of a seventeen-year-old; my teachers didn't know what to do with me. I was bored and needed challenging, but learning was by rote and outliers were trouble-makers, put in the too-hard basket. Thus I preferred the public library to school, where instead of listening to teachers moan, I'd sit alone, quietly devouring geography and history tomes. I'd study German and French, and even bought one of those Linguaphone kits. I found books that taught you how to disarm when in combat; these interested me particularly. I learned the basics of self-defence, like using people's weight against them and exploiting their sensitive body parts like their throat or testicles. Then I'd come home and pretend I'd been at school all day.

Life unravelled when a child welfare officer called Gault started calling around home. G.A.U.L.T. Mr Gault. When you're a kid everybody looks big, but he must have been about six foot. No uniform; civilian clothes. The school must have got on to him. I hadn't taken that many days off — maybe ten half-days — but in a little town like Masterton child social welfare officers took it seriously and investigated as intently as if someone had died. Gault alleged that I'd been truant.

My parents had a hell of a go at me, particularly Dad. Mum pleaded, 'You'll never learn anything if you don't go to school.' To show her otherwise, I'd sit her down and say 'Test me.' At the dining room table, we'd sit with these encyclopaedias while she grilled me about capital cities and I'd rattle the answers off. I don't even recall her being surprised that I knew the answers; she was just petrified of getting into trouble with the authorities, and extracted a false promise from me that I'd go to school. Without fail, Gault would get wind that I was absent and would visit the house while I hid. The days I took off telescoped together, and the results were catastrophic. It slowly dawned on me what a big deal truancy was, but by then they were carting me off to Epuni.

Epuni Boys' Home turned its children into highly trained, fit little offenders. Maurie Howe was the boss of the prison-like grounds, 1.5 hectares of sterility that had housed hundreds of institutionalised kids since 1959. Howe's reign over the home was absolute. He lived in the house behind the grounds, and if anything kicked off he'd be straight over. His omnipresence cast a long shadow. In my eyes, he was a bully, a blasted bully.

Instinctively, I knew that things weren't right with the place. Unlike my peers at Epuni, my home life had been idyllic and I came from a healthy home. Stepping foot into the boys' home, I could feel the shift in atmosphere. This wasn't a good place. Kids wet their beds and were terrified to go anywhere alone with the people in charge. It's been over 50 years now, but I still remember the look of fear in the eyes of one particular Māori boy who was frequently plucked from our group. I told Howe, 'There's bad things happening here' — and he wasn't interested. Much later he would reportedly say, 'I guess I had a sort of gut feeling, but I had no proof.' Christ.

Epuni's grounds consisted of three residential areas, innocuously named Rata, Kauri and Totara, plus a gym, fields, a recreation centre and a TV area. It sounds lovely, but the year I was taken in they had just finished refurbishing the blocks where we slept, reinforcing them with concrete because of all the escapes. It was a bona fide cellblock. There was no warmth. A single dormitory housed very young kids aged eight to ten, another wing held older kids, and then another wing was for the most senior. I had my own room with a little bed and that was about it.

Some of the kids were orphans, or wards of the state. Others had committed all sorts of serious crimes. Of course, I didn't know that then; I believed I was the worst. The day after I arrived, I was interviewed by one of the headmasters and issued with some more clothes, but I wasn't told anything about how long I'd be there. He said my crime was 'wagging', and that if I wanted to talk to my parents I'd have to write to them. And so I did — I wrote to them and asked them to come and pick me up.

I clearly remember the ongoing threat: 'If you're not good, you'll be here longer.' I was also told not to talk too much to the others. When we went out to the gym a couple of nights after I arrived, one of the kids asked me what I was in there for. I thought, 'Jesus, wagging school must be such a terrible crime I better not fucking say it.' I made up a story about my parents splitting up, and that I was just there until it was sorted. Of course I'd later find out that while some of the kids were homeless and needed the care, others had committed serious crimes; and some, similar to me, had been imprisoned for the mere crime of sneaking chips and lollies from a local cricket club — misdemeanours taken to by way of a sledgehammer.

The irony for me was that there was no school at Epuni. Years later they built one, but not while I was there. Life was mechanical. 7.30 a.m.: Wake up. Shower. Cast your eyes down and pretend not to notice the kids carting damp sheets to the cleaners. Collect the medication you were issued. WeetBix for breakfast. If we were lucky, we'd go on an excursion. Some days we'd tramp the Eastbourne coast, pointing out the debris from the *Wahine*'s lifeboats, wrecked on the rocks. Otherwise, it would be chores all morning.

Afternoons were for napping, reading comics, more chores (I was bestowed the job of dishwashing, and given a broom and made to sweep) and exercise. We threw medicine-balls around, climbed ropes, and puffed through push-ups, sit-ups and star-jumps, as if we were training for combat.

Night-time was dinner, followed by instant pudding mixed up from a packet. I missed Mum's baking. Back on the farm we'd cook on the range, and make wine out of wild blackberries. We picked grapes, plums and peaches from trees, and used dripping fat instead of butter. Bedtime at Epuni was 8.30 p.m., every day. Kids cried themselves to sleep.

Television was a treat — the black-and-white TV sat in a leisure room, and if you'd earned enough points for completing chores or showing good conduct you could watch a bit. Saturday was movie-projector night. Sometimes we'd trade movies with the Miramar Girls' Home, and us boys were allowed to trundle over from the Hutt in Epuni's van to swap films. On the way I'd eye the bush and the roads, and finally the towering Wellington city. I'd imagine what it would be like to yank the handbrake on the van and make a bolt for it. It was a rare glimpse of life on the outside. I thought I'd do okay out there on my own.

About two months into my stay, the Education Department's psychological service reviewed me. The report is filled with foreboding. On the Peabody Picture Vocabulary Test I had a mental age of eighteen and an IQ of 140 to 150. At age eleven (nearly twelve), I'm described as warm-hearted, good-natured, co-operative and easy-going, but impulsive at times. I was sentimental, emotional and artistic. I liked people, the report says, but I could be disobedient and reject authority. I was self-effacing, and depressed, with 'incommunicative tendencies'.

At Epuni the fighting was prolific; a constant maelstrom of violence. This is where I started to learn to defend myself physically — for real, not just in theory this time. Once, one of the nastier kids leaped on me out of a bush and I was forced to scrap. I saw and heard kids beating other kids up, but the teachers turned a blind eye and seemed not to care.

The teachers doled out punishments, too. We were made to cut rugby fields with a push-mower, in bare feet, rugby shorts and a singlet. Failure to comply led to the housemasters beating you with leather straps, leaving ugly red welts. I still strongly recall one day being called out of the shower by a headmaster. 'Out', he snarled. Another headmaster followed me into a room. I was dressed only in a towel. One of them held my hands while the other laid into my back with a strap, the leather snapping into my soft skin. The pain was horrendous, and I was left with painful searing marks. To this day I can't remember what I'd done to deserve such a punishment.

Other kids also bore signs of abuse: bruises, black eyes and tear-stained faces. One favourite punishment of the ruling class was making us all stand in a line for hours. If a kid moved, got tired, laid down, they'd be taken off and strapped. Usually it was just the 'crime' of a single kid that led to a whole group of us being made to stand on this invisible tightrope for much of the day.

These kinds of people shouldn't have been let anywhere near the door of a place like Epuni. They probably should have been locked up in prison themselves. Teacher Vincent Calcinai, whose bald head bore a patchwork of freckles on top, arrived the same year I did; he was later revealed to be a sexual abuser. Fortunately I was never abused like that. In large part I think it was because of my family — kids without mums and dads had nobody to rat to. Even from afar, my hovering parents, particularly Mum, seemed to save me from much of the worst treatment.

I desperately missed my family. In the absence of access to a telephone, they tried to visit regularly. They'd leave me comics to read, and I was later amused to learn that I refused to share them.

A note on my file said, 'He insists on keeping them to himself.' I clearly valued and treasured my parents' gifts.

Seeing them leave again was horrible, but I'd learned to put up a barrier and hide behind it. Dad, Arthur Taylor — whom everyone called Sandy (I have no bloody idea why) — had been particularly stoic about his time with the New Zealand Army in World War 2. Dad was mute on the topic, but his photo albums revealed pictures of burnt tanks and smashed artillery in the desert. At the heart of his strong silence lay an insistence on how to do battle: endure and survive.

Dad's time in the war made me curious about combat and fighting. I pored over history books about the war, and grew up on *Hogan's Heroes*. I remember when we first got TV in Waiotemarama — we couldn't get reception where we were, but a guy further up Pine Hill Road, Benjamin somebody, he got TV and I remember watching a show about World War 1, and seeing the trenches. Later, in Masterton, we used to watch *Hogan's Heroes* as a family. From my reading and watching I learned that people weren't meant to be locked up, and that there were two types of people: the ones who surrendered, and the ones who didn't. Guess which side I fell on? It was a duty to escape. All the shows said: escape from your enemy.

The first few at Epuni times I risked running. I'd be brought back and threatened with being sent to the infamous Kohitere Boys' Training Centre in Levin, where, the headmasters informed me, violence was rife and I'd have to do Physical Education every day. Threats of further punishment, however, only served to trigger an instinct in me to leave more often.

Some of the other kids showed me how to break into cars. Minis were particularly easy: you smashed the handle off to get in, or you could get a bit of Flexiband and shove it down the side of the window to pop the lock open, and then, once you were inside, through trial and error you'd introduce the various wires to each other. I was shown how the key interrupted the power circuit, and the next turn of the key connected the starter motor, but without a key that if you found the wires, you could connect the two together that way. It was very straightforward, and a skill I'd keep with me for life.

My first stint at Epuni lasted three or four months, and then they sent me home on the train with a welfare officer. The archangel himself, Gault, met me at the train station, took me to his office and made me sign papers. They had been charging my parents board — while taking the child welfare benefit off them. I'm livid to think of it now. Before they could have me back, Mum and Dad were forced to agree that they owed the Department of Education for my stay at Epuni. Thinking about that, I feel quite emotional — not for myself, but for my family.

My darling Mum was pretty distraught at losing me, but her sadness came secondary to the rapture of seeing me again. The whole family, not just Mum, was rapt when I came back.

I returned to school, but things weren't any easier. All I'd been trained for was a disdain of authority and how to push off when I wanted to. I'd glimpsed a world that I knew I'd run from forever. The kids knew I'd been at the boys' home and treated me like I was a criminal, so in a mixture of embarrassment and defiance I continued bunking off.

If anything, Epuni had taught me to rely on myself, perhaps to my detriment. The Education Department's report catalogued my issues: unsettled and maladjusted, a tendency to control emotional expression, a capacity to guide and coordinate my own behaviour based on my own concept of who I was, lack of self-confidence, severe depression, great anxiety, and withdrawal tendencies. I was hostile to adults, who I thought of as unfriendly outsiders. I was restless.

Mum's joy at my homecoming was short-lived. I was having to report to Gault every few weeks, and invariably he'd find out that I hadn't been at school; most likely I'd been fishing up the river instead. I was sent back to Epuni repeatedly, eventually serving three stints over three years. In later years I was allowed to attend the Hutt Valley Memorial Technical College, travelling there from Epuni and back each day, which allowed me some normality. I was lucky; I was smart and caught up quickly when I wanted to, but most of the kids at Epuni were cheated out of their schooling, and their potential.

By 1970 Epuni had built what seemed like actual cellblocks — for children! — which many years later I could compare to being the same as a tiny police cell. They'd put new entrants in these cells, which they called 'the secure block', after first ordering them to strip so that they could be covered in delousing powder. I'd be put in these cellblocks once I began escaping from the institution, stealthily boarding trains and heading back home to my parents'. Along the way I'd sneak into people's backyards, nicking carrots and drinking their just-delivered milk, or taking some warm clothes off the clothesline. I would only take what I needed, but it would become a way of life for me. If I was cold, there was a warm jersey. If I was hungry, there was some food. Means to an end. If the police caught me, I'd be put in the police cells with nothing to do, and no visits, until I could be taken back to Epuni. Every now and again, beady eyes would peer in at me through slats in the door.

L ife at Epuni ended with an escape that sowed a lifelong distrust of hospitals. I was mowing Epuni's rugby fields in the pelting rain; it was cold, but I was only allowed to wear shorts and a shirt, no shoes. One of the housemasters ordered me to rake all the grass up; a massive job. I was cold, hungry and tired. I'd endured months and months of asking when I was going home, only to be told nothing. I'd had enough. I threw the rake at his head and took off. If I hadn't, I'd probably still be there now, raking it all up.

A rallying cry went up from the staff and I was caught and manhandled into the secure block; they twisted my arms up behind my back as they went. I spent the day in one of those small cells on my own, and then was put in a car and taken to a local doctor. I remember being asked a steady stream of questions, and then I was shuttled off to the Porirua psychiatric hospital — formerly the lunatic asylum — on the other side of Wellington. Its sea-adjacent location was removed from the rest of society to protect the public (and allegedly so that patients could get fresh air), but its English-Baroque architecture frowned at visitors and patients alike.

Built in 1884 to relieve patient numbers at other sites, by 1890 the original building had been damaged in an earthquake and it was rebuilt, with a brick, turreted Queen Anne wing for patients. Originally housing around 1500 patients, it grew quickly, housing around 2000 at its peak. At Porirua, too many New Zealanders were diagnosed as 'insane', and initial 'treatments' were primitive and dealt out by inexperienced or untrained staff. By the 1960s, stories of ECT (electroconvulsive therapy) being used as punishment were widespread. It was hardly a friendly place for a boy.

Mum stormed over that very night, where she encountered me drugged to my eyeballs. The hospital staff had given me some pills. I couldn't even stand; Mum was horrified. Obviously, they hadn't sought parental permission.

Over the ensuing week other patients warned me against those drugs, and I began hiding them under my tongue and spitting them out later. Thank god; I would have become a zombie. However, injections were difficult to avoid. The side-effects of fluphenazine or paraldehyde — injected into your butt by way of a massive needle — lasted two weeks, earning me a gait dubbed the Porirua shuffle. The paraldehyde, in particular, used to really hurt; the huge needle caused an ache for days. I'd sleep all day. 'Consciousness' was a stupor.

I was in a mixed ward with adults for about a week before they transferred me to a youth wing. For months that's where I was kept; again with no schooling. I'd spend my days at the library, reading, but if I returned to my wing late they'd threaten me with ECT. The orderlies treated the patients as badly as the headmasters at Epuni treated their charges. Violence ruled; slapping, kicking. Small children were thrown into solitary confinement in bare rooms. I had no psychiatric or psychological treatment while I was there. It was just another place to imprison me.

There was a dormitory of about twenty kids, boys aged from seven to teenagers. Some of the more unwell kids there were unruly, making noises after lights-out. I was angry — I was here because I'd thrown a rake! — but by this point the only thing I was terrified of were the drugs, because I had no control when I was under their influence. I saw how the other patients, kids my age, responded to those drugs. Their minds were stuffed, and I instinctively knew that I couldn't risk losing my mind.

The staff would threaten me with electric shock therapy more as a punishment or to encourage me to behave than because they thought I needed it. Other residents would tell me horror stories about being held down, and clenching their teeth. The thought of this was so horrific that I did toe the line a bit.

Once again I learned to disappear, running away to my parents' place, which by then was within walking distance in Porirua. The hospital would send the police to bring me back; I was there for three or four months before they released me back home.

Eventually, I'd get a ruling that Epuni had had no right to inter me at the psychiatric hospital, and the Ministry of Health's Historic Abuse Resolution Service paid me a modest sum in compensation.

Many years later I described my experiences at Epuni to the Royal Commission of Inquiry into state care abuse. I told them how I was taken into the boys' home without so much as a court hearing. At that time there was no such thing as a lawyer for a child, and my parents certainly didn't have one either. Even if they knew how to get one, there was no way we could afford one.

Thousands of boys would trudge through those front doors

at Epuni, like I had, and emerge as beaten souls. As a boys' home, Epuni ceased to be in 1990, transforming itself into a centre for youth. In 2000, lawyer Sonja Cooper had seen so many references to Epuni in abuse claims made by its former inmates that she took a case against the Social Welfare Department, with the Court of Appeal upholding a ruling that the government was liable for any abuse inflicted in state-led institutions.

Today the site has been commandeered by Oranga Tamariki, a stark black sign at the front of the drive welcoming you, and former Child Youth and Family signs aptly farewelling you at the exit. A rope swing hangs from a tree across the road, and on a sunny day with cicadas chirping it would be easy to forget the site's history. Ugly yellow and brown prefab buildings next to some former state housing are the only hints of what it was.

The events of my time at Epuni have burrowed deep into my psyche. I have post-traumatic stress disorder, a state where I'm hounded by flashbacks, stress and anxiety. Prison certainly made that worse, but the original ache that grips me was planted the year I arrived at Epuni. The unfairness of it came to plague my whole life.

CHAPTER TWO

TAKING TO CRIME

Wellington Youth Court, 1972: FORGERY. Convicted
and sentenced to six months — one year probation.
Criminal record, Arthur William Taylor

Lower Hutt, 1972

I left Epuni a different person. I am absolutely certain that had I
never been there, I would have had a very different life. After leaving
I was on to my next 'adventure', I suppose you'd call it. I gave up on
school altogether, and free from its shackles I turned my attention
to what I'd seen my parents chasing for years: money.

Aged sixteen, I was working at Griffin's biscuit factory in Lower
Hutt as a machine operator, fitting parts for the best part of a year.
But the pleasure of making money eluded me, and I was intrigued
by what was going on across the ditch. The Vietnam War was on,
and a friend of mine who was living in Sydney told me that the
place was really exciting, full of Americans on R&R. I thought, 'Shit,
this sounds good.' New Zealand was a quiet little backwater where
things shut down at 6 p.m. and on weekends.

By then I had a government Post Office Savings Bank account
that was leisurely accumulating funds. Studying the passbook with
its recorded entries, withdrawals and balances, one day the idea
crystallised that I could easily make myself wealthy. Forgery, I
think they call it. An absolutely successful lark.

At that time there were no computers, so to check whether you
had enough funds the post office tellers would have to make a phone
call. But toll calls were expensive and if you were withdrawing
under a certain amount they didn't bother. Tellers noted your
financial details by hand and embossed each entry with a stamp. I
bought a rubber stamp and used a Stanley knife to carefully cut out
the outlines of 'P O S B'. Using a pen, I then initialled the name of a
branch, and the date, and embossed it with my stamp. It looked real.

It looked good. The next time I visited the bank, I experimented by cashing something small, maybe $20. The teller handed over the money and I slipped out the door effortlessly. No police chased me down the street; it just seemed too easy. Over about twenty occasions I took about $1100, which was a hell of a penny back then — about $14,000 today. The average wage was $95 a week.

Of course it all came crumbling down. I had made different stamps for different post offices around the country, one of which was the Porirua South branch — which had been robbed. There were alerts out on any stamps or entries from it. One day I went into the Manners Street post office, in Wellington central, with a passbook that had the fake Porirua South stamp on a substantial deposit. The staff called the police.

The CIB marched down to the post office, and a detective escorted me to Wellington Central police station, took me upstairs and started questioning me. With images of Epuni foremost in my mind, when the detective turned his back I ran out the door.

That's when I went ahead with my plans to leave New Zealand as soon as possible. I wanted to fly, but they'd be watching the airports. However, there was no security on ships so I forged a letter from my parents saying that I could leave the country and bought a ticket to Sydney on the SS *Northern Star* passenger ship. I told my parents I was going to Auckland, that I had a job there, and they believed me. They knew that I was very independent and could look after myself, so they didn't raise an eyebrow. They knew I'd keep in touch with them.

I packed my bag, said goodbye, and away I went.

When I arrived in Sydney, sometime around August 1972, I moved into a hotel just behind Kings Cross fire station and had a bloody ball partying at the Kiwi Hotel, a seedy place with a lot of working girls. From up on the balcony I helped them bargain with the American soldiers — $10 a time was the going rate.

I befriended some cops from the criminal investigation branch, who were crooked as fuck. Here were people ostensibly in authority who were treating me like their best friend, telling me where and when to knock over places so we could split the proceeds. For a teenager it was such an adrenaline rush. The risk and the excitement convinced me that it was all a bit of a game and, with the police turning a blind eye, also foolproof. At the time the New South Wales police were known as the best police that money could buy. People drove around with $10 in their pocket so that if they got pulled over they could buy their way out of trouble.

My parents got a hell of a fright when I eventually contacted them from the General Post Office in Martin Place to confess that I wasn't in Auckland. I'd regularly book calls to New Zealand, $3 for three minutes, and while the cents ticked away Mum would say 'Are you safe? Are you alright? What's going on? You've *got* to come back home.' I felt bad for what I was putting my parents through, but the truth was I was stuck. I was fairly certain the New Zealand police were looking for me and I couldn't fathom how I could return. I hadn't been had up for forgery before, but I thought it was probably pretty serious. Memories of Epuni filled my dreams, and the thought of stepping foot anywhere near Wellington filled me with dread.

And besides all that, I was having a ball.

I ended up staying the best part of twelve months, until things got too hot. The coppers took me off the work I'd been doing because someone had identified me as a burglar. I high-tailed it north to Queensland on the train, and ended up in Woolloongabba in east Brisbane, where a lot of down-and-outers were filling in the days in a lazy haze of 'Brisbane water' — meths and water. Coming from Northland, I felt an affinity with the local Aboriginal people and was shocked by how horrendously they were treated. Once, at the central railway station, I watched, horrified, as two police with batons bashed the hell out of one man in front of dozens of people who just walked past, turning a blind eye.

Our New Zealand cops, back then, didn't do that kind of stuff. I mean, they pulled your hair — people used to have long hair, especially in Christchurch — but this level of violence filled me with disgust. It was my earliest experience of observing people who were supposed to be upholding the law abusing it instead, and it fuelled my distrust of law-enforcers.

My time in Australia came to an end when I was picked up for throwing rocks off a bridge onto a boat on the Brisbane River. Someone must have rung the police, because the next thing I knew the Gestapo were storming up. I ran onto some nearby mudflats, but was caught and taken to Woolloongabba police station. They sat me down in a chair, wrapped a baton around my throat and were pressing me, asking me who the hell I was. 'You're fucking lucky you're not an Abo,' they said, 'because you see that panel there?' — they pointed to this door — 'We strangle them and throw them down there.'

They got my name, and the fact that I was a Kiwi, then locked me up in a juvenile institution and contacted New Zealand. They wanted New Zealand to pay for me to get sent back, but New Zealand refused because they knew that sooner or later Australia would deport me as an unaccompanied minor.

Being underage, I was sent to Westbrook Training Centre, in Darling Downs, near Toowoomba, for three months. Up until 1966 it had been called the Westbrook Farm Home for Boys, and was a reformatory school for boys with a focus on farming. It was as bad a place as Epuni — a 'haven for sadistic warriors', it was later called. The culture of abuse was rife at Westbrook; so bad that in 1961 a mass escape was launched by its detainees by way of lighting a haystack on fire. The superintendent was removed following an inquiry. In 1971, the year before I arrived, there had been a second inquiry into the punishments doled out.

Mum and Dad managed to get a phone call through. They said, 'We'll get you home, things will be alright.' Dad promised what seemed like the obvious solution to them: he'd get me a job.

One Sunday, without warning, I was driven into Brisbane with a child welfare officer and put on a plane back to Wellington. The guy who took me back worked for the Queensland Children's Services Department, and over a meal on the plane he confided, 'I've got to tell you, Arthur, the police will be at the other end.'

He was right. The New Zealand police were most keen to talk to me and rolled out the red carpet. The CIB met the plane and took me straight to Wellington police station, where they questioned me about what had gone on in Australia, and about the forgeries. This time, recognising the seriousness of my situation, my parents called a lawyer. It would have cost them a fortune.

In Wellington Youth Court the next day, the prosecution tried to get me remanded in custody because they reckoned I was a flight risk, but the lawyer got me released into my parents' custody. When I heard I was going home to my parents' on bail, I breathed a sigh of relief — I wasn't going back to Epuni.

My uncle, a motor vehicle assembly foreman, scored me a job installing door panels on cars at the Todd Motors plant in Petone. When I returned to court the job was a gold star, so I was sentenced to probation for six months to a year — sort of like a good behaviour bond. I lived with my parents in Porirua and took the bus to Todd Motors every day.

I ended up returning to Australia a year later, in August 1974. I was there when Prime Minister Norman Kirk died, and when, that December, Cyclone Tracy flattened Darwin. My memories about these stints across the ditch — what would ultimately become my OE — have become hazy, but unlike other people's OE years mine weren't spent sightseeing. Instead, I incurred a collection of misdemeanours that would ultimately form part of my criminal record. My time at Epuni meant that by now I was a seasoned car thief, and my theft of a mini in Sydney saw me impounded in the Albion Street remand centre — but not for long. When I'd had a gutsful, I volunteered for kitchen duty so that I could be unlocked away from the other prisoners.

I'd befriended this Croatian guy, Boris, who reckoned he had a big stash of cash buried in the walls of his Kings Cross flat. One night we shoved one of the screws into the kitchen chiller, climbed over the jagged corrugated iron on top of the walls, and fled. However, there was no money at Kings Cross; Boris had been bullshitting. Instead I travelled to Adelaide, got into trouble again for stealing cars and was locked up at McNally Training Centre, South Australia's maximum-security centre for youth.

I escaped. Although I was in the maximum-security wing, I had a job in the brickworks outside, which gave me access to the outdoor woodwork building in which prisoners used to work. One afternoon I wandered into this building with a plan in mind. There was no one else around. I fashioned a make-shift ladder from a large plank of wood with some smaller ones tied to it to make rungs. Using this I smashed my way into the ceiling, and got out onto the roof. The building was basically buttressed up against this massive wall with barbed wire at the top — the only thing that stood between me and freedom.

I threw some clothes over the barbed wire to make it look like I'd gone over already, and then went back to the ceiling, where I continued to hide. It wasn't quite time to go — leaping over in the daytime would be too dangerous. I wanted them to think that I was long gone so that they wouldn't search anywhere else. Sure enough, when the alarm was raised they thought I'd gone over the wall. I could hear them interrogating one of my mates from where I was sitting in the dark ceiling space: 'Where's he gone? Where's he gone?'

Using stolen vehicles, I made my way to Renmark, a small town on the Murray River in South Australia. I was nearly caught one day when I was sitting in a cafe having a drink with my stolen car out the front. A police wagon pulled up outside, so I went out the back door, abandoning the car.

I hid out in scrub along the Murray River for at least a week.

Although I didn't realise it at the time, it was a prolific breeding ground for brown snakes, and I had bare feet. I was self-sufficient out there, bathing in the river, unperturbed at the nipping of unknown creatures on my feet. When I'd had enough of the bush I took another car and went to New South Wales, where I bunked in a boarding house and got myself a job with a scaffolding business. This lasted for a few weeks, but then the stolen car attracted enquiries from the cops and one morning I was arrested outside the boarding house on my way to work.

They locked me up in Yatala, a labour prison in Queensland, where I started being dealt with as an adult, as I'd turned eighteen. In October 1974, on charges of car theft, vagrancy, and possessing stolen property, I was sentenced to three months for each charge, to be served concurrently. Yatala had massive fences around it, with armed guards stationed around the place. I had a job in the garden. I'll always remember one day asking one of the guards, whose eyes were glued to me, 'Do you fire warning shots?'

'Yeah,' he replied dryly, 'after we've shot you.' Makes me laugh, even now.

The other inmates called me Kiwi, for obvious reasons, and cricket was the rec activity of choice; we'd be let out of our cells especially to play. Every morning there'd be a big parade of the inmates, the armed guards watching from an elevated position as we lined up outside and had prison officers inspect us and our uniforms, as if we were soldiers in World War 2. During the day, if they wanted you then a call would go up over the tannoy system: '27349 Taylor.' That was my prison ID number; it's burned into my brain.

It sounds intimidating, but I didn't find it scary at all. The Australians had a progressive prison system, and they fed the prisoners well. The wardens went on strike once, which meant that we were locked in our cells for three or four days, and the state gave us the same amount of time in remission — time off our sentence — as a sort of compensation. I was quite impressed.

When it got closer to my release date, and getting wind that

I'd be deported as soon as I got out, they transferred me to a job inside the prison, where I delivered percolated coffee around the wings with a silver bucket with a lid. On the day itself I'd arranged to be released very early in the morning, and fortunately for me the prison didn't tell the federal authorities. Although I knew they were planning to deport me anyway, I wanted to pick up some money I had stashed away. So at 6 a.m. I hightailed it to Melbourne, stole a car and headed to the airport to go home. A tyre punctured just as I limped into Tullamarine Airport.

Many years later, New Zealand received a letter from Sydney, saying that the New South Wales Police were seeking me for escaping from the Albion Street remand centre but wouldn't bother extraditing me. 'If he ever returns to New South Wales, he will be arrested and charged with escaping,' they said.

Blenheim District Court, July 30, 1975: Unlawfully carried a firearm, stole a motor vehicle, burglary, discharge of a firearm, escaping from custody, resisting police, endangering. Convicted and sentenced to borstal training, disqualified from driving for two years.
Criminal record, Arthur William Taylor

Which all brings me to Goose Bay. On my return to New Zealand in June 1975 I set sail to the South Island. Having stolen a Torana at Picton, I then saw some poor bastard's caravan and thought, 'That'll be nice digs for me.' So I hooked it up and headed off down the West Coast.

By this time it seemed just too easy to take what wasn't mine. Unconsciously, I'd watched my parents scrimp and save for every dime, and in a profoundly and clearly irrational line of thinking I'd become both preoccupied with the idea of making money and averse to actually doing the work required. I was always looking for a quicker way of getting from A to B, always looking for the short-cuts, not thinking too hard about the consequences. My time around the crims in Australia at Westbrook had convinced me that this was actually an independent way of living — a fun way of living. Life is nothing if you don't have any stories at the end of it, after all.

The unfailing support I received from my parents was unique. So far, it didn't seem to matter what I did — they'd love and support me anyway. For years to come I'd find myself returning to them for help, and they never slammed the door in my face. Perhaps that constant support was both a blessing and a curse.

The money to be made in the South Island off competing for gold was appealing. After leaving the ferry I stopped at Murchison and knocked over a general store. After scoping it out during the day, I broke in at night after filling up the alarm with foam expander. The foam hardened as it came out of the can, and effectively muffled, then silenced, the screeching. I pulled some sheets of iron off the roof and dropped in.

I grabbed a .22 rifle, ammunition, and hunting equipment, fishing gear and clothes, and headed off to Westport, stopping at the Buller River to swim and fish. Eventually I made my way through to Hokitika where I parked at a local caravan park.

What happened next is one of my favourite stories. The police couldn't check number plates on weekends because the motor registration centre was closed then. Instead they circulated lists of stolen cars, which were obviously never up to date. One night, on State Highway 6 south of Hokitika, I'd accidentally backed out of a driveway down and over a bank. The Torana and I were fucking stuck. And guess who came along? The local police. Fortunately I knew of a sergeant in Pahīatua, a small rural town north of Masterton, who had recently been transferred to a nearby division in Hokitika, so I said, 'I'm friends with so-and-so.'

That softened them. These cops started calling me Arthur and commiserating with the pickle I was in. Blow me down, they retrieved a rope and towed me up the bank and onto the road! We had a yarn, I dropped some rugby chat in — cops love rugby — and then I said, 'Thanks, officers, tell so-and-so Arthur said hello.' They said they'd tell him when he came in on Monday.

'Yeah, yeah, and thank you for giving us a tow.'

And then I fucked off to burgle a sports store in Hokitika in my stolen caravan.

The guns I'd looted so far were no good for taking down heavy game, just possums, and I wanted something high-calibre. From the depot I took what the police would now call a Bushmaster, a Colt AR15, which is the same as the M16 except that it's semi-automatic. It fires exactly the same round, and this one had the carrier handle that an M16 has and a telescopic sight.

By the end of my looting I had a massive cache of weapons. I was fascinated by them, fuelled by my interest in war, and my hunting experience. People didn't associate weapons with terrorism because it just wasn't happening then. Nowadays it would be mayhem and murder if that sort of kit disappeared.

Unfortunately, I left a fingerprint at the store. I had been wearing gloves but I must have taken them off. The cops also knew that someone had taken some blasting gelignite from one of the coal mines nearby. I thought it would come in handy for fishing. So I took the gelignite, and detonators, and blasting fuses. I drove off the next morning to Christchurch.

The cops were spooked.

The AR15 is a funny sort of rifle. There's a funny way you gotta cock it to get it just right. A few weeks after my burglary spree I was sitting in the caravan, parked up in a more or less empty motor camp in Spencerville, just north of Christchurch, where I'd been pissing about quite happily for a few weeks. I thought the gun was unloaded; I thought it was fucking unloaded. I had it pointed at myself as I examined it and I nearly pulled the trigger, but then

I pointed it the other way and *BANG!* it went out the side of the caravan. The bullet pierced through fibreglass and aluminium, the caravan screeched, and my heart dropped. It makes my blood run cold just thinking about it.

In Christchurch I'd got a job at an electrical assembly plant, piecing together electronic equipment. I used an alias and had no trouble getting a job. They didn't check you out in those days. If they thought you could do the job, they'd hire you; there wasn't all this shit about having to produce IRD numbers. If you wanted an IRD number you could ring up, easy. You just gave them a date of birth and a birth certificate and all that. They didn't know if people were dead.

When the newspapers started reporting on the burglary at the sports store, and all the guns going missing, I decided to make a move. I headed north, to Kaikōura, to Goose Bay.

'Taylor, throw out your firearms and come out with your hands above your head.'

The police even knew my name. They knew *exactly* who I was. They must have shown my photo around the place. I told them to fuck off. And then the bastards hit my caravan with massive spotlights. My shelter lit up like a stage as waves crashed on the shore nearby, and I quickly started to think. Walking out and surrendering wasn't an option; that was too easy.

'Don't come near, I've got explosives in here. I'll blow the bloody place up.'

The backwards and forwards went on for about two bloody hours, me telling them to bugger off or I'd blow us all up, them pleading for me to come out. They knew I had explosives, so they were being very cautious. In the meantime, as I discovered later, part of the Armed Offenders Squad was creeping through the dark down a slope behind the caravan.

They threatened to start lobbing tear gas, so I fired a couple of shots through the roof with the Bushmaster — *CRACK CRACK*

CRACK — so that they fucking knew they were up against weaponry just as good as theirs. I know what you're thinking: senseless shooting on my part. Someone could have been killed, or injured; maybe even me. Why not just give up? Most people would be mentally exhausted just thinking about doing a runner from the cops. But I was a fighter. And the boys in blue were reminiscent of the bogies at Epuni.

The police only had .223 bolt-action rifles and .38 revolvers. I was better armed than they were, and in any case I wasn't convinced they'd use their guns. In the early '70s, it wasn't common for police to shoot to kill. Between 1949 and 1971 only two people had been shot and killed by police. So I guess that just wasn't on my radar.

They did begin firing tear gas, which was like a fire from a shotgun — hot as hell if you got hit, and potentially lethal. They'd evacuated the camp, which was basically empty anyway, being winter. One tear-gas canister came slamming through the side of the caravan, hit the table at the back and ricocheted through the back wall. It must have landed back with some of their boys on the bank because the next thing I heard was: 'WITHDRAW WITHDRAW WITHDRAW.'

I took the opportunity to hastily wrap newspaper around my arms and legs, and threw on a heavy coat. I put a wet towel around my head, and as the gas canisters landed I threw the door open and chucked them back out again.

'COME OUT, ARTHUR, WE'VE HAD ENOUGH OF THIS.'

'What's the deal if I come out?'

'What fucking deal?'

'You're not going to fucking shoot me, are ya? If I come out?'

'No, we promise. Throw your guns out first, then come out with your hands above your head.'

So I started throwing the collection of weapons out, and they said, 'We know you've got more than that.' I threw out the rest.

I finally emerged, hands above my head, and they rushed me. The dogs came rushing, too, sinking their teeth into the newspaper.

They drove me nearly two hours north to the Blenheim police station, and charged me with stealing the Torana. More charges would follow. I appeared in court the next day, Wednesday, before a justice of the peace, Mr D.C. Gibson. Detective Sergeant D.R. Alexander opposed bail, so they held me in custody.

I had to appear in court the next week, so rather than take me to the remand wing at Christchurch, they held me in the tiny local police cells. I struck up a conversation with a guy sitting in the cells next to me, both of us mithering about the loss of our liberty. Standing outside in the exercise yard one afternoon, we noted the rickety wire fencing.

'How about we get you out of here?' he offered.

After he was let out, he returned with a hacksaw and threw it over the fence to me when I was in the yard unsupervised. It didn't take long for the wire to give way, and then I slipped through to freedom. My instinct was always to head for my parents' home, no matter how far away they were. This became a common thread in my life, but with us being separated by water it was no easy trip this time. I figured that if I could at least get as far away from Blenheim as possible, I could work out how to return to the North Island.

The break wasn't to last. While I was making away on foot at haste, the cops did a routine 7 p.m. check and noticed that I'd cut my way out. They scrambled to set up road blocks all around the district, brought in reinforcements from Nelson and began patrolling the streets. They caught me about 6 a.m. the next day, down an alleyway near Alfred Street where I was considering taking a getaway car.

I appeared in the Blenheim Court yet again later that day. By then I was facing sixteen charges relating to incidents in Murchison, Hokitika, Christchurch, Marlborough Sounds, Picton and Kaikōura. My arrest became front-page news in the *Hokitika Guardian*; the locals were obviously still pissed off about my antics there.

When the cops forensically examined my caravan, they found a shot through the side of it and deduced that I'd fired at them. I knew that the only shots I'd fired had been through the roof so that nobody would get hurt. Of course, that shot out the side was the one in the fucking caravan park when I'd nearly taken myself out with the AR15.

I pleaded guilty to four charges but decided the rest should go to trial, and so then they decided, 'Right, we're not holding him *here* anymore.' They flew me to the North Island, to the closest prison, Mount Crawford in Wellington. Flying a prisoner was quite a big deal in those days, but they didn't want to risk transporting me in vehicles.

At Wellington, prison staff took me up to the jail on Miramar Peninsula. It was to be my first taste of an adult prison. Little did I know then, but it wouldn't be my last. Not for a very, very long time.

CHAPTER THREE

IN AND OUT
OF PRISON

Until the mid-1990s, the person in charge of each prison was called the superintendent and the prisons were run by the penal division of the Department of Justice. Other divisions within the justice system ran the courts and the Probation Service. The prison muster for the whole country never went above 3000, and at least in the '80s hovered around 2500. Now, of course, we're sitting at 9000 after decreasing from 10,000.

Back then, the superintendent of each prison was God. Consequently, the flavour and character of each jail was very much influenced by who the boss was. My arrival at Mount Crawford gave me the early impression that prisons were run with an air of integrity. Les 'Bully' Hine — a round-faced, thin-mouthed, dull-eyed man — had his officers line up every morning so he could inspect the thread on their uniforms, the shine of their shoes. He was a man's man — if he had a problem with you he'd go out the back and punch it out with you. Screws weren't like these pricks now, who basically sit in the background pulling strings from Wellington.

Mount Crawford was a remand prison (for people waiting to be sentenced), housing only one or two hundred prisoners at a time. The original prison opened in 1915, initially only for women, then became the reform school for both sexes in the 1920s. It was supposed to be a place where men and women would work. It closed in 2012. The last I saw, it had been slapped with an 'earthquake-prone' sticker and was covered in weeds. It's supposed to be haunted, of course. Four men were hung there: George Errol Coats, for bashing his girlfriend and burying her alive; George Edward James, who killed his partner and her son; Edward Tarrant, for killing a man with an axe; and Charles William Price, who bashed a woman to death.

My court date was two weeks away, which meant I was to be on remand in Mount Crawford until then. On my very first day I was chucked in the pound — sort of like a mini-prison within the prison where you're on your own, in segregation. When I asked Bully why, he said, 'I know your father, Taylor — he was trouble and you're fucking trouble. I'm not putting up with it.' He was mistaken — my father was never in prison, ever. I assumed that the police had told him so much about me that he'd figured it couldn't have all been done by just one young man.

Imagine the trappings of prison and you'll typically picture a concrete dungeon, but my first taste of adult prison wasn't too bad. In many ways I felt at home. I recognised some of the old Epuni boys, who'd heard of my escapades, so I walked into a welcoming environment: pats on the back, and 'Kia ora, Arthur.' They were different kinds of inmates, not the sickos and devos and child molesters you get now. They had principles, shall we say. They wouldn't steal out of other inmates' cells, for instance. If they had, they'd have had their fingers slammed in the cell door.

There were no gangs, just camaraderie. You were a prisoner first, a gang member second. Now it's completely different: gangs in prisons divide and rule. But back then they didn't do standover tactics, and they didn't steal other inmates' property. There were no big-mouthed arseholes knowing that there's CCTV and screws watching who'll come and help you. You had to stand on your own two feet. I suppose you could call them good baddies. Unlike the lack of control I had in Epuni as a child, something about prison suited me. I fitted right in.

The squalor of jail grub would be a nightmare for some, but in the 1970s it was at its best, and at Mount Crawford we were fed properly. This was obviously before people got hankerings for fast food, when they could only sit in their cells and dream of Big Macs or fish 'n' chips. (One thing they don't often tell you is that a combination of getting older, having little opportunity for exercise and being on flat ground all the time means that your propensity for stomaching big meals reduces. Even now, when I can eat whatever I want, I can't stomach much.)

Every Sunday we had bacon and eggs for breakfast; the kitchen butcher, an old Māori guy called Tua Brown, who was a mate of mine, made sure I had stacks of bacon. The bread was baked on-site and we spread it with actual butter, not watered-down margarine shit, and proper home-made jam that reminded me of the fruit trees in the Hokianga. The milk came in pint bottles, and if you were quick you could ask the kitchen boys to tip the top of their milk into your bowl so that you had cream — not that we needed to scrounge for cream, because dessert was served every night.

The year I arrived, the penal division did away with using food as a punishment for unruly inmates. A bread-and-water diet as a punishment had been eradicated in the 1960s, but pared back diets as discipline remained. One was a menu of starch: bread, milk and potatoes and another had a bit more variety, with oatmeal, salt, sugar, cheese and dripping. They were then banned in 1981.

My cell consisted of a single bunk, a locker and three shelves; no TV, but we were allowed a radio if you could get one sent in. The stripping away of my privacy, which invaded many corners of my routine, was one of the first things I had to get used to. With no toilets in the cells, every morning I, along with hundreds of others, lined up at a piss pot — a little brown plastic potty — to shit and piss. Afterwards you'd empty it into a big slush pile. The smell was appalling, but I soon got used to it.

A fter my two weeks of remand, they had me back in Blenheim for sentencing. I was handcuffed to a police officer during the whole hearing, which seemed like overkill. By then I'd pleaded guilty to sixteen charges, including escaping, taking cars and burglary. However, it was important to me that I made it clear that at Goose Bay I did *not* intend to endanger anyone when I fired. I was vehement about that.

My lawyer, Mr Radich, told the court that I was introverted, a person who wandered from place to place offending; which I suppose was true. Magistrate Watts — a broad man with a nice smile who went on to become a long-serving judge in Palmerston

North — deemed my record appalling, even then. Sentencing me to corrective training, he had a word of warning for me: 'You should get a job and stay out of trouble, otherwise you'll spend most of your life in prison.' It didn't sink in.

South Island. 1975

They flew me, together with a cop, to borstal at Invercargill to serve my sentence. There were just two borstals in the whole country. Anyone south of Palmerston North went to Invercargill, and anyone north of Palmerston North went to Waikeria. Borstal had taken its name from an English town where the concept of a youth reform school was born. Invercargill's borstal had opened in 1917; its Liffey Street location placed it just a few blocks from the infamous hanging site of the wicked Minnie Dean, who was convicted of infanticide.

In New Zealand, young offenders (aged 15 to 21) could be sentenced to borstal for up to two years. This had reduced from three years in the early '60s after authorities began to form the opinion that long-term incarceration of young people would do more harm than good. Six to twelve months was the average. They had a borstal parole board which decided when you got out, based on what the screws told them about you.

The borstals had had their genesis in the earliest iterations of 'rehabilitation' where inmates at reformatory centres were put to work. Because I'd escaped a couple of times already, I was regarded as a bit of a security threat, so instead of getting a job out on the farm like the others, I was stuck in the prison laundry. There were plenty of characters about the place. One day I was pulling jeans out of the machine, and a pair of pink lady's panties came flying out. I thought, 'Where the fuck did that come from?'

One of the boys said, 'Oh, that's that tranny's. The screw is fucking her.' The prison officer had brought these pink panties in for her. It was a bit of a shock to a young lad like me.

B y the end of 1975 I was thinking 'Fuck this, I don't like this Invercargill. It's too far south, my family can't visit me, it's a cold, windy hole.' I felt the distance between my parents and I acutely. Although borstal inmates were supposed to see a psychiatrist or have access to counselling, I'd had neither.

I had become adept at fleeing when situations didn't suit me, so much so that this action had become ingrained; my flight or fight mode was switched to one gear only. How to escape was an equation to be solved — how to outwit the bastard guards — but in other ways it was just so bloody easy to get out. Security wasn't like it is now; and even now it's still not hard to figure out how to leave, if you really want to. One of the earliest notable prison escapes happened in 1944 when two prisoners escaped from Mount Eden after using gelignite, smuggled in from a quarry, to blast open a wall in the exercise yard. As the prison population climbed in the 1960s and '70s, so too did the number of escapes. At Mount Eden someone escaped in 1962 by hacksawing through a bar and scaling the perimeter wall.

My cellmate, John from Ruatoria, and I didn't have explosives, but we did have one resource at our disposal. Every week each prisoner could get a fig — an ounce — of tobacco, prisoners were charged about 14 cents. I didn't smoke so I saved it, and paid people in tobacco. This was how I got a hacksaw blade — by paying a guy from one of the farm work parties to bring me one from the workshop. The windows in my cell would only open a certain way and to a certain distance, so first I had to cut the hinges off the top before I could get at the bars. John kept watch while I hacksawed through the brass hinges. This wasn't a quick operation. It took ,days, because I had to saw at night. The screws performed daily bar checks, of course, but I guess they were looking at the bars instead of the hinges.

Eventually the hinges surrendered, and I turned my attention to the white-painted bars. At the end of each hard night of sawing I'd take soap mixed into a paste and cake it onto the little tiny cuts, pushing it in until it looked solid. We carried the hacksaw around with us during the day when they searched our cells.

One night we decided 'Tonight's the night.' We both went out the window pretty easily. It was quite a tight fit but I was slim then. We dropped down onto the street, then stole a Land Rover.

I'd figured that when word got out that we were gone they'd block all the roads out of Invercargill, and the main one was State Highway 1, which passes through Gore. On a map, I plotted a course via all the back roads through Tūātapere and that night we screamed through all these little towns, Riverton, Pahia, Te Waewae, heading west, until we eventually circled around and arrived at Waipori Falls, near Dunedin, home to the hydroelectric power station — and some quite heavy bush. We'd only stopped briefly at Tūātapere to siphon some diesel from a tractor. At night we headed into the quiet, picturesque port town of Port Chalmers, broke into a beach house and spent a few days there, winding down from prison and revelling in the free life again.

Our error was in deciding to drive north to a little town called Palmerston. Not Palmerston North. *Palmerston*. We broke into some shops and stocked up on food and supplies, and then took a Triumph, which could really move. Unfortunately, when we continued north towards Temuka the police spotted us. They'd discovered the burglaries in Palmerston. It must have been the bread guys delivering early in the morning who'd alerted the police, who then put two and two together: it's them borstal escapees.

The first indication of pursuit was flashing red and blue lights in the rear-view mirror. I could see the patrol car encroaching on us from way back. John panicked and waved an air rifle we'd stolen from the beach house out the passenger window as a warning: back off. They dropped back a bit, but must have phoned ahead for reinforcements. We realised that when we came across a bridge only to see it blocked by a bunch of cops.

We roared off down a side road, only to come up against the Temuka River. There was only one thing to do.

'Right, we're in the river,' I said.

Jesus Christ — worst mistake I ever made. Fed by ice coming straight from the Southern Alps, the river was freezing. John jumped in, and he was screaming. I jumped in after him and pretty fucking quickly turned into a bar of ice. We swam out to a patch of rocks in the middle of the river and wouldn't come off them. The cops didn't want to jump into the river, so were yelling 'Come on! Come onto the banks!'

They were standing on the bridge, pointing weapons at us. I threw a couple of rocks at them, which actually was a bit risky. But we were pissed off. Freezing. Our teeth were chattering. With little choice, the cops eventually started wading out to us. They leaped over the rocks and laid punches on us, but I couldn't feel them land.

We got dragged back to the river bank, chucked in a police car and taken back to Timaru police station. They put us in the women's cells, because they had a bath we could use to thaw out. After the adrenaline had stopped flowing, it was lovely. They gave us a hot drink and kept us there for a couple of days. The owner of the Triumph came by to get his car. I could hear him, out the back with his son, cursing at the cellblock windows: 'You bastards stole my car!'

Most of New Zealand's prison escapes have been short-lived. Perhaps the most infamous escaper, long before me, was burglar George Wilder, who was a recidivist runner. In 1962 he hid from police in the bush for more than two months after breaking out of New Plymouth prison. The following year he took off from Mount Eden, in Auckland, after chiselling out of his cell, assaulting a prison guard and stealing his keys, then making it out over the wall by way of a knotted sheet. He escaped again after another inmate, John Gillies, helped him hold up five guards by pointing a gun at them. Generally, people were escaping because they hated the prison conditions, which were becoming more and more crowded. When effort was put into the education and rehabilitation of inmates, when they had something to do, escapes and escape attempts appeared to reduce.

I didn't, and don't, condone violence against innocent people. If you look at all the times I've escaped, it was through thorough planning to avoid the one-trick-pony getaway of assaulting your way out.

Having had such a short-lived escape, I wasn't quite done with freedom. Following our recapture they planted us in Christchurch's Addington Gaol. A smallish compound built in 1874, it was once a 'lunatic asylum' and one of the oldest cellblocks in the country. Its Gothic-style architecture designed by Benjamin Mountfort, a nationally renowned architect who was credited for the design of many of Christchurch's early buildings, including Canterbury College and Christchurch Cathedral, was a reflection of the correctional thinking of the times. For the prisoners this meant damp, dark and crowded.

It turned out that Addington was even easier to exit than Invercargill borstal. My drive to return to the North Island remained, and I was undeterred by the threat of recapture and more charges. I was a lone soldier on this journey, though; the other inmates weren't up to it, and John had had enough.

Addington had a big external concrete wall, but its internal wooden yards had been damaged when someone had set fire to the exercise yards earlier in the month, and they were still rebuilding. It became a weak link in the compound. The temporary exercise yards were surrounded with corrugated iron. It was a cage, basically, with wall-to-wall corrugated iron and mesh over the top, and a guard sitting there, watching. But they'd made the mistake of putting lead-head nails on the inside of the corrugated iron. We had real steel knives in jail, so I would go out to the yard, back up to the walls and slowly saw the heads off the nails. Out of the corner of my eye I'd spotted that one of the workmen fixing the yard had a ladder. So with the guard watching us, I'd just be leaning, hands behind me, slowly cutting the heads off, with one eye on the ladder and the other on the guard. I knew that once those lead heads were off you could just rip the iron and it'd come off straight away, because the lead heads weren't holding it on.

The time came after lunch.

As soon as the boys were all in the yard, I walked up to the iron, ripped it off, ran straight through the gap, grabbed the workman, pushed him out of the way, grabbed his ladder, propped it up against the wall, and leaped over, dropping quite a way down. Gone.

> Police mounted an intensive hunt in Christchurch last night for a prison escaper described as dangerous and 'likely to shoot a policeman if he ever got a gun.'
> The New Zealand Herald, *19 November 1975*

Well, that's fucking bullshit, isn't it? Of course I wasn't. I don't know where they get this stuff from — I didn't even have a violence conviction, but of course the public was taught to fear. As expected, there was a massive manhunt as I ran through the streets. I cut through a school, because I knew the dogs would be after me and I thought they'd be reluctant to send dogs through there. I hid under a house way down the road and waited for dark.

At sunset I stole a car and headed north. I remember seeing in the paper later that it was a court reporter's car. I headed north to Kaikōura; didn't stop at Goose Bay, though. At Kaikōura in the early hours I stocked up on bread and milk that was sitting outside shops waiting to be delivered. Unbeknownst to me, however, a delivery driver spotted me. A short time later, as I threaded through Blenheim, I came around a corner and discovered armed police gumming up the road. They lifted and pointed their guns as I swung the car around.

That early in the morning there was little traffic on Blenheim's streets, so while I slingshotted round and round and round a roundabout trying to get my bearings and figure out where to go, the police were right behind me, all flashing lights and blaring sirens.

I ricocheted out of town and reached a farm, where I jumped out of the car and ran through a field of chickens. It was futile. The police caught up with me, tackled me to the ground, and I was back to the Blenheim police station again. Familiar territory. The cops must have been exasperated. It was time to give it a rest.

I was jailed for nine months for escaping, stealing a car, and burglary. The magistrate said something like 'Jesus Christ you've had a bad start for a young fella, but it's obvious you've got a very supportive family.'

He was right. Mum and Dad were in court. They'd taken time off work and travelled all the way from the North Island. The magistrate had clocked them sitting in the public gallery and said, 'What I'm going to do is recommend to the justice department that you get sentenced to a prison in the North Island.' This was a bit of pragmatic thinking from the magistrate, and showed some compassion. He was saying 'I'll put him near his family and then maybe he'll stop ripping off walls and jumping through cell windows.'

Mum and Dad were relieved at the prospect of having me closer, but it wasn't all good news. I'd been serving a borstal sentence, and he struck that out and replaced it with a sentence of jail. Despite my stints at Mount Crawford and Addington, this was my first actual prison sentence. 'In order to protect the public interest,' the magistrate said. But the term was short, to see whether I behaved myself. I was in danger of becoming institutionalised. 'You have to learn to obey the rules.'

North Island. 1976

Waikeria Prison, south of Te Awamutu, proudly displayed framed sections of the Penal Institutions Act 1954 on its walls. All prisons did. Like a set of house rules, the document glowered down on the prisoners whose rights it was supposed to protect, but the portions of the legislation that the prisons showcased were those that were more favourable to the prisons. The Act set out things like our right to be paid for work, how long we could be detained for in certain types of institutions, and our rights if we needed medical treatment or dental treatment.

I arrived at Waikeria by way of transfer on an overnight ferry from Christchurch to Wellington, locked in a small cabin with the guards where the air quickly became stale, mixed with the smell of pies that the sympathetic stewards kept bringing us. We landed in Wellington in the morning, and then police escorted me on a train to Waikeria. Despite my sentence of jail, they'd decided to hold me in Waikeria's borstal because the conditions were a lot better than those in the adult prison. The justice system was continuing to give me another go. The borstals were better than Epuni because they didn't abuse you. The screws didn't indulge in that sort of thing — it would be a punch-up instead. I'd sooner be in a borstal than Epuni, put it that way.

Waikeria was the country's biggest borstal institution at the time. New Zealand's earliest prison classification system grouped like-minded offenders together in designated prisons. The system was quite simple; something like Waikeria and Invercargill were reformatories (borstals), Paremoremo at Auckland was for longer-term, dangerous offenders, Rotoaira was for military defaulters and the like, and the remainder housed short-termers or South Island inmates.

At Waikeria, high-security prisoners wore jeans with white stripes down the side and were called white-stripers; the next level down were blue-stripers. The white-stripers were treated really badly. They were locked in their cells most of the time, and made to scrub the concrete floors until they could see their faces in them. Cells had no furniture — inmates slept on thin mattresses on the floor — and there was little to no exercise. It wasn't right. I could see crooked from a mile away.

In the receiving office they questioned me, and I was told 'Around here you call us "Sir".'

'You weren't knighted by the Queen, were you?'

It was cheeky, but I wasn't scared. I was tired from the journey, and fed up. Fight or flight, remember — and if you decide to fight, well, you just get on with the fight. And that's what I was thinking when five or six screws chucked me in a cell and came at me. I emerged a short time later with bruises, bloodied marks and red shoulders, but I was pleased to have given one of them, who thought of himself as a real tough guy, a black eye. The other screws ribbed him about it for weeks. Because of this I found myself dressed in white stripes.

Waikeria's superintendent was Louis Harder (who, funnily enough, would be given a Companion of the Queen's Service Order for public services a couple of years later), and after this ruckus with the guards I requested to see him. The Penal Institutions Act gave every prisoner the right to have an interview with the superintendent within seven days of asking — but they refused to let me. Nursing my bruises, I kept telling them I wanted to see the superintendent, to lay my grievances before him. The question I wanted to ask Harder itched: 'If I beat your staff up I'd get charged and imprisoned, so why the hell should it be any different for your staff?'

The refusal to let me see Harder went on for a few months. The way Harder probably looked at it, if he had to see every single crim who made a fuss he'd never do anything but hold fucking interviews.

One day one of the boys, having seen me pointing out the Penal Institution Rules to other inmates and sensing that I was already prickling at the conditions, came to me.

The head cook was a guy called Joe Fry.

'You know that Joe Fry? We actually tipped a whole tray of mince on the floor one day, and Joe Fry told us to scrape it up and put it back on the fucking thing and feed it out to the crims.'

My indignation was mottled red. 'You go and tell that fucking Joe Fry I want to see him.'

Fry had the guts to march over to my cell — along with a whole lot of his kitchen boys — and try to intimidate me, the prick. 'From now on, it's minimum rations for you,' he taunted. So it was war between me and Joe Fry, which was a really bad war to be in because he controlled the food. Back then, the screws were thieving pricks. Cars would back up to the kitchen and they'd get all sorts of rations put in the boot. Rations that were meant for the inmates.

After that carry-on with Joe Fry I talked to the guys about their rights. The prison didn't like it. Suddenly, I was a 'bad influence' on the other inmates. I was loud, I knew the rules, and I wasn't afraid to speak up when we weren't being treated to the letter of the law. The final crunch came when some officials visited to give talks, as they did from time to time. One day the health department was in from Hamilton. Scores of prisoners were listening intently to this health department official when I interrupted.

'Excuse me, who inspects this prison's kitchens?'

One said, 'We do'.

'Well, wouldn't you like to know about a big tray of mince being tipped on the floor and then being spread out as food for the prisoners?'

The next thing I knew, the chief officer came down to see me and said, 'Taylor, I'm getting rid of you.' Truthfully, I was glad to see the back of the pricks.

One morning they turned up at my cell door and escorted me all the way from Waikeria to New Plymouth Prison, an adult prison in Taranaki, which quite suited me. However, the screws there had got word from Waikeria that I was a real bad bastard. When I arrived, they had an attitude on them that I could see from a mile away. And this is what bothers me to this day: people believe the hype. You tell a kid there's a bogeyman under the bed, and for the rest of their life they won't dangle their legs over the side. Tell a guard there's a problem prisoner who's so nasty he's being transferred, and it starts a vicious cycle of disrespect. This has affected my entire life.

I served the rest of my sentence at New Plymouth, and I was just appalled at the conditions. We weren't being let out to exercise, and the pent-up energy drove me nuts. My disdain of injustice increased. I'd had it hammered into me — by Gault, by Epuni, by the courts, and by the state —that life was about obeying rules. If there were instructions they should be complied with, they were there for a bloody good reason. Not window-dressing. And that should have included the instructions included in the Penal Institutions Act on how prisoners should be treated. For many prisoners, the maltreatment they received would just whittle them down until they were nothing. In me, however, it stirred something up.

The last time I'd seen my parents was when they'd driven to my sentencing. While they weren't happy, obviously, they rationalised the situation. I was still young; I had time to turn my life around, and they just wanted me to be happy. It makes me sad now to think of that.

While I was serving my sentence my parents moved to Mangatainoka, north of Pahīatua, where the famous brick Tui brewery lords it over the otherwise rural community. During that sentence former prime minister Keith Holyoake was our local MP, and my parents went to see him about my being beaten up by the screws at Waikeria. He wrote Waikeria a letter saying that he was aware of what had happened.

When I was released in 1976, I wrote to New Zealand's first Ombudsman, Sir Guy Powles, who in turn told the justice department to shape up. I remember that Harder wrote a nasty letter in reply, saying 'This is Waikeria, we do things our own way here.'

Powles was a decent man. He knew what was what, and he told Waikeria, 'You have to comply with the law. The Penal Institution regulations says every prisoner is entitled to an interview with the Superintendent, not his bloody delegate, within seven days of requesting one.'

I was determined to go straight, and stay out of trouble. I'd had enough of prison and borstal. I wanted peace for my family. I wanted to get out and get a job and get on with things. Never in a million years did I consider at that time that I'd be spending most of my life in the can. You just don't envisage that sort of thing. I often picture me telling my younger self, 'You're going to have to be a bit more careful what you do. Your freedom is far too valuable to be risking this sort of caper.'

At age twenty, in 1976, I became a trainee linesman with the P&T (Post and Telegraph) department — the predecessor to Telecom. Mostly I lived with my parents. Dad was working in Pahīatua. The legend goes that Pahīatua derived its name as a place to rest from your enemies. Dad worked as the local ranger, telling people when to rein in their weeds. Occasionally I stayed with my darling younger sister Sandra and her partner Tony a few kilometres away in Mangatainoka. People tell me that Sandra and I look alike, and we're very close. Having seen my parents' unfailing support for me, she took up the mantle and has always been one of my biggest cheerleaders.

After my stints on the inside, I loved being outdoors. I'd missed the smell of grass. With my P&T workmates I got out into the country, fixing the phone lines and touring around. On wet days we'd travel to the nearest telephone station, at Woodville, and park up until the rain stopped. I'd brew the billy and we'd play cards.

It was all going well until one day the cops pulled a little stunt. We were way out in Mākurī working on the phone lines, and on our return in the truck the cops had blocked the bridge. I can't even remember what it was over, maybe traffic offences, but they put a big act on to make it look like I was some hard-out criminal they needed to nab. They hauled me out in front of all the boys, my workmates, arrested me and took me to Palmerston North. When I came back to work, it was 'We've had orders, Arthur, we have to let you go.' I had to hand in all my wet-weather gear, all my equipment, and lost my job because they thought it would give the P&T department a bad name. In a small place like Pahīatua, word travelled fast.

That stunt set me on a bad path. I was pissed off — life had been starting to turn around, I was enjoying myself, and the cops' proclaiming to all and sundry that I was a bad bastard was like a terrier incessantly nipping at my heels. It meant war. I ripped out plants in front of the police station, slashed the tyres of their patrol cars and shone big torches in front of the police station windows at night.

I figured I could outwit the police by committing crimes under their noses, so I burgled all the shops in Pahīatua. They knew it was me. At the Dudley Arms Tavern in Mangatainoka, a grand old hotel built in the early 1900s, they stationed pricks to watch me. One night they tried a honey trap. I was drinking in the pub, and this woman called me over. Women couldn't really drink in the public bars then, so she lured me into the lounge bar. Then she started asking me about buying stolen goods.

All sorts of alarms were going off in my head, so I shot out to the car park and checked all the cars — and sure enough there was a car with a police radio in it, which was hers. She'd been sent over from Palmerston North. She probably thought that a young, gullible lad — like they must have thought I was — would be overwhelmed by her. She was quite a pretty policewoman.

I was making good money from stealing all sorts of shit. At the Pahīatua railway station one night, Tony and I broke into a container that was stocked with Tuis from the brewery. We spent all night shuttling through the silent town, with the bottles going 'clink clink clink', taking them to our hiding place up in the roof of our house. We were stocked up for weeks after that. Another night we opened up a container in the railway yards and were nearly smothered by a sea of grain that came flying out.

I also had a good line going in wool. I'd cruise around visiting isolated farms during the day, seeing who had wool, then come back at night to take it and sell it to a broker. I could get four bales of wool on the ute, and each of those bales was worth $300–$400.

I burgled shops and took electrical gear. I'd try not to burgle private homes unless it was necessary, like on some of my escapes. I knew that stealing from people who worked as hard as my parents did was wrong, but I figured that the farmers had plenty of money because they were getting all these subsidies from the government.

Around this time, farmers were struggling to export sheep meat for a good price, and stocks languished. I leased a slice of paddock covered in bush from a farmer who couldn't use it for anything useful. At night, Tony and I cruised for sheep. Have you ever tried to chase sheep? You can't catch them. The only way to do it is if you corner them in a paddock. That was too much fucking work, so I devised a new plan. I'd cut a fence and wait for these sheep to wander off. When they did I'd leave food for them in the middle of the road, and they'd idle down and start munching away. Tony would drive along, and bump them. Gently. That'd sort of stun them a little bit and I'd leap out and grab them.

We had a cage on the back of the ute, and we threw the sheep in there, collecting them until we had about six or seven, then we'd keep them in the bushy paddock until Tony could butcher them. He'd cut their throats, skin them, then cut straight down the backbone with a chainsaw, and cut them into chops. We raffled the meat off in pub car parks.

When I wasn't looting I was working on farms — cutting mānuka scrub and fencing — in the hilly country to the north-east of Pahīatua. This involved dragging strainer posts, packs of fencing batons and rolls of No. 8 wire up hill and down dale, crowbarring post and strainer holes in the rocky terrain. I was weed-spraying, too, backpacking a motorised weed sprayer with a massive tank full of 2,4,5-T (one of the components in the Agent Orange they used in Vietnam — long since outlawed). I was on the sides of gullies on tops of hills where you couldn't get road access to take out gorse. There were many cold, wet winter days where I'd lose my footing and crash, arse-over-tit, down the side of these gullies.

The sidelines were doing really well, though, and I was making good money. I had a nice car and nice girls. Tony and I were having a ball — and the cops were as annoyed as hell. They saw me with all this money and linked it back to all the district's burglaries. I had a store for the goods, however, and whenever they started asking questions I'd hide them.

My rustling enterprise came to an end thanks to my dad. As the ranger for the Pahīatua county council, he had to sort out any stock that escaped on to the road. His mate was Bob Walker. Dad took Bob out one day, and was saying 'My son has got a good job and he's doing a bit of farming.' Well, Bob had recognised some of his sheep in my rustling holding pen. Dad made me shut it down. He said, 'I'm the fucking ranger — you can't go rustling sheep in my county.'

So that was the end of that one.

One November night, my fists were ablaze at the Mangatainoka hotel pub. When we left — Sandra, Tony and me — the police tried to pull us over. I refused to stop, so they turned on their red warning lights. I swerved, which forced them to pull back, and then I shone a spotlight to try to blind the driver. A traffic officer joined the chase.

Eventually they got in front and blocked the road, and I smashed sideways into this police car. *Crunch*. I ran off and tried to jump over a bridge into the Mangatainoka River, but the police grabbed me. They later alleged that I'd kicked one of them in the groin and broke another's rib, but they never charged me. They just wanted an excuse to pummel their batons into me before chucking me in the Pahīatua police station cells.

Enraged, and still handcuffed, I smashed up the toilet pan and cistern, and ripped up the rubber mattress and its cover. They tried to calm me down by talking to me from the other side of the cell door, but I just told them to fuck off. My night had been ruined. I was a caged bird.

I was convicted of endangering, receiving stolen goods, resisting police and fighting in public, and jailed for two years. I was twenty, and off to live with Bully at Hotel Mount Crawford again.

This time the screws gave me a job in the kitchen, and I learned to bake. One day Bully came running through the bakehouse. He used to keep trout in the big freezers, and was upset because the kitchen boss's assistant, an ex-navy guy, used to steal the fish. Not all of them, but enough for Bully to notice. Bully was purple.

'Taylor, who took my trout?'

'Fucked if I know,' I said. This navy guy was giving me all sorts of perks and there was no way I was giving him up.

'I know it's not you, Taylor.'

And then, Bully imparted a hidden warning. 'Taylor, you're reasonably honest, so I'll give you a tip: there's another Taylor in this jail, Norm Taylor. I've had some information about him. He's converting FM band radios to pick up police bands.'

My ears pricked up. I knew exactly what he was talking about. We didn't have police scanners then. The police were on the 75 and 76 megahertz frequencies but the FM bands started at 88 to 108. By putting a variable tuning capacitor on the radio you could drop the start of the FM band from 88 down to 74, thus picking up the police on a standard FM radio.

All police communications were done by radio. When they were going to jobs, they'd put the address out over the air because they didn't think people could listen. I'd worked out how to import FM radios, which was a hell of a job because you had to have an import licence, just for radios.

'I'm going to go and have that Taylor's cell raided,' Bully said. He was just giving me a tip: 'Cut that shit out — I don't want all my crims to have police radios.'

Bully raided that other Taylor's cell just to make a big beef out of nothing. He knew it was me all along.

A nother time I was itching for a day out to see my girlfriend. There were some maintenance workers from the Ministry of Works up in the kitchen ceiling, fixing pipes and shit, so I pinched one of their hacksaw blades. They reported it to Bully, who made a beeline straight for me.

'Taylor, a hacksaw has been reported missing. We need it, it's a security risk.'

'Well I don't know anything about it.'

'You know everything in this jail, Taylor. I'm warning you now, I want that fucking hacksaw blade back.'

'Tell you what, Mr Hine, I'll start searching and talking to everyone . . . How do you feel about me getting a day out? I'll get picked up early in the morning, I'll go out with my family, and I'll be back that night.'

'I know you'll be back. I'll see what I can do.'

Shortly afterwards I produced the hacksaw like a magician pulls a rabbit out of a hat. And this is how much push Bully had: he got straight on the phone to head office, and said, 'Taylor has just performed a very valuable service for me. He wants a day out; I recommend he gets it.'

I got picked up at 7 a.m. and went roaring up the main highway to Paraparaumu with the wind blowing in my hair.

A year into my sentence, in August 1977, the screws at Mount Crawford were blithely unaware that over a period of months several sharpened spikes, dust pans, hacksaw blades, ropes, a couple of coal shovels, overalls and hacksaws had been secreted into East Wing's cell 18. Nor did they notice that after lights-out a thin, seemingly innocuous strip of light would appear at the bottom of my door, which belied the massive operation going on inside.

I was tunnelling to freedom.

I'd come to the realisation that being in prison could be a good alibi. I could be out building up a bankroll, and the cops wouldn't think of me because I was in jail. As I've mentioned before, escaping — especially in those days when security was in its infancy — was quite common. One inmate told me a story of breaking out of Christchurch so many times that the screws made him wear pyjamas after a certain hour as a deterrent. He told me that the last time he broke out from Paparua Prison, he posted his pyjamas back to the superintendent with a note saying 'I won't be needing these anymore.'

I'd learned that there was a drainage hole outside the prison, and if we could tunnel out to that we could come and go from the prison as we pleased. Underneath the native-timber floorboards at Mount Crawford there was a bit of a gap between the floor and the earth — a good metre and a half — so that became our digging pit. The floorboards were easily sliced through, then put back together again and polished like nothing had ever happened. The screws were supposed to look through the peep-hole in the door in those days, but they didn't bother.

Lights were shut off at about 8.30 or 9 p.m. and we needed to work at night to avoid the screws, so I bypassed the light switches to give us constant power. Then I hooked the power up to lights down in the tunnel, so we could see. It was dark as hell in there, underneath the cell. I dug out a massive pit in the work area where we could rest without having to get back up into the cell.

It was easy getting equipment. Getting stuff into prison was no problem; you could just get stuff thrown over the wall. One time a guy persuaded his missus to throw a rope over the wall from outside, and he climbed out and they both left in a taxi. It was fun and games back then.

The tunnel began under my cell and linked up to that of my next-door neighbour, a Wellington boy called Hombre. We branched the tunnel out to the prison's basement records room, to see if we could exit the building through there, possibly by way of getting into the ceiling, but that wasn't possible so we gave up on that. Our biggest problem was keeping what we were doing a secret, from even the other inmates. I tried to sleep as much of the day as possible because I was tunnelling every night.

It was hard, dirty work. We wore overalls and home-made balaclavas to keep the dirt down so that we'd appear normal at morning unlock. My cellmate Alan George (from Āpiti in the Manawatū) pitched in. Stored in our tunnel rest area we had grappling hooks, ropes made out of plaited sheets, and hacksaw blades. George had pillow cases tied on a rope, and he would pull as I filled them with dirt which we'd then pack against the back of the cell. The wing had scores of cells, and underneath them, inside the tunnel, there was hollowed space — about half a metre — under each. Sort of like a concrete ridge. We packed the dirt in there. In a sack we kept our tools: a 14-inch sharpened meat skewer, a sharpened table knife, a narrow chisel, and an oilstone for sharpening them.

The operation was progressing like clockwork, and we expected to be under the prison wall and into the storm-drain exit within a few days when Colin Burt arrived on remand for murdering a barman while robbing a tavern in Masterton. The police informed Bully that Colin was planning to escape, so they stepped up security and we had to suspend the tunnel operation. We figured we'd bide our time — we knew that Colin was slated for maximum security in Auckland Prison at Paremoremo as soon as he was sentenced. In those days, all lifers and prisoners sentenced to more than two years were sent to Paremoremo (which we called Pare) to start with.

Then, Hombre learned that his partner was in strife on the outside and all patience evaporated. On the night of 27 August 1977, he used one of our hacksaws to cut through the bars of his cell and got on to the East Wing roof, from where he was planning to swing a grappling hook onto the top of the wall and go over it.

Alan George went through the tunnel into Hombre's cell to help him out the window, and I issued very specific instructions to ensure that the tunnel entrance from Hombre's cell was properly concealed when he came back through. I'd told Hombre to use a mirror to look out the window in all directions to make sure there were no screws around. But he didn't, and as luck would have it a patrolling screw spotted him getting onto the roof. Alan came back through the tunnel and assured me that when the screws searched Hombre's cell there was no way they'd discover the tunnel entrance.

The screw who saw Hombre raised the alarm immediately, so he was trapped on the roof, more than 10 metres above the ground. He panicked, then fell, was pretty badly injured and was taken to Wellington Hospital. The next morning, the screws searched his cell looking for anything he might have used in the attempted escape, and then locked the cell door. Normally, within a day or two they would weld the cut bars back in place so that the cell could be re-tenanted. But while they locked his cell up, they left the cell bars cut for a week.

My hackles were up. Something fishy was going on.

For the next few days all appeared normal in the East Wing but then staff began reporting that there was tension amongst inmates, especially the East Wing cleaners and some sentenced men. Experienced staff working in the wing said that they were able to detect an uneasiness throughout. Reports of whispered conversation by small groups and silence when staff approached were being observed by staff. They were instructed to remain observant and all staff were made aware that all was not well within the wing.
Report of Superintendent Les Hine to the Justice Department, September 1977

Alan George hadn't covered up the boards properly — they'd found the whole thing. Over two days they inspected the tunnel under Hombre's floorboards and decided that it didn't go anywhere, but thought that if they left the bars uncut, whoever came through that tunnel would try to escape. So for a week they had a screw up in the watch-tower, constantly observing the walkway by that window. After that week, Bully launched a raid.

One afternoon they moved us all out to the yard, brought in cadets from the prison officers' training school and sent them down the tunnel. We were kept out there all afternoon, and then one by one we were called in. I was taken straight to Bully's office where I was surrounded by over a dozen of the biggest screws in the place. Bully opened with: 'You better not be fucking trying to break a murderer out of prison.'

Bully would tell the Department of Justice that I had been paid to break Colin Burt out of prison, which simply wasn't true. I mean, if Burt had produced money then I would have let him use my tunnel. But it wasn't built for Colin Burt's fucking use. It was built for *me*.

They chucked me in the holding room and refused to feed me. One of the screws tipped me off that Bully had a special escort of eight screws ready to depart with me at 6 a.m. the next day for Paremoremo. I wasn't in the best of humours, knowing that it would be a shit of a trip with who-knows-what waiting at the other end. Pare screws had a reputation.

The cell they'd put me in had heavy iron brackets secured by steel retaining bolts into the concrete wall, which had held the original folding beds against the wall. Those beds had long been replaced by steel bunks, though Bully had had the bunk removed from the cell I was in that night, and there was only a couple of blankets and a mattress for me to sleep on.

I spent hours pacing, dwelling on the situation, when one of the screws Bully had doing fifteen-minute observations on me peered through the peephole and started getting mouthy — no doubt resenting having to spend his night keeping tabs on me in the freezing cold. Anyone who's ever spent any time at Mount Crawford will recall how cold it could get. I thought, 'Well, Bully, if you're transferring me to Pare I've got nothing to lose.' We ended up in a massive argument, abusing the shit out of each other. I couldn't get through the door to him so started wrenching one of the iron brackets off the wall. I worked on it for over half an hour and finally got it free — a length of heavy iron about a metre long which I duly began smashing the door with. Sparks went flying every time the bar hit the door. The room lit up like fireworks.

The whole place awakened and screws were called in. I later found out that the local police were put on standby to come to the prison in case I managed to break through the door. Bully arrived and tried to get me to throw out the bar and come quietly. I was really worked up by then, however, and other prisoners were yelling out encouragement. I kept smashing at the door, and the screws were too scared to try to come through it.

Bully decided on a massive show of force and had screws outside the cell window threatening me. They even brought in a megaphone to drown out the noise I was making, and ordered me to surrender. This uproar went on all night. By about 5 a.m. I was stuffed, completely worn out, so lay down for a few minutes. The screws took their opportunity and pounced. The door crashed open. I thought it was the police, because the lead guy coming at me had a riot shield with 'POLICE' emblazoned across it, but Bully had just borrowed the riot gear from the Wellington station.

I was overpowered, handcuffed behind my back, gagged with masking tape and dragged to a holding cell near the receiving office. 'When staff entered the cell Taylor was lying in bed and did not get a chance to resist,' Bully later wrote, 'He was handcuffed and tape put over his mouth so that he would not create a disturbance.' Bully had me put face-down on the floor; everything except for my underwear removed, and one of the biggest screws in the place — this 19-stone fat fucker Townley — sat on my back for a couple of hours. They wouldn't even let me up for breakfast.

Instead Townley fed me a sandwich, morsel by morsel.

I'd lose three months' remission (equivalent to three months more jail), have three months' loss of privileges and sentenced to fifteen days of solitary confinement. Later Bully wrote a detailed report into the whole thing. One phrase always sticks out in my mind. He described all our digging as a 'comprehensive tunnel system'.

When Bully later became the superintendent of Auckland Prison at Paremoremo, from 1985 to 1987, I joked to him: 'Bully, how about a reference for the Parole Board?' He said, with a smirk and a raised eyebrow, 'Fuck off, Taylor, I'd have to write it on thermal paper.' He reckoned his words would blister off the page otherwise. Bully took early retirement in 1987 after gang tensions in the prison began to rise.

CHAPTER FOUR

PARE

On 16 September 1977, I was driven the length of the North Island to Paremoremo with a screw handcuffed to an arm on each side of me, and an extra one in the front passenger's seat for good measure. The drive was forced upon us: Air New Zealand wouldn't carry me.

A car full of screws followed behind the vehicle, and as we passed through each small town with a police station a cop car would fall in behind. It felt like being royalty. The only stop was a toilet break at Taupō police station, where I was given a very late lunch consisting of a couple of bread rolls.

It was well after dark when we arrived, and the superintendent, Jack Hobson, had left instructions that I was not to be able to talk to any other prisoner and was to be taken straight to the pound to serve fifteen days' solitary. That meant they'd take your mattress off you in the mornings but keep you locked up except for one hour a day in the exercise yard.

New Zealand's only specialist maximum-security prison, Auckland Prison at Paremoremo, or Pare, is located north of Auckland in what was then a mostly rural area. It was purpose-built in the late '60s, and opened to much preview and scrutiny. A 1959 Department of Justice report had practically sighed about the need for such an institution as Pare, but said that until a way of knocking out crime altogether was found it would at least protect the public. In 1960 Secretary of Justice John Robson had travelled as far as Europe to study overseas prison systems, and by December of that year plans for Pare were afoot. The justice department reckoned they'd be able to reconcile security with humanity, and that their prison would be a humanitarian institution.

In March 1961 New Zealand's justice department started planning the new, million-pound prison, scouting Auckland for a potential site. By 1962 they were considering south Auckland and Paremoremo, and soon Cabinet agreed to fund the purchase of 276 acres. That was just the beginning. New Zealand watched as other countries experimented with prisons and punishment. San

Francisco's Alcatraz was emptied in 1963 when the US government decided it was easier to build a new maximum-security institute than try to reform its existing ones, and in the UK, after the escapes of train robber Ronald Biggs in 1965 and spy George Blake in 1966, the whole of England's security system was revised. An official was sent from New Zealand to Sweden, England and the US to study prison designs, and all of the department's studies produced a blueprint for what was supposed to be a new, state-of-the-art prison.

Consisting of five wings of 48 cells, each modelled on the 'school house' system, Pare would house 248 inmates. While security was the priority (much later, I would test its systems), authorities vowed that the jail would work hard to avoid institutionalising people. Plans for non-institutional thinking included greenery and a pool. An athletics field was considered, but abandoned. The walls would have picturesque murals.

The government had to convince the public that it was worth spending a million pounds on a new prison, and given the moral panic about crime, the department talked a big game: closed-circuit televisions, bullet-proof trappings, and bars of steel. While some overseas prisons relied on armed guards observing the perimeter, the justice department initially vetoed this.

Fifty-nine inmates — the guinea pigs — started to trickle in by March 1969. The pool hadn't eventuated but prisoners had a gym and exercise yards, a weight room, workshop, library, study room, visiting room, chapel, kitchen, laundry, psychiatric division and hospital. Cells of 3.2 metres by 1.8 metres occupied second and third levels on top of recreation floors, and had running water, a flush toilet, a chair and a writing desk. The front of the cell was barred, to expose inmates' movements. The interior was depressing concrete.

The units were designated A, B, C and D, each for a heightened classification of prisoner. In A to C inmates could come and go, from 7 a.m. to 8.30 p.m., and ate in dining rooms. In unit D, where I was, we didn't leave our wings unless under escort, and we spent most of our time inside our cells with cold meals delivered to the door.

Compared with Mount Crawford, the Pare pound was something else — clean, with mod cons I'd never seen in a prison before: a flushing toilet and running water, although the water was turned off after 4 p.m. so the cells couldn't be flooded by protesting prisoners, and the lights went off at 8.30 p.m. The doors were electronically operated, something no other New Zealand prison had.

> For the aspiring escapee, the minimum physical
> barrier between himself and freedom is always at
> least one 7-metre concrete wall with a trip-wire on
> top of it and two, 7-metre close-mesh perimeter
> fences, also equipped with trip-wires. The windows
> of the institution are of shatter-proof glass in steel
> frames and are guarded by steel-reinforced concrete
> mullions. The bars of the cells and grilles are made
> of tool-resistant manganese steel, each reputed to
> be able to resist the action of 1000 hacksaw blades
> or a press of several tonnes.
> *Greg Newbold,* Punishment and Politics, *Oxford
> University Press, 1989*

Eddie Buckley was the first superintendent to preside over Pare. Jack Hobson took over in 1972. The son of a policeman, Hobson had arrived in New Zealand from England after World War 2. He had served as a gunner in the navy and was a formidable-looking figure. Aged 47, and fit and tall with a classic Prince Philip-looking face — like a Navy admiral, prisoners liked him. It was well known that he'd rather have a tussle with prisoners out the back than record a dispute — a bit like old Bully.

Jack Hobson didn't consider himself above the rest. He walked around the jail and talked to inmates. Prisoners were allowed to see him whenever they wanted. Unlike the faceless prison bosses of today, Jack made a point of touring the prison every day, and meeting his prisoners. If you had a problem, he would make decisions on the spot and sort it out then and there — and he was a man of his word.

Jack came to the front of my cell most mornings and asked how I was, and that was my opportunity to raise complaints or problems and get them sorted out before they festered. I quickly learned that in the pressure-cooker prison environment, things that seemed minor or inconsequential rapidly assumed outsized importance. I've seen prisoners almost kill each other for something your average person on the outside wouldn't consider worth bothering about.

A couple of years after my initiation at Pare, 22-year-old child rapist and murderer Keith Hall had his throat cut in A block. Nobody had had any objections. Prisoners have got the same sort of feelings as people on the outside. If a potential child rapist thinks 'Shit, I'd better not do that because I'll go to jail and be killed' then all the better.

Despite the promised best efforts of officials, however, it wasn't long before Pare gained a fearsome reputation. Nearby villagers, 320 people who were the families of officers who worked at the prison, lived in fear, and for good reason. Within two years, 30 officers were attacked by inmates, four were held hostage, a prison block was flooded and a .22 and ammunition was found in cells. The locals were at their wits' end. Women worried about their husbands going off to work in the morning, and prison officers walked in the purpose-built village bearing wounds and bruises.

One officer, Kenneth Smith, was beaten so badly by a prisoner that he needed reconstructive surgery. One riot saw four men hold prison officer Wayne Wills hostage. He was beaten by a group of prisoners that included a convicted murderer, and later said that the prisoners left him alone only when they thought he was dead.

The prison was also never properly maintained. Its security

features were considered state-of-the-art technology when they went in, but they became outmoded and expensive to maintain. I think they worked out that it was cheaper to build a new prison than keep maintaining Pare, because it cost tens of millions a year.

A fter all the tunnelling drama at Mount Crawford, and the journey to Auckland, I was out like a light as soon as I lay down. I slept soundly until just after 8 a.m. the next day, when the door burst open and two screws bowled into my cell while a third waited outside, looking on. I'd come to know these two as Mr Monk and Bryan Christy, Pare's hard nuts. Christy was a big motherfucker. Although he and I would have many ups and downs, we later came to respect each other — he was the Pare prison boss when I eventually returned on another lag, but has since retired.

'Welcome to Pare,' they said, waving fists and pointing fingers as they explained the prison rules. They gave me a paper plate of porridge, two pieces of toast and a plastic mug of weak prison 'tea' while Christy said, 'I've heard about you. You won't be digging any tunnels out of jail — Paremoremo is built on about 200 metres of concrete.'

After I'd clocked my time in the pound they moved me to D Block, the most stringently controlled block in the prison — perhaps the whole country — where we were only let out for a few hours during the day. This despite the fact that I was only a petty criminal. Maximum-security prisoners are not those the public might think of as dangerous, but those who the jailors consider present the most risk to them or 'the system'. Their crime is that they are a threat to 'the good order and discipline of the prison'.

I got on with everyone quite well. There were some real hard-case good blokes up there. Among its famous inmates was Dean Wickliffe, who'd first arrived there in October 1969. Dean was alright, a solitary sort of guy and the first to ever escape from Paremoremo. He was serving time for all sorts of shit, a bit like me;

a burglar, a thief, a conman. A Bay of Plenty boy, Dean's upbringing was different to mine in that his parents pretty much abandoned him, but he also got a taste of crime young and bouncing around borstals taught him the rest. In 1972 he committed his worst crime, killing Paul Miet while robbing a jewellery store in Wellington, and received a life sentence.

By the time I arrived, Dean had already tried to escape from Pare once — and later became the only person ever to do it twice. He said he'd trained, because you had to be as fit as hell to escape from that place, to clamber up the 15-metre-high walls.

Drug convict Greg Newbold, who became a criminologist, was also a resident for a short time, though we didn't meet until I was embedded at Oakley Hospital in 1981. He would go on to write books about his experiences in prison.

Being around these hard-case blokes filled me with a sense of awe, and we exchanged yarns like kids in a playground. While the conditions at Pare were grim, the camaraderie between me and the other boys was something to enjoy.

I did my time, and on my release in 1978 continued to stay intermittently with my parents and with Sandy and Tony, this time in the Kāpiti coastal town of Raumati South. I worked for Winstones, a place that made tiles, in Plimmerton a bit further south. My job was stacking the tiles onto pallets, and unloading bricks and tiles by hand from the kiln wagons once they'd cooled. Two of us did this wearing thick gloves. When I'd got the job, they told me most only lasted a few weeks before quitting. It was a prick of a job. We had a quota of wagons to empty, and once that was done we could knock off and still get paid for the full eight hours. I'd go like hell in the morning, sleep most of lunch and be finished by 3 p.m., which gave me time to shoot down to the Colonial Arms tavern in Paremata for a few beers before heading back home with the boys in the van.

One night I was at the Arms drinking with Tony. He worked near Whenua Tapu cemetery north of Plimmerton, so if there was a girl I was trying to impress then Tony would give me the pick of the discarded flowers. We were just having a yak, enjoying ourselves, when three cops barrelled in and straight over to me. One grabbed my arm and said, 'I know who you are, and what you get up to.'

'Really? Do you? Fuck off, I haven't done anything wrong.'

'I don't think you're old enough to be in here — get outta here unless you've got some evidence of age on you.'

If they knew who I was, they also knew my age. I didn't carry a driving licence, so he ordered me out.

And so it all started again. Police would frequently follow me home, lighting the whole street up with their flashing red lights. One night they pulled me over and insisted on searching my car to check the spare tyre and make sure it had the right tread. I opened the boot, and then the hood, so that an officer could fiddle about underneath. When they buggered off, I flicked on the ignition only to hear the sounds of my car dying. It wouldn't go. They'd swapped the spark plug leads over, but I didn't know what was wrong and had to walk home.

Kāpiti district was quiet, and pretty much crime-less; I was a Big Kahuna in a small pond and the police were surrounding it with a net. Only really bad bastards went to Pare, a cop once explained to me. They spread the word around, too.

One Saturday, Tony, Sandra, a girlfriend Julie and I ended up drinking up at the Paraparaumu Hotel, which was managed by a bloke called Debreceny. Tony wore his gumboots into the lounge bar and Debreceny ordered him out. I told Debreceny to piss off; he assembled a posse of regulars and there was an all-out brawl, which ended in us retreating across the road and fending them off with fence palings.

I didn't fancy drinking at the only other pub in Pram, so I tracked Debreceny down at home and tried to change his mind. He was surprisingly accommodating, and said he would lift the ban as long as Tony promised not to wear gumboots in the lounge bar again. I thought that was reasonable, and apologised, and Debreceny said: 'You know, the cops have painted you out to be an arsehole, Arthur, but you don't seem like that at all. They told me you'd come in the middle of the night and probably burn my house down or shoot me.'

The ill-feeling between the police and me culminated in a fight with a local constable who I remember as being called Murphy, at the police station when he locked Sandra up one Saturday night. Murphy was obviously trying to make a name for himself.

Sandra, Tony and I had left the pub just after 10 p.m. closing when the Ministry of Transport pulled us up in one of their black and white patrol cars. They must have been mounting a drink/drive operation, because we were surrounded by three cars with flashing red roof lights. One got on the PA and said, 'Do not get out of your car, the police are on their way.' I'd had this happen before. There were alerts on their system indicating that if the MOT pulled me over they'd probably need police backup.

I thought I'd have some fun. I got out of my car and started banging on their car boots, and they really went into panic mode. When the police turned up they escorted us to the Ministry of Transport base and put me on the breathalyser. Nothing. I hadn't actually had that much — I've never been a heavy drinker — and it was amusing to see their reactions. I heard them saying, 'What the fuck? He must be on drugs or something.'

Meanwhile, a drunk Sandra started taunting the cops so Murphy arrested her and took her to the police station. After I'd been breath-tested I wandered over. The station consisted of two large houses side by side and a cellblock out the back. The place was locked up, but Sandra was yelling from the cellblock to get her out.

I bashed on the door. Murphy eventually came over and said she wouldn't be released until she'd sobered up, and that if that wasn't soon she would be transported to Porirua and probably held overnight.

I told Murphy I would take her straight home and take responsibility for her — and he just laughed and said he wouldn't trust me to take responsibility for anyone. Things got heated.

'Open that door, Murphy, and get the fuck out here and we'll sort it out.'

Murphy was really wound up. Lo and behold, out he came, taking off his jacket and equipment belt and hanging them over the fence. He started shaping up, and throwing haymaker punches at my head. I deflected.

The young cop who Murphy had left at the station had seen me and him disappearing into the school grounds and became worried. He radioed Porirua, and when they heard that one of their men had disappeared into the dark with me they called the Armed Offenders Squad. I don't know exactly what Murphy told his bosses when he got back to the station, but it wasn't enough to stand the AOS down. They got the idea in their heads that I was going to break Sandra out, and arrived about 45 minutes later wanting blood. I climbed onto the roof of the railway station and watched as the convoy arrived.

They'd brought a dog unit and began carefully searching the whole area. State Highway 1 was blocked and cars were being searched. I thought I'd put them out of their misery, so jumped down, crossed the railway lines and found a phone box by a dairy. I phoned the police and asked to speak to someone about the AOS emergency.

They seemed pretty surprised to get a call from me. I said: 'I'll come in if you let Sandra go.' They didn't want to spend all of Saturday night on this and they'd had heaps of complaints from the public, so a deal was proffered. They said, 'We can't just let her go. We'll have to arrest you for something.'

If you look through my record, you'll find the conviction: 'Otaki: Speaks threateningly.'

CHAPTER FIVE

THE LAW

I find I'm so excited that I can barely sit still or hold
a thought in my head. I think it's the excitement
only a free man can feel, a free man at the start of a
long journey whose conclusion is uncertain ...
Red, character in The Shawshank Redemption, *1994*

LOWER NORTH ISLAND, 1978

Later that year, I was passing through Palmerston North on my way
to the races in Feilding, with a robbery kit in the back seat: a duffel
bag holding a pistol and a balaclava. An off-duty cop saw me going
by and recognised me, but he didn't have a radio in his car so he
shot back to the station and checked out the vehicle. An alert went
out to all Palmerston North units: be on the lookout for this stolen
Vauxhall being driven by Arthur William Taylor.

The car was parked outside one of the fast-food joints just
outside the TAB when the cops swooped.

I jumped out. 'What's the problem?' I was thinking 'This is
going to end up in court one day — I better fucking make it look like
I know nothing about what's going on.'

Sure enough, six months later I found myself sitting across
from prosecutor David Ongley at the Palmerston North High Court
as he held up some lengths of coloured wires to a police sergeant
sitting in the witness box, while twelve jury members looked on.

'What are those wires for, Sergeant?'

After the police had found some wires in my bag and presumed
they were for stealing cars, I'd been charged with possession of
instruments to use for car conversion. At the trial an idiot cop
gave evidence to this effect. He had no formal qualifications or
expertise; his parents just used to own a garage and that was his
expert witness qualification, apart from being a cop. He told the
jury that the wires could be used for stealing cars by running them

between the ignition and the coil.

When we got a spare minute, my lawyer turned to me, a look of concern on his face. 'What are we going to do here, Arthur?'

The answer was obvious.

'Look, the fucking wire is bare — if you hook that to the coil, and that to the battery, the fucking thing would short out. Lies, see?'

When it was time to cross-examine this rookie cop, he stood up tall and said, 'You can't use that for car conversion, can you, Sergeant? I'll put it to you that it's a bare wire, it's not insulated. If you put that on the coil, it'll short out.'

My lawyer was very sceptical that we could defend the case successfully, but I said, 'Here's how we're going to do it.'

Number one: I've got a witness to say I was picked up in that car and that we were on our way to the Feilding races. Number two: I didn't know it was stolen, and I didn't know what he had in his duffel bag in the back seat. I knew nothing about it. Number three: he was driving. We'd stopped for some fast food and, obviously, when he saw the cops he wasn't going to come back. He'd fucking done a runner!

The cops were spewing as I gave evidence.

'How come we haven't heard this story before, Mr Taylor?' Ongley asked.

I'd anticipated this. 'You have heard it before. Two detectives came down to the cell block to see me, and I told them exactly what I'm telling you now.'

Not too long before this, I'd read an article about Arthur Allan Thomas in the *Listener*. News that police had planted evidence against him was big at the time, and I produced that story as an exhibit to the jury during my defence. Arthur had said something like 'If I'd only shown the police the door the day they came around to see me, I wouldn't have done a day in jail.'

'I'm taking it as advice,' I told the jury. 'The man is innocent, and *I'm* fucking innocent.'

To the cops' horror, I was acquitted. They couldn't believe it. They saw it as a personal insult.

It was the first major case where I'd essentially told my lawyer what to do, and was a good grounding in successfully arguing a case and establishing reasonable doubt.

Was my story true? Was there another passenger in the car? Let's put it this way. I was acquitted. I was found not guilty.

When I inevitably found myself back in court for another offence, I defended myself.

Ōtaki and South Island, 1980

I'd met Ivan Sic at Mount Crawford. He was serving time for drug offences, burglaries and robberies; when he escaped, one of the first people he contacted on the outside was me. We were both in our early twenties and I'd enjoyed Ivan's company in prison, but I certainly wasn't ready to take on a caretaker role while he was at large. I bedded him in with a female friend of mine, but it wasn't long, maybe a week, before he was whining that he had no money and needed to get some.

Desperate to get him off my back, I agreed to help him carry out a robbery so he could get some money. While on paper this looked like a significant escalation in my offending, to me the truth was much simpler: I wasn't in the business of violence, I just wanted the money. I was in the business of making money.

Ivan had robbed the local rifle club already. I'd worked out that the TAB in Ōtaki, on Wellington's Kāpiti coast, had the best means of making a quick getaway. On the morning of 13 October 1980, a Monday, Ivan and I — both wearing monster masks and blue overalls — strode into the Ōtaki TAB with a gun and walked out a few minutes later with $6700. When we walked in, we were expecting to see a man opening up, but the manager was a woman. Events unfolded quickly, with us threatening her to get her to hand over the keys to the safe. We handcuffed her to a stanchion holding up the bench with cuffs I'd brought back from Australia after one of my trips there.

Two days before we had also robbed Western Park Tavern, on Wellington's Tinakori Road, because Ivan wanted to recover some wages owed to his sister. I'd gone into the storeroom and the manager had sprung me. I had a gun.

It was a while before the police caught up to us. We broke into an Ōtaki beach house and hid out there for a period, then made it down to the South Island. While I was breaking into some houses at Picton and Lake Rotoiti, either to get supplies or as somewhere to hide, police started hounding my family. The handcuffs had helped identify me. Not being able to recognise them, police put a picture of the cuffs in the paper and Customs got in touch with them — they'd questioned me about them when I'd returned to New Zealand. Mum worked at the New World supermarket and the police would follow her up and down the aisles, demanding to know where I was. This set up a relationship between my parents and the police that was equally as combative as mine. As the year unspooled, they'd be subjected to numerous early-morning raids, with police tipping the house upside down, but rather than blaming me — I don't recall them ever telling me to cut it out — they blamed the police for having such a hard attitude towards me. They blamed the state for taking me away from them all those years ago, and for installing me in Epuni, where I'd learned to fight and steal cars.

Ivan and I split up, and I was eventually caught in Greymouth. We were charged with aggravated robbery; I also faced some burglary charges.

Some people accept custody, others run. While I was being held in the Wellington District Court cellblock waiting for my case to be heard, I spent the lunchtime adjournment picking the lock to the cells with a paperclip that I'd carefully twisted this way and that. The door led into the courtroom, paving the way for a quick getaway while everyone was out having a sandwich. I'd been working on it for quite a while, on the off-chance, and sure enough the door popped open. I was quite amazed. I disappeared through the courtroom, then ran onto Lambton Quay and was up the Terrace and into the Botanic Gardens in short order.

This led to much of Wellington being locked down while they searched for me, eventually cornering me at gunpoint near Victoria University. One of the cops pointing a pistol at me was shaking like a leaf while I prayed that he didn't accidentally shoot.

While I was in Mount Crawford waiting for the robbery charges to be heard, I met a well-known bush lawyer, an old Māori fella called Bob Coombridge. We used to call him QC Coombridge. He was a rogue and a fraudster who used his knowledge of the law to rip people off. He knew Arthur Allan Thomas, and had gone out collecting money for him and kept it for himself.

Coombridge was a painter and he drove around with a typewriter in his back seat and a legal book he'd poached from a lawyer called *Police Law in New Zealand*, by John Luxford. Sensing my appetite for justice, one day he gifted me the book. 'This will be more use to you than it will be to me,' he said. He'd made notes about his own cases in the margins of the pages. It was a bloody handy book. I learned the basics of criminal law, like the principles of evidence and the elements of different charges; the ingredients to make a cake. I learned that to prove aggravated robbery it's got to be two or more people together, or there's got to be an offensive weapon involved. Burglary has to involve breaking and entering into a building or enclosed yard with an intent to commit a crime, or it's not burglary.

I devoured *Police Law*, read it day and night for years, until I just about knew it off by heart. Here it was, my Bible.

By the time the TAB matter got to court I'd had two lawyers withdraw. Peter Boshier (who is now the Ombudsman) withdrew after depositions, which was a laborious series of hearings where the Crown and defence discussed their evidence and the judge decided whether there was enough to get to trial; they don't bother with it anymore. Pat Grace withdrew before the trial. I was basically told by the court 'You will have to soldier on, lad' — so I thought 'I will, and you know what? I can do this case better.'

And so, bolstered by my win in Palmerston North, I did my research.

Because I was defending myself, Bully let me have an Imperial 80 typewriter in my cell. The screws had the same type. Even though Bully was a proper arsehole on certain matters, he had a sense of fairness about him. Even when I was in the pound, I had that typewriter. The book, the typewriter and typing paper became my tools.

The woman we'd threatened in the TAB really couldn't identify either Ivan or myself, as we were both wearing masks; all she could guess at were our heights. She only knew that whoever had put the cuffs on her had been very pleasant, and she made a point of saying I'd been very nice to her. I like to remind people of this when they bring up my aggravated robbery offences. Ivan Sic was happy to say that I'd had no part in it.

In New Zealand we have this thing called reasonable doubt. It's a relatively simple concept that I think people forget about, or perhaps don't care to dwell on. If there's reasonable doubt, you should be acquitted, plain and simple. I believe wholeheartedly in reasonable doubt. I know that most people think it doesn't matter, but we have to look at a higher value: the protection of the law. The law says that there should be evidence beyond reasonable doubt; and as that simply hasn't happened in some of the more contentious cases, it's dangerous for others. I like to trot out that old saying that 100 guilty men should go free lest one innocent man be convicted.

Take Scott Watson, for example. Scott is serving life for the murders of Olivia Hope and Ben Smart, who disappeared in the Marlborough Sounds on New Year's Eve 1999. Their bodies were never found and it's been widely speculated that police have the wrong man. I used to think Scott was innocent, and then one day in Pare's B block he came around and was yakking away. I sort of ribbed him and said, 'Scott, if someone was to incapacitate two young people, how would I fucken do it?' He replied, 'Rollies, Arthur, rollies.' Which means Rohypnol. The way he said it, I thought, 'You've fucken done this before.' Regardless, I don't think he should have been convicted on the evidence that was presented at trial.

Another contentious case was Mark Lundy, convicted of the murders of his wife and daughter, who were bludgeoned to death in their Palmerston North home; I never met him but I think he is as guilty as fuck. I'm pissed off with him because he undermines the case of genuinely innocent people.

In the case of the TAB robbery, I tried to show the jury that there was reasonable doubt. Nobody could put me in that building.

The twelve jurors weren't convinced. Ivan and I were both found guilty, and on 24 July 1981, at the High Court at Wellington, I was sentenced by Justice O'Regan to four years and six months in jail, my longest term yet. I represented myself at sentencing. A month earlier we'd been sentenced for the Tinakori Road burglary. During that hearing Justice O'Regan commented that it appeared I'd decided to make burglary, robbery and theft my career.

When I returned to Pare that year, Jack Hobson was still the superintendent and again I was sent straight to D block, where I bristled about the verdicts. I was bored, annoyed and angry, and feeling powerless. In late 1981, still in D block, I set two mattresses in my cell on fire.

I regretted it the second the flames leaped up at me and I inhaled the toxic fumes that started to permeate my tiny cell. This was a bad idea. The sprinklers weren't working. Realising that I was running out of oxygen, I crawled to the toilet, where I thrust a tube (I had it in my cell to pass things to my neighbours) right down into the bowl to suck on the air below. There was no water in the toilets (many years later, I'd start hiding phones down them). My nose was clogged with black soot and I was starting to become unconscious when the screws burst in to rescue me.

They assumed I was suicidal, and under section 42 of the Mental Health Act 1969 I got carted off to the Oakley Hospital in Point Chevalier, also known as the Whau Lunatic Asylum among many other names. It was 2 December 1981. The hospital was an imposing brick building set on vast grounds and housed several hundred patients, down from a peak of 1200 in the 1970s. The site had housed a mental health facility of some kind since 1867, and its buildings as they stood then were built during World War 2. Until 1960 it was the called the Auckland Mental Hospital. It had been under the microscope by way of official inquiries dozens of times in the intervening decade as a result of failings in its care of patients, and its ongoing inability to improve.

On my arrival I was welcomed by the medical superintendent, Dr Pat Savage, who immediately realised I wasn't insane.

'You just need a rest from prison,' he said.

Like my time at Porirua Hospital during the Epuni period, the patients at Oakley had their own distinct shuffle. I was held in a high-security ward called M3, where I met a fellow resident, a delusional Pommy called Keith, who'd killed his wife.

Keith managed to convince me that his family would get him out of the country and back to his homeland if he was able to get out, and reckoned they'd pay my way out of the country too. While I wasn't sure about leaving my family, I *was* keen to get out of the place.

My parents had moved north from the Manawatū to Tuakau,

a small settlement in the rural Franklin district on the fringes of south Auckland. They'd moved for work and to give my younger siblings better schooling, with a bonus that they were closer to me in Paremoremo and could visit more often, particularly Mum, who came regularly. As much as she could. I thought it would be fairly easy to get to them, so Keith and I made plans to leave.

More than two months into my stay, on the afternoon of 28 February 1982, Keith and I picked the lock to the building, broke out and threw plaited white sheets up over the barbed wire. Time was of the essence. I started climbing first. Once I'd clambered to the top it was Keith's turn, but the poor bastard — six foot four and heavy with it — wasn't fit enough. I was desperately trying to pull him up but it wasn't working. He recognised this, and quite valiantly — though I saw the deflated look in his eyes when he realised he wasn't going to make it over — said, 'Just go. Leave me.'

I felt bad, but I had to go. I ran to the nearest shopping centre where I found a timber yard not too far away. I hid there until I was able to get to a payphone and call a mate to pick me up. We travelled south, to a local campground near Tuakau — Ramarama Motor Camp — where, much like my time at Goose Bay, I holed up in a stolen caravan that I'd taken from Pauanui, a nearby resort town in the Waikato. This caravan was much nicer, a double tandem with an awning. I visited my parents frequently, which ended up having consequences for them.

I managed to evade the authorities for months, but one night in May, after I'd visited my parents, police followed me back to the campground and then barged in. I managed to confuse them for a few minutes when I produced a passport in another name, one from my graveside-name-pillaging days. They couldn't believe it; they said, 'You're definitely Arthur Taylor.' They kept looking at the photos they had of me on file, comparing them with my face, then looking at the passport, taken aback. They soon recovered, though; by this time they were used to my exploits.

I was arrested and charged with escaping from a penal

institution 'in which [I] was lawfully detained' (the wording of this really matters), and taken back to Oakley as required by law (I remained there for another few months before being returned to Pare). They also charged my father for aiding and abetting me after they discovered he'd given me money during my time out.

B y this time the asylum was heading for yet another inquiry after the death of Michael Percy Watene, a 25-year-old Māori patient, during electroconvulsive shock therapy back in February. Just a few days before he was taken to Oakley he'd been sentenced to a week's imprisonment in the district court at Whangārei for disorderly behaviour. On Valentine's Day he barricaded himself in his Mount Eden cell, and was deemed 'sullen', 'morose' and 'uncommunicative'. Jailers claimed to have found a knife on him, which Watene said was for protection.

The following day he was taken to Oakley where a doctor noted his uncommunicative nature and wrote that he seemed dangerous, suicidal and impulsive. The doctor prescribed several options for medication, including paraldehyde, the same drug administered to me many years before at Porirua Hospital. It was used to treat patients with anxiety or convulsive disorders.

When Watene shuffled into the secure ward M3 he was accompanied by half a dozen prison officers and he was handcuffed. After hearing from the screws about their 'considerable' difficulties with Watene, the psychiatric nurse in charge of the ward put him in Strongroom 7, an isolation room where nothing but a mattress and a pot greeted him. He was locked in.

The following day other staff members, including one fluent in te reo, attempted to speak to Watene, who either didn't respond or simply asked for a cigarette. Ongoing patient notes recorded that Watene, while saying little to nothing, could be unpredictable and should be watched. One thought it looked like he was listening to voices.

On 17 February, the day that Watene's prison sentence should have expired, he refused a meal in his room, and appeared to recoil from staff members if they came too close. Medication wouldn't work, staff decided. Electroconvulsive therapy might, and would be administered with urgency at 2 p.m. Watene was not told. Although staff planned to transfer Watene to Strongroom 5, which had better light and a mattress on the floor, he was so agitated that this was not possible, and the treatment was administered in Strongroom 7. Normally an anaesthetic and a muscle relaxant were injected into a patient before ECT, but the doctor present decided that this also was not possible. Watene was forcibly restrained — there were eight or nine nurses present — and the ECT was administered. Watene was then given paraldehyde and left locked in his room. Further medications, including more paraldehyde, were administered that evening.

Over the next few days, Watene was given multiple sessions of ECT, initially without anaesthetic or muscle relaxant but later with these, and was sedated heavily with haloperidol. He continued to view staff with suspicion. By 21 February he was considered to be improving, though his two-hourly medications were continued. The following morning, further ECT was administered from which he appeared to recover quickly, but he was found unresponsive half an hour later, and could not be resuscitated.

The coroner concluded that Michael Watene hadn't been properly observed during his treatment, that the ECT procedures undertaken were alarmingly deficient, and that there was insufficient medical monitoring of the haloperidol, the effects of which accumulate over time. There was an outcry, followed by the inquiry. By then, Māori were already disproportionally overfilling our prisons.

During the Oakley inquiry, the investigating committee strode through the halls of the building, including its ECT chamber, visited Lake Alice Hospital to enable a comparison, and also visited Mount Eden and Paremoremo prisons. Oakley, the inquiry report said, had been expected to take challenging patients that other hospitals considered disruptive or unsuitable. Watene's death, and a subsequent action brought by me, gave pause to the justice department who were blindly institutionalising people in asylums so that they didn't have to deal with them — like in my own case.

I defended the charge of escaping from a penal institution on the basis that at Oakley I wasn't in lawful custody of the kind covered by the Crimes Act 1961. When Judge Augusta Wallace found me guilty in the District Court, I appealed to the High Court at Auckland. Justice Jeffries overturned my conviction on the grounds that the hospital wasn't a penal institution, but replaced the conviction with one of escaping from lawful custody — with the same cumulative (on top) sentence. I took that to the Court of Appeal in 1984, which resulted in my first victory in what was then New Zealand's highest court bar the Privy Council.

In overturning both my conviction and my sentence, Justice McMullin said that my submissions had raised questions of public importance.

I'd like to take a minute to explain this. Under the law, patients who had been committed to a psychiatric institution were allowed to take leaves of absence and could be recalled from such leave. Where they were absent without leave, they could be 'taken and returned', but if they had been absent without leave for longer than three months they were deemed to be discharged. There was no provision under the law that made it an offence for a committed person to escape from a psychiatric hospital. Justice McMullin didn't perceive this to be an oversight — remarking that in the spirit of the legislation it did not make sense to prosecute a person for escaping from a psychiatric hospital.

Aged 26, I'd argued the case myself, all the way through. Word reached me that several of my old police foes were far from happy that I was acquitted 'on a technicality' (their words, not mine) and were planning to make sure that my freedom was short-lived. As for my dad, he got his charge thrown out as well, following my acquittal.

A world away, events were unfolding that would become an inspiration for me. On 5 May 1981, Bobby Gerard Sands, an IRA bomber, had died in prison on hunger strike while protesting the removal of a special status that gave him particular rights in prison.

I'd begun serving my sentence (at Pare) for the TAB robbery about a month after he died. Then a witness came forward saying that she'd seen the robbers taking off out of the Ōtaki TAB and reckoned that I wasn't one of them. I thought this was a good avenue for getting a new trial. Reasonable doubt, eh? But the courts wouldn't give me a hearing. The fight dragged on for over a year. I petitioned the Governor-General, Sir David Beattie, for deferral of my sentence and conviction back to the Court of Appeal, and even smuggled a letter out of jail to Prime Minister Robert Muldoon.

When that didn't work, I tried another tactic. The law required that I had to be 'legally represented' before I could be jailed and, obviously, I'd had to rely on my own legal representation. Technically I shouldn't have been in custody because under the Criminal Justice Act in force at the time, the court couldn't sentence someone who wasn't legally represented to anything other than periodic detention. And yet I was in jail.

On 3 November 1982 I wrote to *New Zealand Truth* reporter Don Farmer and sent him my original arrest warrant. 'Please have this warrant examined by a solicitor, he will tell you it is wholly invalid,' I wrote.

But nobody listened. My complaints fell on deaf ears.

I remembered Bobby Sands: how he'd stopped eating for 66 days. My own hunger strike started on 13 December 1982.

The first days were the worst. Dessert was paraded into my cell to try to tempt me. Every meal time a tray was placed right by my head, which I ignored as the food sat there going cold. It was coming up to Christmas, too, when they trotted out the best meals, like steak. I didn't touch any of it. After about four days I'd sleep most of the day; drifting in and out of consciousness, which numbed the pain. My body felt like it was feeding on itself.

Jack Hobson was nice enough, but he told the *Auckland Star* he couldn't understand what all the fuss was about. He said that regardless of whether I was serving time for the TAB robbery, I was serving a sentence for other burglaries and so I'd be locked up until 1984 anyway. To me, that wasn't the point.

A few days before Christmas, a psychiatrist evaluated me and concluded that I was hydrated and articulate, so they weren't worried. Hobson publicly speculated that prisoners were passing me food through my cell doors at night (they weren't). On Christmas Day they put me in the prison hospital, and I thought 'Fuck, I'll probably end up dying here', as I was taking nothing but water. I knew that Bobby Sands had died after 66 days without food.

Mum and Dad visited. They were very worried, and knew that I was headstrong enough to see it through. Margaret Shields, who was our local MP in the Kāpiti electorate, offered to fly up to Pare to sort it out.

Eventually the Court of Appeal agreed to hear my appeal, and I hired John Haigh (who later became a QC), who agreed to work pro bono. The court ended up dismissing the appeal — but at least it was going through the process, so I didn't quibble about that. At least I got a hearing.

Having secured my hearing I started eating again soon after Christmas. I stayed in the hospital for another two weeks, though, because I wasn't in a fit state to leave. I was fed Complan until I got my strength back. In Pare they didn't have baths, just showers; I had to sit down in the shower because I was so weak. My first glorious mouthful was jelly and custard. I'd only have a couple of spoonfuls before it would come back up.

One other good thing came out of this. There never used to be portable stereos in the prison, but I knew there was one in storage. When I was in hospital, Jack Hobson said, 'What do you want, Taylor?'

I said, 'I wouldn't mind having something to listen to.'

When I left the hospital and went back to D block I took the stereo with me, and nobody said a word. It became a *fait accompli*, shall we say.

To get my strength back up, I started working out and training harder than ever in D block, getting fit mentally and physically. Having experienced what felt like targeted profiling from the police every time I was released, I knew that once I was released this next time every cop and his dog would have their ear to the ground looking for me.

In particular, I'd had a message from prominent detective John Rex 'The Gardener' Hughes, an ex-navy boxer who regularly ran marathons. Everyone called him 'The Gardener' because he was known for allegedly planting stuff. Hughes told me that I would be met at the gate and escorted straight through Auckland, as he wasn't having me on his patch.

My first run-in with him had been years before, when he had me handcuffed to a chair in an office on the sixth floor of Auckland Central police station and questioned by other cops trying to get a confession to a jewellery robbery. Every now and again the door to the office would fly open and he would rush in and hit me over the head with a telephone book, leaving the room just as quickly without saying a word. Later he led the double murder case against David Tamihere.

Hughes was of some use to me in the late '80s when I managed to obtain his police computer QID (query identification) number. He had been interviewing me, and when he left the room I saw the number on a document he'd had in front of him and memorised it. In those days, police accessed information by calling a special number to get through to an operator in the police control room. So long as they gave their name and the correct QID, the operator would access the computer and tell them whatever they wanted to know. I would phone up the control room operator and give John Hughes's name and QID. If I wanted to know whether the cops were looking for me, or interested in anything concerning me, I'd call through and say 'JR Hughes QID JH 1079, I need a QP [query person] on PRN 183643' — my Personal Record Number with the police — 'Interest W.' W stood for wanted. They would come back and say something like 'Arthur William Taylor flagged for assaults police, escapes custody, firearms user, not currently wanted. Need anything else on him, John?'

I could find out whether they were investigating me because every computer sub-system held the file number of every open police file, along with a brief summary of what it was about and the name of the cop who was responsible for it or was holding the paper file. There were many times when this saved me from arrest. It was also very handy if I needed to locate someone. I'd say 'QVR [Query Vehicle Registration] on [whatever the rego number was].' Back would come full details on that vehicle, including the address of the registered owner — even if it was in the registration agency's confidential vehicle register.

When personalised plates came out, I bought QVR ME and still own it. It's a sure-fire way to make sure your vehicle is less likely to be stolen, because it's like a red flag to a bull for every cop you pass.

I had one more run-in with authority before I left Pare in October 1984, albeit of an unlikely sort. With a strict training schedule and my mind fixed on getting released, I wasn't happy to one day be summoned by Jack Hobson to his office. He got straight to the point.

'Taylor, I need your help. We've got an old bloke in the prison hospital who was received at Mount Eden on remand about a week ago and began a hunger strike four days ago.'

They were really worried because he'd been refusing all liquids and had been transferred to the hospital. (Pare Max was then, and is now, the only prison in New Zealand that has its own fully equipped hospital, with X-ray facilities and surgeons even coming in to do routine operations.) 'Can you go and see him and talk some sense into him? We don't want him dying on us.'

I asked for assurances that he wasn't some real bad bastard, like a paedophile, and Hobson replied that he'd never had so much as a parking ticket — until one day he got pulled over by a traffic officer and given a ticket for speeding. He'd considered it an injustice, and had stewed over it for ten years before stabbing Helensville local politician Dail Jones in his electoral office, in June 1980. Jones survived. The old bloke had later gone to court in Whangārei, and had thrown petrol at the judge.

'He's from Tindall's Beach just north of here and his family are very well respected in the district. His name is Ambrose Tindall.'

Prepared to go to the edge to stand up for what he believed in; I liked the sound of this guy, so I said I'd do what I could. Apparently when he'd first arrived at Pare he'd asked if he could see me as he'd heard about me getting my Oakley escape conviction chucked out. (It's almost impossible to beat an escape charge — you've either escaped, or you haven't.)

Screws escorted me to the hospital wing at Pare where I'd been during my own hunger strike. Sound asleep in bed was this frail old-timer, looking like he was at death's door. I asked the screws to leave, sat on his bed and started talking to him. After a while his eyes opened and fixed unblinkingly on me. He tried to talk, but could only croak.

I went first. 'Look, old mate, I'm Arthur Taylor. I will help you if I can, but first I need you to be able to tell me what the story is. Please, at least sip some water so you can talk.'

After a while he nodded, so I asked the nurses to get some iced water, and put it in a plastic beaker that I held to his lips while he slowly sipped. After half an hour — and more than half a litre of water — I could see the life flowing back into him and he became quite animated.

I listened carefully to him.

'Right, first thing is we've got to get you out of here — you can't fight your battles from prison.'

Up to this point he had steadfastly refused to have anything to do with lawyers, as all his encounters with them had been bad. Consequently, he hadn't applied for bail. I broke off my training schedule, and Jack arranged things so that I could spend as much time as possible with Ambrose in the hospital. After a day I had him taking food, and his eyes began to sparkle. The nurses were quite surprised when they heard us cracking up with laughter after they'd given him up for dead.

I took my Imperial 80 down to the hospital and typed up an application for bail along with an extensive memorandum detailing supporting reasons. Jack had it delivered to the Whangārei Court. Ambrose was granted bail on the condition that he go home and reside with his wife, and not travel within 10 kilometres of the judge or any courthouse, unless appearing on the charges he was facing. Ambrose's family picked him up and took him home.

Ambrose was a stubborn old bugger, but the salt of the earth. A few days later I was thrilled to receive a beautiful card from him and his wife, thanking me for my help. When I was released a couple of weeks later, he called me to say thanks, that he had been able to put it well behind him and get on with normal life — much to the relief of everyone, not least his family who had been hellish worried about him.

I've seen a lot of people get twisted on a certain bend and it becomes an obsession; their total focus in life to the exclusion of everything else. I don't want to see people dying — I don't care who they are. If you were drowning out there, I'd jump in the harbour and save you while other pricks would be standing around saying 'What do we do? Where's the life-raft?'

I took The Gardener's advice. My parents had moved from Tuakau to remote Ohinewai, just north of Huntly, so when I left Pare in 1984 I went straight down the line to bunk with them. Dad got me a job at Te Kauwhata research station helping to maintain the national grape collection. They held a sample of every variety of grape grown in New Zealand, and also a lab where they experimented making different wines.

However, life became a kaleidoscope of ducking in and out of prison. I mostly stayed out of trouble aside from the odd burglary. In June 1986 I was charged with receiving stolen office equipment and law books from a Thames solicitor's office.

That year I was also charged with my most violent offence yet. Although I'd been involved in aggravated robberies and carried weapons, I never intended to use them; they were just for show, to get things going. I've never been a fan of knocking someone over, and the furthest I'd ever gone was the odd dust-up with a cop, or with a crim. I've always thought: Outwit with your smarts, not your fists. But on this particular night, I had no choice.

In May I was staying at my girlfriend Tania's parents' place, just up from a nightclub at Paraparaumu Beach. I'd met an already pregnant Tania at a party; she knew my brother John, and I was immediately drawn to her. She was younger than me, about twenty I think (I was approaching 30 by then), with blonde hair, dimples and a great sense of humour. Her family was lovely. Tania and her mum, Ruby, both worked at a local chicken farm, and her dad, Gary, drove a concrete truck. We clicked, I suppose. I liked her spirit, and as the father of her child wasn't in the picture, I decided to step up. I was there when she delivered her daughter, Patricia, at Wellington Hospital several months later, and we moved in together in rural Waikato, at Whitikahu. I raised Patricia like she was mine. Her middle name is the same as my mum's, Shirley.

On this particular night staying at Tania's parents' place in Kāpiti, I was out running when I happened across Wiremu 'Beaney' Webber and his gang. Beaney was about six foot something, and pretty mouthy. His relative Jack Webber was a well-known local drug dealer who disappeared in 1999, presumed drowned. The family lived in an expensive house on Motungārara Island off Kāpiti Island.

I watched as Beaney punched a guy to the gutter in front of his girlfriend. I slowed and stopped to give him grief. While somebody called an ambulance, Beaney got lippy to me, threatening me as he produced a knife. His three henchmen dived into the boot of their car, returning with iron bars.

I thought 'I can't fuck around with this.' Luckily, Beaney was pilled and drunk and I was trained in unarmed combat, so as we began to scuffle I grabbed the knife off him and went *bang, bang, bang, bang* — six times in all. The knife went in and out like I was cutting cake. I'd never stabbed anyone before. It all happened so fast.

Beaney was a very, very lucky boy, because at the very moment he collapsed to the deck, the ambulance came tearing around the corner to pick up his victim. They diverted to Beaney while his bloody idiot mates started banging on the door of the ambulance abusing them and carrying on. They soon abandoned any ideas of attacking me. Beaney got carted straight off to intensive care with wounds to his lungs and bowel.

The cops turned up and there was a hell of a melee; his mates were screaming and yelling, but wouldn't come near me. A policewoman and a constable from Paraparaumu started dispersing the crowd. More police arrived, but only uniform, not CIB. One of them got talking to me and said, 'He deserved exactly what he got — he's a fucking local thug rat here.'

The police said they'd have to take me to the station and get a statement because they'd spoken to some witnesses. They didn't know who I was then. We headed up to the Paraparaumu police station and then they buggered off again, to control the situation, and left me there with just a lone policewoman. Then I heard it over the police radio: 'CIB are en route to Paraparaumu from Porirua.'

I thought 'Oh fuck.' As soon as they arrived they were going to realise who I was, and the pleasantries up until that point were all going to change. So I said, 'See you later love, I'm off.' Gone. Not to be seen for some time. Out of the Paraparaumu police station, over the railway tracks and gone! Tania and I travelled back to the Waikato.

The next thing I knew, there was a warrant out for my arrest.

When they heard I'd been involved, the Armed Offenders Squad followed me to my parents' home, then trailed me all the way back home to Whitikahu. They surrounded the place and called on the loudspeaker for me to surrender. So I did. Tania was there with baby Patricia. The cops were going to tear-gas the place, and I couldn't have that with Tania and the baby there.

September 1986

They took me down to Hamilton, and questioned me. Then they put me on a plane to Wellington. I went up on a downgraded charge of wounding with intent to cause grievous bodily harm. The maximum penalty was up to fourteen years' jail. This was serious.

Initially, the deputy Wellington Crown prosecutor, Ken Stone, was put on my case. I represented myself. By that time I'd learned that most cases are won before you even get into the courtroom, and that preparation is everything. You have to map your defence out, and not believe that bullshit about not asking a question unless you know the answer. I can work out what the potential answers might be, and I frame things in such a way that either way it will benefit me or advance my case.

We were at the depositions stage, and in chambers, when the justice of the peace suggested 'Look, Mr Stone, this case appears to be self-defence. If you offer Mr Taylor a lesser charge like injuring, maybe Mr Taylor will plead guilty.'

And I would have, because I was in custody on remand. But Stone was adamant. 'No, it's a very serious case, your worship. Mr Taylor is a dangerous criminal, we have to bring him to justice.'

One week later — this has got to be the quickest time from committal to depositions to trial in New Zealand's history — I was on trial in the High Court in Wellington. This time I was up against Jim Larsen, who had taken over the prosecution. Larsen was the cream of the cream, who normally did murder trials. A nice bloke, actually, but they brought him in to try to nail me.

My parents sat watching from the public gallery while Larsen said, in front of the jury, 'Now come on, Mr Taylor — one stab wound, maybe, in self-defence, but six?'

I wasn't troubled. 'Listen, Mr Larsen, when you are in a situation like that, and I hope to God you're never in one, you don't stop to think: Is one enough? Is two enough? You want to disable your opponent as soon as possible.'

In my defence I called as a witness the guy who had been bashed to the ground in front of me that night in Paraparaumu. He told them what a thug Beaney was.

Up until that point Beaney Webber had been recuperating on Kāpiti Island, and the Crown had to fly him over by helicopter because it was too rough for sailing. When Beaney turned up in court he spun his bullshit, trying to paint me as the aggressor.

'Listen, Mr Webber,' I said, 'you simply got what you were asking for, didn't you? You're a thug — you've bashed fucking defenceless people.'

Of course he didn't agree with that, no way. When he got off the stand I stood up and gave evidence, and then Larsen started grilling me again about how many times I'd stabbed Beaney. I was ready.

'Look, Mr Larsen, I am going to put it like this: aren't we lucky this happened? Only a few months ago a police officer in Auckland shot and killed a man. The man was pulled up in his car, and the police officer leaned in with a revolver and fired all six rounds into the man because he claimed that he had a gun. That police officer didn't stop to think: Is one enough, is two enough, is three? Similar situation here.'

To the jury I said, 'Look, ladies and gentlemen, you are lucky you didn't run into Beaney that night — he might have killed one of you. This is self-defence, it's as simple as that.'

Standing up in that courtroom, talking to the jury, I felt empowered. For most defendants sitting there, it's meant to be about them but they're just like an ornament on the wall. It invigorates you to be able to speak up for yourself and get your point of view across. I find that I have a good connection with jurors.

I had to be at my sharpest, though, because with just one week since depositions to prepare for trial, and without any copies of statements or anything, I was flying blind. Normally you would have months to prepare.

When the jury went out to deliberate on 1 October, they came back ten hours later with a 'not guilty' verdict. It was one of the first cases Jim Larsen had lost — and he lost to me. Later I heard that Mike Bungay, the renowned criminal lawyer, had been peering through the doors, watching my case. Dad had seen him and thought, 'He's come to watch my son'. Dad said that Mike Bungay thought it was one of the best cases he'd seen.

The last I heard, Beaney was still living on the coast — with Tania's sister in fact. They've had a few kids together. One day, many years later, when I moved back to Paraparaumu, I went looking for Beaney. When I walked down his driveway, his sister came bowling out. 'Arthur, I haven't seen you for years.' She said he wasn't there, but I reckon he was hiding under the table. He thought I'd come looking for him to finish the job. I never did talk to him again.

Despite the not guilty verdict, I wasn't exactly free. There were other charges — they'd found guns on my property when I was arrested, and I'd also been sentenced for the offences relating to the solicitor's office burglary. I'd been held at Mount Crawford while the Beaney trial was unfolding, but was to be sent to Waikeria. I'd heard that the conditions there were so terrible that the year before 50 inmates had barricaded themselves in the yard to protest. It was the last place I wanted to be, having just been acquitted and on a high because of that. I thought 'I need to be out celebrating with Tania', so started hatching a plan.

On 9 October they put me on a prison escort bus to take me from Wellington to Waikeria. That bus limped up the central North Island, turned off at Tūrangi and crawled through the back roads until it came into Waikeria, near Mangakino.

I had people owe me favours from all over the place, and if I wanted something they could usually get it to me. Thus, I'd smuggled a hacksaw out of Mount Crawford. As we plodded up the backcountry on this nice sunny morning, I set to work on the bars on the side of the bus when the screws weren't watching. Remarkable that the screws didn't notice, I know, but I had fans within the Department, too. In the movie *Shawshank Redemption*, old Andy Dufresne used to give the prison officers advice on tax. They'd come looking for legal advice from me, too.

A couple of other guys on the bus were supposed to escape with me, but they dropped their guts. They didn't have it in them to do the jump onto the road, so I hacked away at the bar myself.

I waited until we were going up a hill, and while the bus was struggling I wrenched at the bar and left it just hanging on, then smashed the window out. For a split second, I accidentally locked eyes with the driver in the rear-vision mirror. He looked horrified. Then I commando-rolled out, onto the tarseal.

I was a bit stunned when I hit the road, and picked up a few cuts and bruises. But I was on a roll. Adrenaline kicked in. I ran down the road while the bus slammed on its brakes and started reversing. The back doors burst open and a screw standing on the footplate stretched out his arm, but I out-ran the bus and escaped into the bush. They weren't going to follow me in there, because, you know, I could pick up anything in the bush, like a weapon, or something to make a weapon. So they called in the police from Te Awamutu. An hour or so later, the bus pulled into Waikeria Prison with the window smashed out.

While I was making my way along the Waikato River, the police called in dogs from Hamilton and blocked the roads. The blades of a chopper thwacked overhead. I stayed low, occasionally trekking up cliffs to try to break my trail for the dogs. After staying out of sight until dark, I then wandered into the town of Whakamaru and stole a quad bike. I roared off down the road at high speed to the dam, threw the bike into the dam waters, and then made a collect call from a callbox and arranged to get picked up to reunite with Tania. The two of us went and stayed with a mate of mine, Ron, up in Whangārei, for twelve days.

When Tania and I returned to Auckland, we were having tea in the old Farmers building near the children's play area when someone recognised me. Next thing, a whole posse of cops came out of the lift heading in our direction. I picked up my knife, stood up and said, 'Back off. I'll surrender, but this young lady here — she's got nothing to do with this, you let her go.'

They didn't want a disturbance with all these kids running around, so they backed off. I chucked the car keys to Tania, gave her some money and off she went. I got taken to Auckland Central and was charged with escape.

They took me to Mount Eden Prison, one of New Zealand's oldest and grimmest, where I met Chris Campbell who was running the Ruatoria Rastafarians. He'd been sent up after kidnapping a police officer. In what was called the basement, next to the former hanging scaffold, we exercised and yakked. We were the only two down there in that dingy, grim place. Then appeared old Brownie, one of the screws from the bus. I knew why he was there. The tradition was that if someone escaped from a screw, the screw could bash them when they got them; but Brownie backed down.

On 30 October I was jailed for a year. Judge A.B. Lawson said, 'A deterrent sentence is called for, not only in respect of yourself, but in respect of discipline in the prisons.' They sent me back to Pare; Tania and I broke up.

CHAPTER SIX

ON THE
RUN

9 March 1988

Dark had descended on Taranaki, and all that could be heard for several hours between Stratford and Eltham was the deep pant of a slow chase that was turning into a marathon. Limping behind was Constable Terry Johnson; Tireless Terry, he came to be known as. In front, a would-be car thief: me.

'Come on, just give up, it's only burglary,' Terry would occasionally yell, his breath turning to cloud in the cold night.

'Just fuck off home to your family, Terry. It's only a job. What are you chasing me this hard for?'

I had been back living with my parents in the Waikato, working in the motor parts business, and a customer wanted parts for a Rolls Royce. I thought, 'Where the fuck am I going to get parts for a Rolls Royce?' Then I found this garage in Stratford, with the exact model I wanted. It was right next door to the Stratford police station.

I was dismantling the parts off the car late at night when Constable Terry Johnson came in the fucking door. The guy I'd got keeping watch had failed spectacularly; a security guard had called Terry.

He said, 'Stop, you're under arrest for burglary.'

I thought 'I'm not under arrest for nothing' and was out the back door, with Terry hot on my heels.

The chase went on for 30 kilometres, deep into the night. Occasionally we'd stop and rest, or cruise along slowly, sometimes falling down holes. I'd say 'Watch out, Terry' as I ran into a fucking electric fence.

'Just give up, mate, I'll give you a good word in court.'

'Mate, I don't give up, Terry. I don't give up for nothing.'

We knew each other quite well by the end. The finish line neared as we passed a farmhouse and Terry crashed his baton against the house, yelling, 'Terry Johnson, police — call the police.' His cry must have reverberated throughout Taranaki. By sheer chance Terry had checked out a burglary at that house a few days before, and they knew who he was. When they heard 'Terry Johnson' they knew it was legit, so they called the police. We thundered on.

Of course all the cops who were whistling throughout Taranaki now knew what was going on, and as we continued to run through farmland, the next thing I heard was this *swoosh swoosh swoosh* — the sound of police cars travelling through grass without their lights on.

I came running into a whole line of them, with dogs.

I was bailed back to my parents' house at Ohinewai to await trial for the burglary. A few months later, on a Monday afternoon, a passing tanker driver began rapping on Terry Johnson's front door.

'The courthouse is on fire!'

Terry raced out to the Stratford Court House. He quickly saw smoke and flames licking outside the windows of the 1903 building. Inside, stacks of documents were burning. The night before defended hearings, staff put all the police files on the desks ready for the next day.

I turned up the next morning, 14 June, for my case. The main street of Stratford was still smoking. There was fire-brigade tape everywhere, and grey plumes of smoke coming out of the courthouse windows. A charcoal mess.

I wandered over to the police station. 'What's going on here?'

They'd drafted other cops in from out of town, and these two didn't know me. They said, 'Our courthouse burned down last night.'

'Fuck, I hope you catch whoever did it! Shit, mate — I've got a case going on here today. I suppose it won't go ahead now.'

'Oh no, it's going ahead — they've brought in a special judge. It looks like there's been an attack on the administration of justice and they won't allow it. All cases are now going to be heard in the borough chambers.'

I bowled up to the council building, and Tireless Terry was there with Detective Inspector Ross Pinkham, who headed Taranaki's Criminal Investigation Branch.

'What's going on, Terry?'

'Some bastard burned our courthouse down last night.'

There had been a headline in the paper saying 'Tireless Terry always gets his man', so I thought 'Right.'

'Terry, you didn't happen to be on duty last night did you?'

'Yes I was.'

'Well, how come you haven't arrested whoever did it?'

Pinkham: 'We know it was you, Taylor.'

I had an alibi — I'd been in Huntly — but they didn't believe me. I returned to the council chambers, after the lunch-time adjournment, at 2.15 p.m. The judge entered, almost relishing the moment.

The sergeant told the court: 'There's been an attack on the administration of justice.' He was looking at me. 'We're now proceeding with a very important case.'

I said, 'Excuse me, your honour, I have a procedural matter to raise. It's most unfortunate that the courthouse got burned down, but my understanding is the court documents went up in flames.'

Blank faces looked back at me.

'I don't want to be too technical, but there's a section in the Summary Proceedings Act 1957 that requires the court to have the original sworn information on a charge before it has jurisdiction to hear the case. If they've all been burned, where is the original information?'

The judge said that the prosecution and police had agreed that copies would be fine.

'Well, I don't agree, your honour. There's no way in the world. I don't trust the police — they might have made some alterations. I need to see the original. My submission is that there is no power to continue.'

The sergeant wouldn't have had a clue what was going on. The judge retired to consider this; he probably looked up his law books and rang another couple of judges, and they would have said 'Well, Taylor's right — you can't proceed.' And fifteen minutes later the judge granted my submission.

It was a strange technicality. I hadn't had the charge dismissed, and the court hadn't adjudicated in any way on the charge — so they could have laid a fresh new one. I was expecting them to arrest me again, but they weren't quick enough. I disappeared.

Nobody has ever been convicted of lighting that fire. Later, Tireless Terry told reporters that a defendant wanting to get out of their case burned it to the ground. It's anyone's guess who he's referring to.

Once they cottoned on, the police launched an operation to find me. The cops were pissed off because a couple of their wives used to work at the courthouse, and cases had to be heard in Hawera after that. I knew they were going to catch up with me eventually and lay fresh charges, but it didn't suit me to be in custody at that time. I had a new girlfriend, Anne-Marie, a petite woman with dark, curly hair. Her family owned a local motors company and she barely worked, but I'd taken a liking to her. A friend I'd met in Mount Crawford, Mark Hall, had introduced us.

I thought a change of scenery would do us some good. At the top of the North Island, Northland's Dargaville Holiday Park was a good place to hide out of sight. I was cashed up at this point, so, calling myself Paul Colin Richardson, I bought the motor camp and started running it with Anne-Marie. I told the locals I'd been opal mining in Australia and I'd returned to New Zealand to take it easy.

Bloody great lifestyle, that was. The proprietor's house was attached to the end of the camp, along with the office, and it was running well. I really enjoyed it. Nobody knew who I was. I was on a first-name basis with the mayor, Peter Brown, Lois Newby from the local tourism board, and the local cop. I was looked up to in the town, consulted by the tourism promotion council; even made honorary ranger for the Selwyn Park reserve next door. The night we took over, Lois Newby came over with a cake.

At Dargaville I was on the right side of the law. The police faxed through the names and faces of undesirables in the area, and I promised to keep an eye out for them. The local constable came and talked to me often, warning me 'Be on the lookout for these thugs — don't let them stay at the camp, Mr Richardson, they're trouble-makers.'

The whole thing lasted a few months. *Crimewatch* got me in the end. I'd learned that I was going to feature on an episode about that Tireless Terry carry-on, and thought 'I can't let the people in this town see this.' I had a plan to knock out the power cables at Tokatoka just before it aired, but I couldn't pinpoint when that would be. One night, I was in the office when my face flashed up on the TV. I raced straight out into the camp to see who was watching TV in their caravans, but everything seemed okay.

The next morning, two cops wandered over to the camp. I watched through the blinds of the office door while Anne-Marie went out to talk to them.

'Mrs Richardson, you're not going to believe this, but we've had several calls from people saying that Paul looks a lot like a guy that was on *Crimewatch* last night. Whangārei has insisted we speak to him.'

She told them I was in Whangārei on business and they were quite happy about that, but then one of them said, 'Well, how about we just take a photo and send it over to Whangārei? Then they'll be happy. Have you got some photos of Paul?'

I watched this cop's face change when she said that she didn't have a photo, because what kind of wife doesn't have a photo of her partner? I was thinking, 'Fuck, this is it.'

I jumped out the back window and headed towards Dargaville Hospital, where I hid out in a little shed. Within about three hours the Armed Offenders Squad was cruising the roads of small-town

Dargaville. As usual, my mind started racing, and the town became a Venn diagram as I thought hard about how I'd slope out without being noticed. That's when a lightbulb went off — they were building a new bridge into Dargaville but so far the police had only installed road blocks, to check drivers going in and out, on the old bridge.

Crossing the unfinished bridge over the Wairoa River was quite hairy, but I managed it. Mark Hall came and picked me up once I was past the road blocks and we high-tailed it down to the Waikato. I figured I'd go to my sister Joanne's in Paeroa, but I wanted to call in and see my parents in Ohinewai first. Unfortunately, the cops were watching their house. They put a trail on me, and within an hour of arriving at Joanne's these flood-lights came shining over the house and they were yelling at me to come out. Tear-gas shells flew in. A few kilometres away, police had taken over the Ngātea rugby headquarters as a place to plot. The whole of Ngātea was sealed off.

The tear-gas was awful, acrid stuff. I retreated into a room and sealed it off with wet towels. My plan was to get into the car in the garage and plough through all of them. I asked Mark to go and check out the garage, but the police spotted him trying to leave. They were yelling 'Come out!' and I was yelling 'Come back here!' He didn't know where the fuck to go. Joanne left the house.

When I finally decided I'd had enough, I thought 'Let's get this out of the way.' I came out, and they rushed me and handcuffed me. I was arrested and sent back to Taranaki to face the case that had brought me there, the Tireless Terry charges.

I was sentenced to three years in jail. While I was in custody, Anne-Marie continued running the motor camp and then I had to get my mother and sister to run it for me. I owned that camp for years, before selling it back to the Kaipara District Council to end their embarrassment at having a criminal running one of their biggest tourism ventures.

I was released in 1991. Anne-Marie and I decided to get out of Wellington and head for the big smoke — Auckland. I'd always liked Auckland, it was bustling, and I was quite keen on buying a house. That June we bought in Te Atatū South. Number 17A Paton Ave was a two-storey weatherboard home set over a double garage with a generous lawn. It was my first home. It cost us $78,000 with a $38,000 mortgage. Although I'd made some money off my crimes then, the majority of the deposit had come from actual toil. People used to tell me it was the safest street in West Auckland because I was there.

Later that year, on 13 August, two people wearing balaclavas and holding a pistol and a sawn-off shotgun strode into the BNZ at Te Kauwhata, a lonely little backwater just north of Ohinewai in the Waikato, in broad daylight at 10.30 a.m. One of the men, who was agitated, fired a shot into the wall of the bank while frightened customers looked on. The manager was forced to open the safe. The police station was just up the bloody road, and as soon as the masked men had started stuffing the cash they got the signal to abort.

The New Zealand Herald related how one of the customers was Judy Wiechern. Waiting in the car outside, her husband, Ron, heard the bang of the gun going off and instinctively turned the engine on, imagining that in a moment's time someone with a stash of cash would run out of the bank and he might be the one to stop them. He didn't. When they did flee, Noeline Gutry, who had also been inside, breathed a sigh of relief after what felt like a lifetime with two armed men.

It seemed like a strange bank to choose, but it was holding substantial amounts of money. There was no EFTPOS; everything was cash. You might think that a little town like that would have had bugger-all money, but there was a retirement home there and the pensioners used the bank all the time.

Within minutes the pair had made away in a stolen car with nearly $40,000. But one of them had made a crucial error. As he fled, a CCTV camera captured him with his mask partially pulled down. When the bank was empty of nothing but customers and good people, the four staff members burst into tears. 'The community is devastated,' Noeline Gutry told the *Herald*.

I'd promoted myself from common burglar to planner of aggravated robberies. This would be my main income for some time to come, and I'd end up meticulously planning half a dozen of them. It seemed like a no-brainer to me — I had no shortage of people coming to me wanting to do the dirty work, and I'd convinced myself that a well-executed, tightly controlled robbery would ensure that the likelihood of anyone getting hurt would be minimal. This was how I justified it to myself. In many ways, I stand by this: nobody was ever hurt on my watch (though now, of course, I recognise that post-traumatic stress disorder and anxiety would have been likely consequences).

The day the BNZ in Te Kauwhata was robbed I was waiting down the road in the car, keeping an eye on the police station while radioing backwards and forwards with Ian Johnson and Manu Royal. I'd met them both in prison; Royal was a convicted killer. I'd phoned the local cop and told him I was calling from a payphone and somebody was rustling some cows — he'd better come quick. That took care of him for a while. Afterwards, Ian, Manu and I split the money equally.

The police began their hunt in earnest. There had been a huge number of other bank robberies in recent months — a High Court justice had called it an 'epidemic' — and the police believed they were connected. An armed hold-up of a security van outside Birkenhead Foodtown had netted the assailants just under $300,000; the police later tried to link me to that one. Māngere's BNZ on Ascot Road had been pilfered of $40,000. A dozen bank hold-ups around Auckland had seen half a million stolen from vaults and registers.

'The bank robberies are well planned, months in advance, and organised right down to the letter,' Detective Ross Walden told the *Auckland Star*. He speculated that they were being committed by hardened criminals with links to drugs, although admitting that the police were '100 miles from proving it'.

Police were tipped off that a suspect might be hiding out in a home in rural Drury, in the very south of Auckland not that far from Te Kauwhata. Road blocks were set up and drivers were questioned. Shops on the main road were shut, people were ordered to stay in their homes, an Eagle helicopter patrolled, and the AOS stormed a house only to find nobody of interest there.

T wo days after the Te Kauwhata robbery, I went to 80E Kerwyn Ave in East Tāmaki and signed a lease on a recently vacated warehouse. The owner wanted to rent it out after the business that had been leasing it shut its doors. Anne-Marie and I came prepared with a pre-signed lease.

It was a single-level warehouse with a roller door. Upstairs was a mezzanine floor, part of which I converted into a room. Downstairs was a bathroom and kitchen. The rent was $433 a month and we gave Ivan Brown a month's advance in cash. We signed the tenancy agreement in the name of Regent Panel Beaters, my brother-in-law's business, which I'd had some involvement in, mainly by way of spinning my money through it. We signed it with our own names, though. We told the owner we wanted to store parts.

Manu Royal's brother, Charles, was living in Papakura and wanted to start a small business, so I had agreed to back him financially. Charles was Māori, six foot something tall and skinny. We'd met the year before and quickly become friends. I was godfather to his daughter, Teone. Charles Royal seemed like a chap worth investing a few dollars in. He had a tree-felling business and was making reasonable money. So when he came to me for help starting his venture, I figured that I would pay for the lease, do the paperwork and advise him. What was the benefit to me? I thought when he got on his feet, he'd show some appreciation; that's all.

But then Charles ended up in Mount Eden Prison, and I was stuck with the warehouse costing me a lot of money. However, I'd met a woman at a barbecue who'd been part of a group arrested for running a large-scale cannabis plantation in Northland. She wanted somewhere safe to grow some seedlings she had left over. I started thinking. A few doors down from the warehouse was the famous Mr Chips factory; I reckoned that the wafting smell of roast potato wouldn't do my newest enterprise any harm.

In 1990 about 43 per cent of the country had admitted to trying cannabis, and in 1992, the year I was arrested, police spent about $12 million on enforcement. It's now more than twice that. Skunk was virtually an unknown then. They didn't start asking in national drug surveys whether people used it until 1998. Some people use the word skunk interchangeably with weed or cannabis, but it's a particular strain of plant, and it's potent.

Like everything I do, I researched. I threw a box of seedlings inside a cupboard in the factory, along with a fluorescent tube, and away they went. The plants grew bigger and bigger, so a friend built a second room on the mezzanine floor. Then the Gro-Lux lights went in, then 200- and 400-watt lights timed to go on at 10 p.m. and off at 6 a.m. to infuse my gardening project. Initially, I was thinking of stopping at ten or twenty plants, but I became attached.

I don't know if you do much gardening, but it was hard to stop. The plants germinated. I should have destroyed the male plants — the books say there's no point having them because they don't contain much active compound — but I left them growing so that I could get seeds. I'm a perfectionist, I suppose.

Towards the end of the year, Leslie Maurice Green needed a place to stay. Les was an old-timey crook who mostly robbed people with his .44 Magnum. He was on the run after robbing a bank and I agreed that he could stay at the factory for the princely sum of $1000 a week. I put in a microwave, a 14-inch television and a bed for him. Les was short, about five foot, with the whitest grey hair I'd ever seen. He wasn't short on energy despite being in his late fifties. We had a common interest in robbing banks, and became friends. After I'd bought my house on Paton Ave I'd become something of a hotel for passing friends. That year Anthony Ricardo Sannd had come to stay in my sleepout; he'd even given it to the courts as a suitable bail address, which Anne-Marie found fishy. She thought the police were just keen to use it as an excuse for them to swoop by and monitor me at the same time. With the benefit of hindsight, I later realised she was right.

My gardening project metamorphosed into one of New Zealand's first major skunk operations. I blacked out the factory's mezzanine windows and lined all the walls with silver building foil, cut a hole in one of the walls and installed an extraction fan. Lights from the ceiling hung about 2 metres from the floor, and each corner of the room housed a large spotlight to bathe my hydroponics. The lights were all looped together, and there were a couple of remote ballasts connected to individual power boxes and an array of multi-plugs. A sophisticated lighting scheme, the police would later say, and an elaborate irrigation system for feeding. Too fucking right. At the centre of it all: 132 beautiful plants. The tallest grew in the main room, some towering at a lofty metre. The small room housed the fledglings, somewhere between seedlings and 30 centimetres tall.

This enterprise went on for months. At a conservative estimate, a mature cannabis plant yielded about a quarter of a pound of dried plant material. I reckon I had about 33 pounds-worth there, and skunk was going for about $3000 a pound wholesale. You do the maths.

Along with the robberies, I'd coined somewhere north of a million dollars during this period. I took to burying money and drugs in regional parks to keep it safe. This would have repercussions later on; one of my associates dug up $30,000 of my cash, which I never saw again. Another time I was doing a dash from the police when I had to make a quick decision to bury some gear under a tree in someone's backyard. Later, I struggled to retrace my steps to find this fucking tree.

All the while the neighbours — just businesses, no houses — noticed motorbikes and cars and vans coming and going at weird hours. What looked like a clothing rack was rolled in. Some orange car doors were walked in. The windows at the top were blacked out, and then the bottom ones. They must have wondered what the fuck was going on.

February 1992

Just four months later all eyes were trained on the factory. The cops' eyes, to be specific. They had a hunch that I was behind all the robberies that had gone down around town, and were watching my house and my factory like a hawk. They'd bugged my phones, too.

They started watching the warehouse late in January, and carried on watching that and my house through February. The last day of surveillance was 25 February because the very next day it unravelled like a ball of wool. A guy who was working next door at unit C noticed at about 3 p.m. that the door to my warehouse had been forced open. The lock on the wooden door had been jemmied, and while the door was still closed it didn't look very secure. (I never did find out who attempted to break in.)

He was a good neighbour, and gave the door a knock to check things out. He stepped inside and yelled out twice — no answer, but he could hear a fan unit and saw a brilliant glow on the top floor. He recognised the Gro-Lux lighting. There was dirt leading up the stairs. He didn't want to go up alone, so he grabbed his colleague to watch the door and up he fucking went, to be overcome by the warm orange light and the fields of magnificent green. He called the landlord. Around the same time, a constable watching the factory also noticed that the door had been tampered with, and went in to check things out.

An hour and a half later, Sergeant Alistair Smart at Ōtara police station was being told by his boss Detective Constable Gould that weed was being grown at 80E Kerwyn Ave. About fifteen minutes after that I was coming face to face with Sergeant Smart and a bunch of his colleagues. Sannd and I were trying to fix the door to the warehouse after being called by the neighbours. I'd had a bad feeling that things were about to turn to custard. I called Anne-Marie, told her what had happened and that things were liable to hit the fan. We'd just found out she was pregnant.

'You're a fool,' she replied.

When the cops showed up, I thought, 'Jesus fucking Christ, how am I going to explain this?'

The first cop asked if he could come inside. I politely declined, and he just as politely told me he could go in anyway. And so he did. The first thing he saw was a radio on the floor turned to channel 2, the Auckland Central police station channel. He stood there listening to his colleagues for a bit, and then asked, 'Whose radio is this?'

Obviously it was mine and I told him so. 'Why shouldn't I have it? It's not against the law, is it?'

Then he headed upstairs and of course I was expressing surprise that there was dope inside. I told him I'd been sub-letting it to someone called Robert and what he was doing there was some surprise to me. There we were, standing among extension cords and potting mix and oxygen cylinders and liquid and dried plant fertiliser. Two specks amid a tide of trees.

'Jesus Christ, officer, I'm just as shocked as you are.'

They cut the plants and dumped them into sacks, then upturned each pot so the soil littered the floor of the warehouse. The pots were removed for fingerprinting and some plant matter was taken for samples.

Police searched both the warehouse and our home on Paton

Ave. They obtained receipts and evidence showing that I'd bought or taken a bunch of camo gear from shops in Auckland. There were photos of me in the gear all around the place. It looked like someone training for an armed robbery. Between the factory and the house they found a 9-mm Luger firearm, 36 rounds of ammunition, a stolen motorbike, an imitation Uzi machine-gun pistol that looked pretty fucking realistic, two balaclavas, two gloves, a gun-cleaning kit, a box of used pistol cartridges, stolen licence plates, more radio receivers tuned to the police channels, a bullet-proof vest, knuckle dusters, and a burglary kit with plastic ties, masking tape, gloves, bolt cutters and spray paint. And a partridge in a fucking pear tree.

It seemed to the police that they'd found their lead organiser of all the bank robberies going on around the place. I was charged with cultivating cannabis, unlawful possession of a weapon, and conspiring to commit aggravated robbery.

Within a week, a snitch had told the cops that I'd masterminded the Te Kauwhata BNZ robbery as well. There was no evidence against me except this jail-house snitch's story. That snitch would give evidence against me in court, for which he'd receive special treatment in jail, including visitors he wouldn't otherwise be able to see; he also had the police write a letter of support to the judge when he was facing jail for another bank robbery. His sentence was halved. He also got name suppression, so I can't name him here.

I was incensed; 30 years later, I still am. Is it wrong to be outraged that I was ratted out for something I'd done? No. Because in this case it made a mockery of our justice system. I might have committed the robbery, but I'd certainly never breathed a word of it to this guy. Everything the jury would hear about the case from this seasoned crook was a lie and it fuelled an inappropriate and ongoing relationship between police an crooks. (I'll go into this more soon).

In addition to the snitch's evidence, the cop investigating the robbery, Detective Senior Sergeant Rex Knight, said that they had eye-witness reports of me handing over a weapon to one of the men. An elderly farmer alleged that he'd seen me in the area at the time. I was held in custody awaiting trial and they also charged Ian Johnson and Manu and Charles Royal. I immediately filed a bail application from behind bars.

T he Ōtāhuhu district court was an overburdened place. Rows of plastic chairs were constantly full, with people waiting hours for their matter to be heard. Lawyers, police and defendants clotted the over-crowded halls like herds of cattle. It wasn't even supposed to be a court. In 1970 a filing room had been turned into the Ōtāhuhu courthouse to help deal with the region's increasing criminal fraternity. It was so busy and bursting at the seams that in 2000 they closed it down and replaced it with the equally busy — but larger and more modern — Manukau District Court.

On 23 March 1992, the deputy court registrar was laden with a pile of bail paperwork. It so happened that two Mount Eden prisoners with the same surname had applied for bail. The deputy registrar signed and dated release papers as appropriate and sent them off to the prison without realising that all was not well. That day, I was sitting on remand at Mount Eden when I was called to the receiving offices. It appeared I was to be let go. The prison officer read aloud the bail conditions and then handed me the bail bond. I was a bit fucking dubious. It had my name and date of birth on it, but one of the addresses given for surety wasn't mine.

'You sure you've got the right guy?'

'No other Arthur William Taylor's in this jail; must be you.'

I collected my box of personal things and my television, and hastily skipped off down the road before they could change their minds. At a nearby store I asked if they would mind holding onto my TV for a bit, as I'd just got out of prison and had nowhere to store it; somewhat dumbfounded, they nevertheless agreed. Then I jumped into a taxi that took me to the Regent Panel Beaters in

New Lynn, where a friend took care of my fare. I spent the next few weeks hiding out.

An hour after I was released, someone turned up to Mount Eden Prison to collect another prisoner, who shared my surname, and who'd been granted bail that day. Prison officers told her to wait ten minutes, but two hours later she made inquiries again. Where was he? Still in custody, as I'd been released instead of him.

The next day, 24 March, the media were told that one of the country's most notorious criminals had been freed. 'He would be one of our worst offenders,' Detective Senior Sergeant Rex Knight told the *Auckland Star*. He believed that I was more of a risk to the police than to the public, and dutifully outlined my history of escaping.

'He is unstable but I don't consider him mental — and he's nobody's fool. He is extremely intelligent,' Knight said.

The following day, police searched four houses, including Paton Ave and my parents' house in the Waikato, all the while telling the public that I was unstable, dangerous and shouldn't be approached. Meanwhile, the Ministry of Justice promised a full inquiry into how I'd been freed. Lianne Dalziel, then the justice spokesperson for the Opposition (now the mayor of Christchurch), called for the resignation of Minister of Justice Doug Graham after it transpired that this had been the third time that year that an inmate had mistakenly been freed. Dalziel told parliament that the three incidents highlighted a disturbing trend and the immense pressure on the courts, prisons and police. Graham ignored calls for him to stand down. 'I can guarantee to you this deputy registrar is unlikely to repeat it.'

I immediately called my mum to reassure her I was alright. She was annoyed, my mum — but not with me. She told the *Herald* that I wasn't the mad, armed lunatic that police were making out I was. 'Police are trying to make him look like a crazy man and the public are falling for it. He knew police thought he was armed, and he knew I would be worried if I heard. He said he definitely did not have a gun and had only rung to let me know he was okay.'

She was right in saying that I wouldn't give myself up. 'What is the good of him doing that now? He's been branded a notorious lout. He's not going to get a fair trial anywhere in New Zealand with that kind of publicity.'

On 29 March I contacted a reporter at the *Sunday News* and told them I was in the South Island, to throw the cops off the scent. They had been harassing Anne-Marie, who, as you'll remember, was pregnant.

The cops eventually caught up to me at Paton Ave two months later. They showed up unexpectedly so I leaped into the closet. Funnily enough, they didn't spot me that time, but eventually returned and found me. I was wearing only my undies. I was arrested and immediately refused bail.

They charged me with escape, but I argued against that in court. I had applied for bail while I was in prison and had been released. 'If the mistake wasn't obvious to an experienced prison officer, it wouldn't be obvious to me,' I told Auckland District Court judge P.J. Evans. 'One who withdraws from custody without intention to escape and thereafter deliberately remains at large does not commit an offence.'

On 11 July, Judge Evans ruled that there was no evidence that I knew there had been a mistake when I left Mount Eden Prison. The judge complimented me on my defence.

Much later, in 1998, when I had escaped from Paremoremo, that same Rex Knight told the media I had escaped using false bail documents — as if it had been my fault. 'We are talking about one of the top ten most dangerous and cunning criminals in the country. As soon as he is out of jail, he will start re-offending', he said then.

Around this time, while I was sitting in the cells at Auckland District Court, the door opened and a senior police detective wandered in. He greeted me with the name I'd been known by at my school in Northland: 'Hello, Butch, how are you?' I eyed him suspiciously before realising that we'd gone to school together. We shook hands, and caught up on the intervening years. 'Jesus,' he said, 'you've gone down a pretty different path. You were always considered the brain box at school.'

Cockiness encouraged me to reply with 'Oh well, them's the breaks', but inside, a sadness was welling up.

Between April and May 1993, the AOS convoy between Paremoremo in the north of Auckland and Hamilton to the south was a captivating scene. The trial for the Te Kauwhata bank robbery lasted five weeks. During the week they'd keep us at Waikeria, so once a week, in the early morning, Ian Johnson and I were escorted from Pare through Auckland's rush-hour traffic, all the way down to the High Court at Hamilton, with the AOS turning their big air-horns on and forcing everybody out of the way. The convoy stopped for nothing. There were lights, armed police, the works. They'd take all sorts of different routes on the way down, through back-country lanes.

After court, at night, they'd light the whole countryside up again as they drove up the middle of the back roads like lunatics. Sometimes there were helicopters, too. The cows were mesmerised. I was held in a special cell block in Waikeria and armed police stood outside my cell window and around the prison at night. On Friday afternoons, the convoy headed back to Auckland.

At the court I was repeatedly searched for weapons in the cells before heading up to the courtroom with my boxes and boxes of documents. I'd enlisted Anne-Marie as my McKenzie friend, which basically meant that she sat next to me in court to help me prepare my defence. She was also searched for weapons by police. Every morning and whenever she left and returned to the courtroom, they'd look through her clothing, footwear, handbag and anything else she was carrying, like documents. Even on weekends, if I got a visit at Pare from Anne-Marie or my parents they'd be strip-searched.

Ian Johnson and I were tried together. Manu Royal was tried separately, and ended up pleading guilty. He was the one who'd been identified via CCTV because his mask had slipped off during the robbery. That was curtains for him. Charles Royal pleaded guilty to being an accessory, for hiding Manu after the robbery.

During the trial, each security officer had a little radio attached to their lapel. These radios softly squawked in the background while witnesses gave evidence. At one point all the lights in the courtroom went off, and the AOS came storming in as if it were the apocalypse, as if it had something to do with me. This sort of thing went on for weeks. It worried me. The jury doesn't normally know about your previous convictions, but if they think they're dealing with a highly dangerous criminal it obviously makes the likelihood of them convicting you higher. They'll think 'Jesus that's a dangerous bastard.' I would, if I was a juror.

I was defending myself brilliantly. My first step was trying to get a bunch of the disclosures made by the informant (the snitch who'd first told police I was behind the BNZ robbery) thrown out. I argued that the informant's repeated references to Pare were pejorative, and that the obvious over-the-top security arrangements were prejudicial. I argued that this was all cumulatively breaching my right to a fair trial under section 25A of the New Zealand Bill of Rights Act 1990. However, these applications were all dismissed.

When it came time for the snitch to give evidence, I ripped him to shreds. I printed a ream of paper and kept it on my desk, and alluded to it as if it were his criminal record. I could see him eyeing it nervously while I had him on the stand for the best part of two days, cross-examining him. He admitted that he'd agreed with the police to turn Queen's evidence, and I was able to show the jury that police later gave a letter to the sentencing judge in relation to the informant's robbery of a bank, saying that he was cooperating on this case and had been given witness protection. Both Charles and

Manu Royal gave evidence in my defence, saying that I was in no way connected to the robbery. Charles Royal said that the Crown's informant was obviously a nark.

I told the jury that this guy had just been arrested for bank robbery himself and was wanting a get-out-of-jail-free card. I put it to him that part of 'turning over a new leaf and accepting God' — as he claimed was his motivation for giving evidence against me — was that he'd tell the police everything he knew about any other crimes he knew about.

He agreed that this was so, and so I specifically put it to him: 'Do you know of any other crimes I've committed?' He said no. We'd been friends for a long time, and this was obviously bullshit. He was being selective in his squealing, that's for sure.

I was so angry that I eventually charged this man with perjury in a private prosecution heard at the Auckland High Court. This was practically unheard of, but many years later it would prove to be good training for me. While the charge was initially accepted, a judge would later dismiss it because it was made a year after the BNZ trial, and he ruled that it had taken too long to come to court — what's called an undue delay.

On 19 May we had a day off the trial and Anne-Marie brought our newborn, Tyrone, to Waikeria, along with Mum and my nephew. We had a special room to ourselves. It was a marvellous break.

Two days later the trial was drawing to a close; all that remained was for Ian Johnson's lawyer to sum up to the jury. I'd already made my final address — prison officers even congratulated me on it afterwards. However, that morning, Friday, something was amiss. Justice Penlington wanted to see counsel privately, without the jury.

In hushed tones, Justice Penlington said, 'Last night one of the jurors in the case, the foreman, received a copy of Mr Taylor's criminal convictions under his door. I'm thinking of discharging him because he can't be impartial and fair any longer.'

The juror had received an envelope with his name and address typed on it, and a photocopy of a newspaper cutting titled, 'Dangerous criminal freed in error', along with my criminal record. We had already lost one juror on account of stress, so this was the last one — if they lost any more after this, the whole trial would have to be aborted and there was so much money being spent on it.

I knew which juror it was. He was an executive who took meticulous notes. He was on my side, I knew it — and whoever had slipped my convictions under his door knew it, too. Justice Penlington ordered a formal investigation and discharged the juror; but the trial went on, despite my protests. The jury went out that Friday afternoon, and late on Saturday it returned with two different verdicts. I was livid. Johnson was acquitted, while I was found guilty. Ian's lawyer credited my cross examination of the jailhouse snitch to draw doubt on his claim that Ian had confessed all to him. I maintain that there was no evidence against us, and that the leaking of my convictions sealed my fate.

I was able to get my own back on the snitch, though, during another hearing, held after I attempted the perjury prosecution. Despite the massive security, one day I was able to break away from the special Pare squad in the courtroom to smash the snitch in the head and jaw. His face went white as my fist connected with his head. The Diplomatic Protection Squad, who were there to mind the informant, pulled their Glocks out and were about to shoot when the Pare screws crashed into my back, flooring me, then jumped on top of me. It actually turned into a bit of a fiasco — I'd taken to wearing a hair piece, which fell off in the melee. The Pare guards and the cops were pissing themselves over that. (I've stopped wearing a wig; I'm not so vain these days.)

I was charged with assault, but Judge Bruce Buckton threw the charge out because the guy refused to come to court and so I was denied the opportunity to cross-examine him. This guy eventually got five years for a bank robbery. He served just over three, and spent it mollycoddled in the supergrass unit, Te Moenga, at Kaitoke prison near Wanganui. The cops even ran out to the prison with a crock-pot so he could cook his own meals after he bullshitted them that I was going to have him poisoned.

I n July 1993 I was sentenced to nine years for the aggravated robbery and cultivating cannabis. My earliest release date would be 17 January 2000. I was sent back to Pare.

A year later, I was also sentenced for a robbery in June 1991 that had caught up with me: my organisation of the hold-up of a Remuera antiques store, Antheas Antiques, where I'd had two people walk in with a sawn-off shotgun and threaten the two staff inside for jewellery worth $250,000.

Before you're sentenced, Probation Services send in someone to interview you about your life and crimes. This is to make the judge aware of your personal circumstances, and any stressors. It's important for judges to know what forks in the road people have faced. Sometimes I would refuse to talk to the report writers. It would strike me as bullshit that they were suddenly taking such an interest, but some reports on my record do give insight into my offences. Although I struggle to distinctly recall this conversation, apparently at that time I'd struggled to forgive my father for what I saw as taking the lead role in having me sent to Epuni. I hated being in custody — being told what to do, when to eat, when to piss, who to see. I hated that my family had to be strip-searched when they visited me during the trial, and I hated that I couldn't see my son whenever I wanted to. I'd become desensitised to offending — you get to a point where you stop caring. I cared about making money, and about outsmarting the police, and if that resulted in another cross on my sheet, then I didn't really care. Of course, you see this in hindsight.

The report writer submitted to the judge that I might actually benefit from being away from prison, that periodic detention along with supervision and counselling might do wonders instead. Given that I had a newborn, they suggested that rehab, rather than prison, might sort me out. It's hard to believe now that they said this. Probation Services would do anything to keep me in, but the report is proof that someone, once, saw an alternative path for me.

Less than six months later, in December 1993, police executed a search warrant on my cell at Pare, which was housing thousands of my court documents. They seized just a fraction of the papers. The police were accusing me of attempting to pervert the course of justice. They said I had organised for the mail drop of my own convictions to this juror. It was a fucking stitch-up. I had no reason to do it — I was going to get acquitted and that guy was my best juror, but the police had every motive in the world to get rid of him.

Again I stood trial, with Anne-Marie by my side throughout, us swapping notes and documents. The police said that while I may not have had the opportunity to send the record myself, I certainly could have had help. I'm vehement about this: I did not do it.

Probably it was some disgruntled cop who wanted me convicted. The cops had a lot at stake. If that juror had stayed, I would likely have been found not guilty. I would have walked — it only needs one juror, and at the very least you get a re-trial.

They fingerprinted this note that had been slipped to the juror and didn't find anything, but a couple of weeks later they re-did it and found an upside-down fingerprint of mine on the criminal record. Later I learned that you could shine a very powerful light through a photographic negative of someone's fingerprint to make a fingerprint stamp. I'm convinced that that's what happened.

Instead of a trial by jury, a lone judge tried me on attempting to pervert the course of justice. Of course, I defended myself. I told the judge that this juror who'd got dismissed was my best juror, that it didn't make sense for me to send him my criminal record.

'He was the one who saw things in a detached and responsible way and would be able to put things in perspective,' I said. 'It was he who I felt would be able to keep the jury on track in confining their deliberations to the legally admissible material and not the other inflammatory, prejudicial and inadmissible matters that came to their notice.'

On 2 March 1995 — nearly two years after the BNZ bank robbery trial — Justice Barker wrote a 30-page judgment finding me guilty.

'Arthur William Taylor: you are a very intelligent man. Unfortunately you have channelled your intelligence into criminal activity,' Judge Barker said. Later that month I was sentenced to another year in prison.

Recently I tried requesting the whole police case file and the court file for the BNZ robbery trial, and guess what? Both have been lost. Isn't that fucking mysterious?

A few months after my sentencing, the oversight of prisoners and people serving sentences in the community was transferred from the penal division of the Department of Justice to the new Department of Corrections, established on 1 October 1995. Mark Byers would be its first chief executive. In 1981 a committee reviewing how penal policy was doing had identified the reduction of re-offending as the main goal, with the idea that regional prisons would help prisoners feel more connected to their communities, and more community-based sentences would help. Then, in 1987, an inquiry had recommended changes to uproot the system, suggesting in-prison rehabilitation and partnerships with iwi and local groups. A programme called Straight Thinking was introduced in 1995 to teach inmates reasoning skills, but it was abandoned in 2006 after three reviews showed no impact on re-offending rates. Mark Byers resigned in 2005. It was around this time that my interest in the law increased. Up until then I'd focused on criminal law, and I thought it might be good to get a proper grounding in other areas like judicial review, consumer law, contract law and property. I enrolled in a legal executive correspondence course through one of the local polytechs at Carrington and completed the eighteen-month programme in less than a year. I was in B block by then, which is not as strict with security as D. It used to be unlocked virtually all day.

Basically, a legal executive can do anything except appear in court and argue cases. There were nine core subjects, including communication, English, conveyancing, property law and consumer law. The correspondence course would send me all the workbooks and I would mail the assignments back. I was passing all the tests and assignments with flying colours. I found it quite easy. Don't ever assume that a lawyer knows all the law; the lawyer knows the *basic principles* of law. A lawyer is just trained to find information, to research and prepare submissions — nothing people can't do themselves.

When it came time to do the exam to gain the certificate, Corrections wouldn't let me. You've got to do it under the supervision of tutors; there was no way I was going to let the screws supervise it, and it was unlikely that polytech staff would come into the prison. The screws could easily have escorted me out there for half a day, but they refused because of security concerns. I'd even got the okay from the Law Society because I wasn't going to be representing people in court.

I've since accepted that I don't need the certificate. An LLB — a lawyer's credentials — is just confirmation to the client, the public at large and the courts that they can do the job. But everybody knows I can do the job without it.

Many years after the BNZ bank robbery trial, the same snitch — obviously seeing the merit in pinning crimes on me — tried to incriminate me in the 1992 armed robbery of the PostBank in Western Heights, Rotorua, claiming that I'd confessed all to him. Two Rotorua cops turned up at Pare one day in 2001 to question me about it. I was only weeks away from being released, and they said they had a 27-page statement alleging that I had robbed the Western Heights PostBank and that on my next appearance they would be seeking for me to be remanded in custody.

I had a hunch who the snitch was, and, of course, I'd committed the robbery. An acquaintance and I had trained hard out for it, scoping the place out during the day and enacting how we'd handle things the day before. My acquaintance held the gun while I demanded the money. We took $80,000. Funnily enough, there was a huge queue of people lining up for their money that day, and I'll never forget this frozen group of people, still as statues, as we ran out the door with the cash.

Just a couple of days before my release, I was surprised to receive a letter from Rotorua Police saying that they believed I was guilty of the robbery, but 'because of the circumstances' (whatever they were) and 'considering the public interest', I wouldn't be charged. I was to take it as a formal warning. This must have been the first time in history that anyone has received a formal warning for the armed robbery of a bank resulting in the theft of $80,000. The real story was that there was no evidence other than this guy's statement, and police wanted to write the robbery off as solved to make their books look better.

CHAPTER SEVEN

BREAKING OUT

15 JUNE 1998. AROUND 7.45 P.M.

Corrections manager John Small was a pale, moustachioed man who'd worked as a prison manager since 1989. Twenty minutes before his shift was due to finish, he was white as a ghost and practically delirious. Another screw, watching Small panic in his patrol room, dialled his number and said, 'What the fuck's wrong, Small?'

'Fuck, you'll never believe it — I've lost four.'

The screw listened intently as Small told him what had happened. At 7.40 p.m., the lock-up call was given over the tannoy and he began locking up 24 cells on the bottom landing. When he arrived at cell 17, in unit three, he noticed that its inmate, murderer Darren Crowley, was missing. After calling fruitlessly for Crowley he continued to cell 18 — my cell — which was also empty. Small raced to the shower-room and saw that the lower windows on the left-hand side had been smashed.

The screw went to check both landings, 48 cells in all. Sure enough, four of the cells in unit three were empty. Small again started calling, 'Crowley where are you?' Another screw locked the upper right landing and then proceeded to the left. 'Thompson?' he called. Their calls reverberated off the cold walls and the prisoners could hear that some of their own were missing. Nobody was surprised.

Small ran upstairs to the unit office and dialled '5' to report missing persons. Watching him sweat, the screw shook his head and thought, 'The worst four you could ever lose.'

Murderers Darren Crowley and Graeme Burton, aggravated robber Matty Thompson — and me, of course.

Corrections officers would later say that they couldn't believe four men had escaped Pare West in one night. They still can't believe it.

Just a few days earlier, John Small had been battling a cold.

He wasn't feeling well and was struggling with his computer, so he called me up to help.

I sorted it for him, and then I thought I'd pull his tail.

'John, have you ever had anyone escape on your watch?'

'No, Taylor, no — it's never going to happen on my watch.'

I wasn't meant to escape. I didn't know Burton very well, although he was seen publicly as a sort of berserker who'd stabbed a lighting technician to death at a Wellington nightclub in 1992. I thought he was just a normal prisoner — in prison he just seemed like a boy from Wainuiomata, although he did put on some big acts later. He was a brilliant tattooist and did tattoos for heaps of prisoners, so he was well regarded. Most people liked him, so I kind of assumed he was alright. Burton might have been big news to the public, but in a jail there are a hundred big, tough bastards and he was quite a way down in the pecking order, although he didn't like to think so. He and Crowley had plans under way and I thought I could probably help them. They wanted to go overseas, but they were like children trying to plan that. They wouldn't have got out without my help; no way in the world.

They needed an expert, so I called in a few favours from my mate Neil Swain. I'd met Swainey many years before in Pare. Typically unshaven, he was 6 foot 2 with frizzy hair. People called him the terrorist, or Bomber, because he'd nail-bombed the Sydenham police station in the '90s. He was one of the rare South Islanders to get sent to Pare. They hated getting transferred to the North Island, and they would do anything not to go. Screws down south would say, 'If you don't toe the line around here, we're going to send you to Pare where all the Mongrel Mob and the black boys are, and they'll eat you alive.' That's what happened with Swainey. He was so scared when he arrived at Pare that they had to physically carry him in and chuck him into B block one day. Out of sympathy for this guy, I asked my friend and fellow inmate Whetu Hansen to look after him, and he did.

Swainey had been paroled the year before the escape, so was

key to the emancipation of the yardbirds. I was due to be released in October and was happy to wait, but around the end of April I got a letter saying my release date was in fact December 1999. The bastards came to me and said, 'Oh, we've made a cock-up on your release dates, Arthur. You're not actually getting out for eighteen months.' I fought it, but they said they'd got my release date wrong the first time. I couldn't face more time inside, so now there were three of us.

Planning for freedom wasn't unlike planning a camping holiday. I called Metropolitan Rentals from a secret cellphone and ordered a van for two days, at $48 a day. I gave the rental office woman my credit card number but told her my mate Neil would give her cash when he picked the van up. For the love of God, I told her, don't charge my credit card.

To Swainey I gave a shopping list: cooking gas, clothes (colour: camo), toilet paper, chippies, chicken, torches, lanterns, canned fruit/spaghetti/sausages, casseroles/stews/risottos/rice, muesli bars, coffee and sugar.

'A very big THANKS very much for all the hard work you've put in on this one, buddy — won't be forgotten!! You're a bloody marvel,' I emailed Neil, just days out, from the computer I had in my cell.

The plan was this: on Monday, after first muster — where guards do a body count to check everyone is there — at 6 p.m., the boys would go through the fence. The bars had already been prepared, so they only needed to undo a couple of bolts and cut through the fence. Ten minutes, max.

'Depending on the exact time of the muster, the pick-up should be between 6.15 and 6.30 p.m. I will be in cellular contact with you throughout, so you'll be updated on progress as it happens so you'll know exactly when to move.'

I plotted for them to pick up supplies on the North Shore, then head through Riverhead, across the Highway 16 intersection at Kumeū and out on the back road to the Muriwai Beach area. I asked Swainey to scout a suitable location for the camp and to leave the gear there. 'And they can then move into the bush and set up, where we anticipate they'll stay for a few days at least while the coppers thrash about!'

Darren had organised a box of his clothes to be dropped off to his family, and I had my mum drop off a scanner and camo gear at my sister's. My darling mum had no idea why I needed my things. She didn't ask questions, and probably figured that it was for my imminent release. She would do anything for me.

'So you'll need to arrange to uplift these and position them with the boys' other gear', I told Swainey, by email. 'Hope that's not too much hassle for you. The scanner's not charged or programmed at the moment, so hopefully you can do that as well; I'll fax you a full list of police frequencies shortly. Otherwise they can do it at their camp site. The boots for G are A [all good]. We also need one US size 10, one US size nine and half or 9 if that's not available, then two size 10 US. Talk to you soon, mate.'

On the day of the escape, the unit guards were unusually busy, with inmates' requests interfering with their normal duties. Curiously busy. In unit three, inmates were coming and going from the gym and their other programmes, which required carefully checking them in and out of the unit. There was an unusual number of queries to the guards about various matters: computers, drug testing, home leave.

We were last seen by the guards at 6.40 p.m., but our plans were already in motion by then. The shower block had a long, thin window with two metal bars that ran across the length of it, fixed with two bolts at each end. In between and behind these two bars was a third bar across the centre. As I told Swainey, we'd already loosened each of the four bottom bolts securing the bottom of the bars so that on the night we just needed to unscrew and remove them before jimmying the bars aside. We'd also partly sheared off the centre bar with a hacksaw I'd been secreting, painting the cut marks in the bar with a small test pot of paint I'd acquired, and had cut out the Perspex window that sat just behind the right-hand side of the centre bar. This bit of Perspex had been reported missing by a prison officer about ten days previously, but they'd done nothing about it. After the bars came away, we were able to drop down outside and head for the perimeter fence.

Something fucking funny happened then — Crowley was working away at the fence — we had a prison kitchen knife with a good sharp blade — when he was called over the prison intercom to get his medication. So he fetched it and returned. By the time we got to the perimeter fence Swainey had had a bit of a go at it. Burton used a great deal of force with the bolt cutters. Too much. They broke and we had to call Swainey out, who happened to have a spare set.

Once we'd finished cutting a small hole at the bottom of the fence, through we all went. The whole thing took about twenty minutes.

Nearby, Swainey was idling in a white Toyota HiAce with no seats in the back. 'You're not meant to be here, Arthur.'

'Yes, I fucking am. I've had a gutsful of these screws. They think they're showing me a trick or two — I'll show them a trick or two when one of the country's biggest escapes goes down.'

We picked up our supplies on the North Shore, including some .303s and ammo. After swapping our prison-issued denim jeans and jacket — mine with the number 112 for washing purposes — for camo gear and heavy-duty boots, Swainey took us out to the west coast to drop us off in the bush.

In the meantime, pandemonium was reigning at Pare. After our absence was noted, the guardroom was told we were missing. They discovered the hole in the fence and the missing window in the showers ten minutes later. At 8.02 p.m. the police were called; three minutes later the manager of the unit strode down. At 8.10 p.m. the crime prevention officer arrived (months too late, some might say), and by 8.30 the senior prison managers and police were congregating.

One poor orderly was tasked with notifying the 94 local residents that two murderers, a career criminal and an aggravated robber were on the loose. A community outreach programme meant that residents were tasked with informing others. After about two hours of ringing up these homes late at night, the orderly kept being told 'Yeah, yeah, we've already heard.' A note on the incident later recorded: 'All key persons were advised at least once, in some cases twice. Comments: Bloody brilliant, the system works.'

As we headed towards the North Shore, Burton was sitting on the floor of the van, cradling a rifle like you'd cradle a woman. At that moment I thought, 'Oh god, this is going to be a nightmare.' I realised then that I had to get Burton away from everyone, because he'd probably kill people. I'd freed a murderer, a lunatic, who now had a stash of guns. Does that weigh heavily? Not really. I didn't know what he was truly like until that moment.

On our way to Muriwai we passed the Kumeū pub and I saw the car of a friend of mine, Joanne Hewetson, who I knew through her boyfriend, Cruz Waipouri (he's doing life now, for murder). I called her and told her to follow us. She was, naturally, a bit mystified. Jo tried to talk me out of going with those three bastards; said she'd book motels and I could stay with her. That would have been good, but after seeing Burton with that rifle I thought I'd better not. I said to Jo, 'Look, babe, I'm going to have to stay with these idiots and keep this lunatic away from fucking civilisation. Then I'll meet you somewhere as far away from here as possible. Start looking for a place.'

At Muriwai, we walked 500 metres into the bush and set up camp with two tents, sleeping bags, camouflage, thermals and food — 'Everything but the kitchen sink,' Detective Senior Sergeant Mike Bush said, after they'd found it. And there we stayed for a few days to let the fuss die down. The next morning, Swainey returned the van. The Metropolitan Rentals staff noted that it was caked in mud.

Meanwhile, one of New Zealand's biggest ever manhunts

TOP My darling mum and I. She was one of my biggest supporters.

BOTTOM Tuakau, around 1981, while I'm on the run from Oakley Hospital.
Pictured with my mum and a friend of my brother's.

ME TAYLOR / Arthur / William
IT 16 . 11. 2006

NAME TAYLOR/Arthur/Will

OPPOSITE TOP Ohinewai in about 1985.

OPPOSITE BOTTOM LEFT Carolyn and I on our wedding day in 2004.

OPPOSITE BOTTOM RIGHT Leighanne and I.

THIS PAGE My collection of mugshots over the years – I've since ditched the hair piece!

TOP Lake Rotorua, 1985. Tania and I were on holiday.

BOTTOM Representing myself at the High Court in Auckland in 2011, arguing Corrections illegally took my DNA. © Stuff Limited

ABOVE Pictured after emerging from the Tairua bush following our
breakout of Pare in 1998. I'm wearing Roger Flowers' vest. © Getty/Ross Land

TOP Armed police scour central Wellington after I escaped on Manners Street in 2005. © Stuff Limited

BOTTOM With Otago University law professor Andrew Geddis.

TOP At Hazel Heal's graduation from her law studies —
from L-R: me, Hazel, Mark Henaghan and Judge Mark Crosbie.

BOTTOM On business at Dunedin's High Court, pictured
with law school graduates who are being sworn in.

ABOVE Pictured in February 2020 after my parole the year before.

was under way. More than 120 police officers assembled. Armed Offenders Squad and Special Tactics Group members from around the country were called in. The New Zealand Air Force was on standby. It makes me smile seeing how loaded-down with equipment today's police are — stab-proof vests, pepper spray, Tasers and guns readily at hand, and a dog unit within radio call. I wonder what the ones I grew up with would have made of it. *They* had to rely on their wits and brawn, and were sometimes on their own, hours from the nearest assistance. No helicopters and air support in those days. To get hold of a gun they had to go through all sorts of rigmarole, as weapons were held in an armoury and proper consideration had to be given as to whether there was justification in issuing them, and then only to experienced and properly trained staff. Nowadays every patrolling police vehicle has at least a .223 Bushmaster semi-automatic rifle with telescopic sight and, usually, a 9-mm Glock 17 pistol on board.

In my cell they had found a bolt and a rag on my bed, a screwdriver, and a grey sock under the mattress with two spanners inside. In Crowley's they found a notepad with names and North Shore addresses. They pulled up visitor and phone records, examined the shower, walked around the outside of the unit and examined the hole in the fence. They went through my computer, too, finding my emails to Swainey. They called my mum and my sisters and checked my credit cards. Detective Sergeant Kim Libby circulated information to cordon and patrol groups: 'I have personal knowledge of (three of) the escapers and consider them to be highly dangerous individuals.'

The tent was smaller than my cell, and colder. Three nights into our camping trip, I woke up in the middle of the night to a ruckus — thumping noises, and breaking glass, and laughing like fucking hyenas. I thought 'What the fuck is going on?' The other half of my tent was empty, and all three boys were missing.

Getting up, I followed the sound of the music about 3 kilometres to the Muriwai Volunteer Fire Brigade station, where Crowley, Matty and Burton had kicked in a door panel to break in. They were wearing fire brigade uniforms, playing pool and downing piss.

'Jesus Christ, you're going to wake up half of Muriwai!' I screeched. And sure enough, they had. The next day, the police got wind that the fire station had been broken into. We'd taken clothing, boots, gloves, medical supplies, radio equipment, alcohol and Moro bars; later on, with a sense of guilt, I helped return most of it. They were volunteers, those firefighters, and a lot of the stuff we took was as expensive as hell. We'd left most of it sitting rotting in the bush, no good to anyone. I was annoyed that the others had broken in in the first place.

Come daylight, there were helicopters purring above our camp.

Abandoning the camp, we ran about 10 kilometres through bush to Waimauku. At one point we encountered a car parked up with two AOS cops in it, snoring their heads off. Unbelievably we slinked past, two of us on either side of the car — and all the while Burton was aiming his gun, prepared to shoot. I had to calm him down. We hid out until dark, and then found a property with a 1989 Ford Falcon parked in the driveway, behind a padlocked gate. We lifted one side of the gate off its hinges and reversed the car out, parking up in the bush for the night.

The next morning, a Friday, we headed off to Tairua, where Jo had told us a friend of hers was cleaning a house for some millionaire who'd be in Hawaii. The place would be ours and she knew where the key was. En route we stopped at a McDonald's in Manukau before getting back on the motorway. Burton was hungry, so I ordered some Kiwi breakfasts plus a banana thickshake for the hulk in the back. The operator had no idea who we were.

The distance between Auckland and Tairua is over 100 kilometres and it takes a couple of hours, mostly through rural farmland, the town of Thames and some winding roads. En route we stopped for gas and spotted our mugs on the front page of the local newspaper. The cashier didn't even twig when I bought a few copies. Before getting to the mansion, I took the guys on a wee tour of the Coromandel — through Hot Water Beach, Hahei and Cooks — because they hadn't been there before. We looked at some houses in Hahei that we considered breaking into, and then we headed on.

Wealthy Roger Flowers spent the New Zealand winters in Hawaii. His plaster and Otago stone home was a two-storey, three-bedroom pad called 'Island Views' and had a 25-metre lap pool and its own private beach access. The steep concrete driveway led to the landscaped garden and entranceway, with a stone-slab path to the front door flanked by eleven motion-activated garden lights — it would have looked really pretty at night, but for us ripping the lights out so that they would stop detecting our movements.

The property was so palatial that cereal company Kellogg's had filmed a commercial there. Flowers had considered having the cleaner stay in the house while he was gone, but instead they had some elderly neighbours, Robert and Annette Dixon, keeping an eye on it. Just a few hours before we arrived, Robert had been around to check on the pool pump.

Jo hadn't yet joined us, so we smashed the lock to get in, and disabled the security alarm. We covered the windows with blankets by spearing them to the wall with kitchen knives, and then basically just chilled out, ate and drank, and the boys spotted cannabis with Jo when she arrived. We were armed to the teeth thanks to Swainey's efforts: a .22 semi-automatic, a lever-action 30/30 rifle, a .22 single shot, a semi-automatic 12-gauge shotgun, and a single-shot 12 gauge shotgun that Burton had sawn down to turn it into a pistol.

The next day, I realised we hadn't actually disconnected the burglar alarm so I tasked young Matty with that. Good lad, actually. He went round with the ladder and climbed up to deal with it; and while he was up there, we heard this *BANG!*

'Go and see what he's shot, Matty, I don't want to see the mess.'

He came back and reassured me that everything was fine, but the swimming pool was leaking.

Crowley had been snoozing in the lounger by the pool. Meanwhile, old Burton had been playing around with the rifle and pulled the trigger. It shot straight past Crowley's head by about a thumb's width. Some big splinters had been taken out of the wood of the deck loungers, and a bullet had lodged in the swimming pool.

I said, 'You're going to become famous as the prick that shot and killed the swimming pool. Now I've got to bloody fill it up all the time.' We had to keep the hose in there to keep it topped up.

Dinner the next night was fish 'n' chips. We took two cars — the stolen Falcon and Jo's — into Tairua. Like a kid with a toy, Burton had his .22 with him. It was dark when we returned, and we got lost and ended up in the wrong driveway. Robert Dixon was walking his pointer dog to its bed for the night and could see headlights facing his driveway — two cars parked one behind the other, motors still running, and people standing around. He came up to us, hearing me muttering, 'It must be here somewhere.'

'Can I help you guys?'

Well fuck. We would have looked a bit of a fright, all of us wearing black lace-up army-style boots with heavy woollen socks, green camo combat trousers, green camo T-shirts, jackets, bullet-proof Kevlar vests, and packs.

Burton, who was standing next to me, walked off, leaving me to do the talking. I needed to think fast because I was pretty worried that Burton was going to lose his shit and just start shooting. I'd already had another drama with him when he nearly killed a whole family in a campervan because he thought they'd seen him. I needed to explain the guns and camo, too.

'I think we might have the wrong place,' I said. 'John Foley said we could come up and shoot possums.' I was really apologetic, and laid it on pretty thick. 'I'm sorry to disturb you — we'll get out of your hair.'

Dixon and his dog definitely knew that something was up. We quickly piled back into the cars and took off. Crowley managed to stall the stolen Falcon and Jo and I nearly ploughed into them from behind, and all the while the fucking neighbour was staring at us.

Dixon later told the police I had the gift of the gab, that I was a good bullshit artist and I was confident and in control. Unfortunately for us, he continued to watch us as we drove up to the Flowers mansion.

We kicked back for a little while, but intuition told me it was time to go. 'Jo, let's get away from these bloody idiots. We'll go out for a cruise, to Hot Water Beach.'

As Jo and I pulled out of the driveway and around the corner, there were police across the road. One police officer was holding a Glock pistol across the roof of his car, but they weren't really tooled up yet because they were waiting for choppers to arrive from Auckland. Jo's a brilliant driver, so I said 'Boot it' and she immediately did a U-turn and shot back to the mansion. I had kept packs loaded with food, clothes and weapons, ready to go at a moment's notice, and I told the boys to evacuate on to the beach.

Burton had been pissing around while we were grabbing the packs, so I said to Jo, 'I better fucking go and see what he's been up to.' I shot back there, and what had the bastard done? He'd set booby traps around the place. We'd planned a couple of these, but only dummy ones, just to delay the police — things like fire extinguishers with wires leading off them into the undergrowth, so that as soon as they encountered them they'd think there was a bloody bomb. I knew about police standard operating procedures; I'd talked to cops, even an explosives inspector, and knew what they'd do in those situations.

When I went back, though, I found he'd gone a step further — he'd turned on the LPG and the gas stove, and shut all the windows. In those days, the AOS would first call on you to come and surrender; then, if you didn't come out after a little while and they didn't hear anything, they'd fire tear-gas grenades in there. Those grenades are hot as hell and can actually start fires. I thought, 'Jesus, as soon as they go through those frigging windows there'll be a massive explosion . . . some of those cops will probably be under cover, but it'll be a fireball, it'll get 'em.' It would kill them — that was his intention. I opened the windows up and turned the gas off, although in my haste I missed one of the burners.

Burton mentioned it later on, and I pretended I didn't know. I said, 'What did you do that for? It's alright for you, you're already doing a life sentence — but what the fuck do you think they'll do to me? They'll claim I was the leader.'

He said, 'Oh, I didn't think about that, but they won't blame you anyway — I'll take the rap.'

'Yeah, yeah,' I said, 'that's if we survive. If we kill four or five cops, guess what's going to happen? We'll be fucking dead.'

After Robert Dixon and his wife called the police, the Special Tactics Group in Wellington had jumped on a Hercules and flew to Tauranga, then screamed over to Tairua. Journalists flocked to the small coastal town. Police stayed in small motels. ('They don't talk much,' motelier Roger Turner later told the media. 'We've got guns and ammunition laid out on the tables in the units instead of hibiscus flowers in vases. The cleaners just have to work around them.')

Jo thought that maybe we should hand ourselves in, but there was no way I was going back to D block. I'd sort of mapped out a track where I'd seen a boat and a boatshed at the bottom of the private path that led to the beach, but the bloody vessel was stuffed and wouldn't start. So we kept going. The mansion was up high, really high, and I had no idea what those cliffs were like. It was also pitch-black — no moon — and you couldn't see anything. Only a lunatic — or a desperate man — would go around there. We were all creeping along bit by bit. Jo was first, as she was the lightest, and I was behind her, then came the other three. Edging along.

We were moving through the bush, and then the ground dropped away and we were at the end of the earth's goodwill — on a cliff. I was tiptoeing, edging sideways along this fucking cliff with a pack on my back and a rifle peeking out the top.

And then the cliff gave way, and I was falling, falling, into the black and the cold.

CHAPTER EIGHT

RAMBO

The Special Tactics Group officers look like combat
soldiers. Tairua locals stare as the camouflaged
figures march past with blackened faces and
weapons swinging. There is an air of mystery about
them . . . these men are considered the 'Rambos' of
the New Zealand police force: brilliantly equipped,
highly trained, and deadly.
The Dominion, *29 June 1998*

I somersaulted into the Pacific, and my boots and pack started filling
with water; I was sinking. I didn't panic — well, I panicked a little
bit, then thought, 'Shit, I gotta keep my bloody senses here.' So I
held my breath and slowly started unlacing my boots, wriggling the
laces apart and feeling a wave of relief as the sodden boots started
to come away and my feet freed themselves. I shrugged off the pack,
feeling suddenly weightless, floated up to the surface, and gasped
for breath. I was struck by how warm the ocean was.

There was blood pissing out of my wrist; I must have gashed
it on the side of the cliff on the way down. A souvenir from that
escapade is a track of long, thin scars along my wrist, as if someone
had taken a thin, multi-bladed razor and sliced it along my arm.

Jo kept going along the cliff, while Burton, Crowley and Matty
branched off up into the forest. I was pleased about that because
they'd been hanging on to me like leeches. Jo managed to get down
and near the sea, and started flicking a torch on, off, on, off, on, off.
Clever girl — I hauled myself ashore and found her. I was stuffed. I
dumped the wet camo gear and put on some clothes from Jo's pack,
including Roger Flowers's grey woollen vest and his track-pants.

It wouldn't be long before the cops were there in force, so we
scrambled up the hill, through the gorse, and crawled into the bush
where we bedded in and kept each other warm through the night.
We'd had a couple of space blankets in the lost pack, but it was no use
thinking about them. Jo's nerves were shot and she started lighting
up, which made me really nervous because I assumed that the STG

had heat sensors out there. They'd see her smoking for sure.

Next morning a chopper was screaming around, but I wasn't giving up. I'd gone to a lot of trouble to get out of Pare; I wasn't giving them the satisfaction of an easy catch. I knew that they'd only shoot if they identified a target, and at that stage, it was theoretically possible that if they spotted us, they might not be able to ID us. We could have been anybody — there were cannabis growers in the area.

After spending the day hiding, night came and we started moving again. I was optimistic that they hadn't seen us, but Mike Bush was in charge and he was determined to find me. He knew me well, old Mike, and he'd brought in massive reinforcements. Michael Dennis Bush had joined the police as a cadet in 1978, a year after I'd been digging out of Mount Crawford. After being on my tail for a few decades, old Bush would become New Zealand's thirty-third police commissioner in 2014. He wasn't the sort of person who gave up easily.

As we started moving across the beach — which was mostly rocks — watching our step while leaping from rock to rock in the dark, an Iroquois helicopter bounced over the cliff without warning and caught us on infrared. Its blades were going *crack, crack, crack* — just like those choppers you see in Vietnam movies. My energy surged.

The Iroquois could only watch us for a little while before it had to return to its base at Tairua to refuel. We scrambled into the gorse for cover, but soon we could hear the cops inching closer on foot, like ants encroaching on two crumbs. They were so close we could hear the chirp of their police radios as they talked to base camp. Later we found out that they'd airlifted people to the top of the cliff to walk down. Lazy buggers.

When the chopper had disappeared I'd thought 'Miracle, this thing hasn't seen us,' but it came back pretty quickly — this time with AOS officers dressed in black hanging out both doors pointing assault rifles with spotlights. I wasn't worried about being shot, though, since they still needed a positive ID. It's ingrained in them — before police are issued firearms, they're issued fire orders: circumstances under which they can shoot. They didn't know we had a woman with us, and that would confuse the identification.

They couldn't land because of the rocks and other shit, so we played a game of cat and mouse — the chopper hovering, while we scurried about, still looking for a way to get off the beach. The cops were yelling out over a loud-hailer, 'Stop! Stop! Do not move, or we'll shoot.' Jo was freaking out.

Actually they were doing us a favour, as their spotlights were lighting up a route up the cliffs. I went for it. The chopper rose up with me as I started to climb, with them leaning out the doors pointing their rifles. If they hadn't had those spotlights, we would have been stuffed.

Despite the AOS and their rifles, I just had to take the chance. You don't think about stuff like that in the heat of the moment; you're full of adrenaline, and that was how I was getting up the bloody cliff.

Jo wasn't as strong as me, and she was trying to hold onto my leg, screaming, 'Don't leave me, don't leave me, they'll shoot me!'

I was exasperated.

'Well, you'll have to climb up, won't ya?'

Don't worry, she came out of this just fine. She's now in Australia and married to a millionaire.

However, Jo didn't have the strength to climb and I didn't have the strength to pull her up. As I got higher, the chopper rising along with me, I was thinking 'Jesus I wonder if these bastards will shoot' — because they were getting more annoyed and yelling, 'This is your last chance.'

I decided that I had to head off without Jo, who was only halfway up the cliff. When I made it to the top, I took off straight into the bush, away from the bastards to where they couldn't land their chopper, and away from Jo. The choice, as I saw it, was either we both get arrested, or at least one of us gets away. I didn't want to abandon Jo, but we didn't really have time to discuss the matter. She's pretty tough, old Jo. I *think* she's forgiven me.

In fact, Jo gave herself up by waving at a helicopter to come and pick her up. She was charged with helping us escape and to avoid arrest, and was eventually convicted of aiding our escape.

When the police arrived at the mansion, they quickly spotted Burton's booby trap. The bomb disposal unit set to work while police searched the cars.

Inside the house, they removed the blankets covering the windows and surveyed the damage. The remnants of our weekend in the mansion were lying on the glass-topped coffee table: an orange box containing items for a shotgun, an empty Steinlager bottle, four remote controls, a tin plate with cannabis on top, a broken glass bottle used for spotting cannabis, a green Primus stove with two knives for spotting, matches, a lighter, a bag of coins, empty glasses, a map book opened to Mexico City, insect-repellent wipes and Burn-Cool wipes.

On the couch there were three *New Zealand Herald* newspapers and a *Waikato Times*. Despite my attempt to turn off the gas stove, one burner was still going, and the toaster had two pieces of toast in it. The bin contained McDonald's wrappers and a shopping list. The fridge contained fruit salad, coconut cream, bacon, leftover fish 'n' chips, mandarins, milk, coffee, eggs, and four bottles of red wine. Surveying the mess and the various items, the police concluded that we'd been there a few days. Later they tried to bleat and moan that I'd put 30-year-old red wine in the fridge. It wasn't me at all, but that's how it's remembered.

Somehow police got onto the beach that night, I think in boats, and arrested Jo. They put her in the chopper and flew her to Auckland. The next day, they interrogated her around the clock;

I was still in the bush, freezing cold. My teeth were chattering like anything. I've never been colder in my life, but my ordeal was about to end.

Suddenly I saw a movement out of the corner of my eye: a fucking dog. Do not make a sound. *Do not make a sound.* I backed up slowly, against a tree. The dog was snarling and baring its teeth, and the cops were seeing this and moving up behind it; armed police with Bushmasters, creeping quietly along. For half a second behind this tree I thought 'Fuck, they might go past me' — because the dog hadn't barked, it hadn't warned them. Then one of them caught my eye. He raised his assault rifle, and at that very moment a TV chopper came screaming overhead.

As he lifted his gaze to the chopper another cop screamed, 'Don't move, don't move — armed police!' About fifteen of them advanced on me. I stayed frozen, otherwise they might have claimed that I'd made a move for a gun. They were fucking pissed off — if Burton had succeeded in killing some of them I would probably have been shot there and then.

On 22 June at 9.30 a.m., they walked me out of the bush wearing Roger Flowers's woollen vest. This battle was over.

T he following day I was back in Pare, and decided that there was no better way of telling my side of the story than giving it myself. I called an associate, Bruce Andrews, whose number was on my approved contacts list, and he had me conferenced through to Paul Holmes's current affairs show. I told him why I'd escaped: my frustrations over the discrepancy with my release date. I spoke to Holmes for ten minutes. Of my comrades who were still hiding, I said 'They're very determined; they'll hold out until the last.'

The broadcasting of that interview sparked another investigation. My call privileges were stopped. Media liaison officer Senior Sergeant Gary Allcock, who was in Tairua looking for Burton, Matty and Crowley, said that he'd had members of the public stopping police on the streets all night asking how they'd let Arthur William Taylor use the phone, having only just returned from whence he came.

The other three stayed in the bush for four days, then broke into a bach on Sailors Grave Road north of Tairua. They used radio and TV to monitor police activity, but neighbours noticed that they were there and the police were called. When the cops came in through the front door, Crowley, Burton and Matty must have been sick of hiding because they called out 'We're up here.'

The operation to recapture us cost $733,000, which was pretty outlandish considering that they could have spent it on a stronger perimeter fence, electronic monitoring or better internal security. Or at least less-overworked screws. Labour's justice spokesperson Phil Goff told the *Herald*, 'If they'd invested it in the first place they probably could have prevented the escape.'

On 4 August 1998, in the North Shore District Court, Judge Bruce Buckton sentenced the four of us to three years for escaping, burglary and stealing a car. We'd pleaded guilty; it was one of the rare occasions when I'd admitted to something straight off the bat. It seemed the right thing to do, to get it over and done with. Judge Buckton was universally recognised as a fair judge, a good bloke, and had been sitting on the bench since 1987. I'd come to know him from his role on the Parole Board, too. Known for speaking bluntly, he hated inefficiency and nonsense and talked to defendants like human beings. Later that month, on 31 August, he sentenced Neil Swain too, to a year's imprisonment for helping us escape.

A month later, State Insurance said that the cost of the damage to Flowers's mansion was more than $30,000. That included $8000 to repaint the walls, $3000 to import fabric for a couch that had been damaged, $2000 to fix a cigarette burn on an antique chest of drawers, $5000 to fix the spa and swimming pool, $5000 to fix two eucalyptus plants one of us had smashed with an axe (guess who), and $600 to dry-clean the linen. 'Because we didn't know where it had been,' Flowers's spokesperson, Noeline Argent, told the *Herald*.

A few days after I'd returned to the clink, Dad died, aged 78, on a Friday in June at a rest home in Paeroa. He'd been unwell, and a lot of people thought I'd broken out to see him. The cops had the place under intense guard so that I couldn't get near the place.

The funeral was held on 1 July, but Corrections wouldn't let me go to it. On a special form they'd calculated that letting me out would involve paying three members of staff for six hours of work each to travel to and from the Salvation Army Chapel with me, and would cost $376.80 — to be charged to my family. Because the funeral was to take place before my sentencing, Corrections staff noted that my escape charge was yet to be dealt with. 'Generally well behaved,' wrote Bryan Christy, 'however if things don't go his way he has the capability of posing a nuisance with his constant requests. This escorted parole is not supported.'

Postscript: Nine years later, in June 2007, Joanne Hewetson was arrested in Queensland, Australia, while trying to board a cruise-liner to the Pacific with a false passport. That same year Graeme Burton, who was on parole, went nuts with a gun and shot Karl Kuchenbecker in the hills of Wainuiomata in Lower Hutt, cementing my instinct that he was a psychopath. During his arrest, police shot Burton in the leg and he later lost it in surgery. He had to use a prosthetic leg from then on.

And what of old Swainey? Many years later, I thought 'I'll reward old Swainey', so I helped him get a wreckers yard near Palmy. To start with he was as good as gold — stayed out of trouble, no problem at all. But then he got tied up in the methamphetamine scene with old Whetu Hansen, who'd once welcomed him at Pare. I liked Whetu. He'd been in D block with me and was highly intelligent. I taught him how to read. When inmates don't know how to read and write, they communicate in other ways — mostly with their fists. I'd compile reading books and stand in the workshop with them, explaining the words, the alphabet.

Whetu was forever grateful to me, but I know what he was like — he could be quite arrogant, and he would have been putting shit on Swainey in front of people, which would have driven Swainey around the bend. Whetu disappeared in November 2013; Swainey was eventually convicted of murdering Whetu, although he claims he's innocent. The body has never been found, although at Swainey's trial it was said that he sealed up a 44-gallon drum and dropped it in the Whanganui River.

Auckland, 2003

A sombre Bryan Christie showed up outside my cell.

'Taylor, I've got some bad news for you.'

The last time he gave me bad news, he alleged that I had handcuffs and he was putting me in the pound, and that's where I stayed for the next six weeks. So I was thinking 'What now?'

'Judge Bruce Buckton is dying.'

I didn't believe him, because I'd seen Judge Buckton about two months beforehand and he was looking as healthy as a fucking peach. Buckton had been a district court judge since 1986 and had also been deputy chair of the Parole Board after that was formed. He used to ring me when I was on the outside and check on me. He was a very, very highly respected judge. He wrote the bible on road transport law, *Brooker's Law of Transportation*, known widely as 'Buckton on Transport'. Lawyers use it in court for traffic cases. It was his speciality as a lawyer. That's where the money was — all those drink-drivers and rich businessmen who want to get off a DUI charge.

I'd read his book and found a loophole in the Transport Act 1962 which meant that they had to change the law. Although the Transport Act obviously intended to have a separate definition clause for what constituted a motorway, they defined a road in such a way as to not include a motorway. No one picked it up until

I twigged that this meant if you were on a motorway then you were not on a road — by their definition — and were therefore not committing a traffic offence. They had to rush legislation through parliament to change it in the early '80s.

Anyway, Christy says, 'Look, fellow, this is an extraordinary event. You know Judge Buckton is well respected by everybody — the police, the Corrections Department, everybody — and he has made a special request that you be able to visit him.'

Of course I wanted to go and see him and, believe it or not, it had actually been okayed by head office. I got all my boys to sign cards for Judge Buckton, and then sent some flowers up to North Shore Hospital. The day arrived, and three screws handcuffed me and escorted me to the hospital. It was low-key; no police escorts or anything.

On the ninth floor, we came out of the lift and there were a whole lot of detectives coming the other way who had just been to visit Bruce. God he was thin, really thin. And only 57. The screws took my handcuffs off; they knew I wasn't going to jump out the window.

Bruce's mind was still as sharp as a tack and we had a few laughs. He'd been a heavy smoker all his life, and he'd got pancreatic cancer, the worst kind, which kills you very quickly. He was just a shadow of his former self. We discussed some cases we had been involved in, then I made my farewells and left. When I got out of prison the next year, Judge Buckton's wife, who had moved to France, sent me a lovely card, thanking me. She said, 'My husband really respected you and had a lot of time for you.'

Some members of the legal fraternity you just click with. They know what it takes to succeed in the circumstances I've been in, so I guess they have a great deal of respect for my work — the fact that I have actually achieved things while coming from well behind the starter's block, shall we say. It was good seeing him, one last time. Afterwards one of the screws told me that when they'd paid their respects at Judge Buckton's bedside, Buckton told him: 'You take care of Arthur Taylor.'

I'd think of Buckton when I was in Waikeria Prison many years later, and a King Country Mongrel Mob gang leader came to me one day. He was in for bashing someone in Taumarunui, and he wanted to know what I thought about going to restorative justice to meet his victim and apologise. Despite the rivalry between the different gangs, I'm respected and can go between them. I'm quite often called in to mediate between them because they all trust me. It saves fights and problems. That's often why individuals sought my advice.

I encouraged him to go, and told him he'd feel a lot better afterwards, and that it would give his victim a chance to not be in fear of him, wondering what the hell he was doing, or thinking. When he came back, he was just about skipping. They had talked, shook hands and sorted it out.

There's nothing worse than fear, which is why I used to say to the guys in jail for beating up their girlfriends: 'What are you doing that shit for? How would you like to be scared and terrified of being beaten in your own house by someone who is meant to love and protect you?' They don't think like that, some of them, and it's rewarding to see a few of them think about it and change. Most of them respect me and listen.

He was quite a big boy, from the ironsands, Tahāroa, although he mainly hung around Te Kuiti, Jim Bolger country. Out of fear, his victim would probably have taken action to harm him, to prevent him from being able to go about their town. Instead, they just met each other and found that they were both humans, just on different sides of the divide. Same as me and Judge Buckton.

CHAPTER NINE

OUT — AND IN AGAIN

A person of his obvious industriousness should be
able to find work. I hope he's sincere about it, but
you can't help be cynical about these things. They
all come out saying they're going to be angels.
*Mike Bush, who'd led the 1998 hunt to find him, on
Arthur Taylor's pledge to go straight (September 2001)*

The day the planes hit the Twin Towers in New York City, *The New
Zealand Herald* had cottoned onto the fact that I'd been released
from prison. I'd served nine years and had been released on home
detention back to Paton Ave with its padlocked iron gate and the
sleepout that Anthony Ricardo Sannd had once stayed in. Anne-
Marie and I had parted company, though I'd always stay in touch
with our son, Tyrone. I had met Leighanne, who had long, jet-black
hair. She quickly changed her name to Taylor, despite us never
marrying.

I'd been let out on the condition that I'd stay away from riff-
raff. The Probation Service was unimpressed when it learned that
I'd been to a trial involving Leighanne, which breached the non-
association order that had been imposed on me. I was temporarily
recalled, then let out again. A few months later, in September, a
curious reporter from the *Herald* came to talk to me. I showed him
the aviary I'd built in the backyard for the budgies I planned to buy.
I told him I was going straight. And I meant it, actually.

I'd set up a business: advising on criminal trials, investigations
and strategies. People both in and out of prison had started coming
to talk to me all the time. They'd say 'Fuck, you're on the wall,
Arthur, about this criminal shit', and they'd be lining up to talk to
me. I had business running out the door. Mainly I was consulting on
drug-dealing cases, along with a few armed robberies and organised
crime. There were some very lucrative offers from gangs, and I'd
started charging for advice. Not much, though — it depended what
it was and how complex it was, and how much time it was going to
take; the same as for a lawyer. But if I hadn't much on, I'd advise

them for free because I wanted to see them get a fair go. I'd request disclosure and concoct a game plan for their trial.

But, of course, plans are one thing and actions another. My return to offending started small: some driving offences, then a few cheque frauds that barely amounted to anything — I had to pay back $1500. But I got recalled to prison.

Around this time I met William Dwane Bell. Willy had been born a year after I'd dug through the soft ground below Mount Crawford prison, and had grown up in Māngere with an abusive, gang-member father. Willy is a puzzle, but he's not entirely stupid. Later, in prison, we'd show much consideration to Willy so hopefully it rubbed off on him. Everyone gets older and wiser. But the story going around Pare is that Willy asks everyone who is getting out of jail to help him break out. And he did it with me the day I met him in December 2002.

I'd had to go to Waitākere District Court on a washing-up charge (a charge that I had to clear up), and the Corrections van picked Willy up from the High Court in Auckland where he was having his trial for beating three people to death at the Mount Wellington RSA and nearly killing a fourth, Susan Couch. We were taking Willy back to Pare with us. Being a segregated prisoner, Willy was in the back of the van and I was in the other part. Willy yelled out, 'Hey listen, I'm trying to get a gun. Can you help?'

I said, 'What the fuck? How are you going to pay for it, son? What are you going to fucken use that for anyway? I've heard of you, Willy . . .'

He said, 'I'm going to break out!'

'I'm going to have to think about this,' I said, 'because I've heard you're a bit of a loose cannon.' His plan was to grab the screws down in the cells at the court and force them to let him out the back door. I knew it was possible, as long as he had a means of disabling them.

'Yeah, I'll think about it Willy. How am I going to contact you?'

'I've got a girlfriend, she's having a baby.' He gave me the number of this teenager and said she'd pay for it.

After I got out again, I rang her and said, 'Look, love, you'd better tell Willy that this ain't going to happen.' There was no *way* I was giving him a gun.

Around the time of my encounter with Willy, the New Zealand Parole Board formed, and I came face to face with a cohort of them in 2002 after being recalled. In December the Parole Board noted a suggestion that I should meet with police, 'With a view to sorting out relationships with the outside world.' I think the idea was that I could try to mend bridges with people I'd come to see as enemies.

January 2004

After being released again, this time on parole, I spent the year living mostly alone at a lovely property on Mazengarb Road, in Paraparaumu, not far from the beach. Leighanne became pregnant, but our relationship was a struggle and by about October it was over and I was living the bachelor life. She had the baby a few months later.

Despite turning my place into a fortress, with security cameras, two massive attack-dogs and high fences, a little bit of light found its way through; and in 2004, life would change in the blink of a buzzer.

Towards the end of the year I was recuperating from a serious car crash that had knocked me around pretty badly. I'd swerved to avoid an oncoming driver on Haywards Hill Road and my jeep had nose-dived down a gorge. I was lucky to be alive, but the aches persisted so I was having acupuncture for weeks. There I was one night, doing my work, when a Toyota Surf pulled into the driveway. I peered at the security cameras; someone was at my gate. The dogs were going nuts, and I was thinking 'Who the fuck is this?'

Over the intercom I growled, 'What's your business? What do you want?'

'Oh I'm Carolyn, Arthur. Mike's friend.'

I knew who she was. Mike Sneller and I had met in Pare in the '80s. Mike was a Hulk-looking guy, all tan and jaw-line and gold chains. Back then, he was in Pare for beating a guy to death in 1983. He noticed the typewriter I had for my legal work, and soon had me typing away, creating labels to stick on all of his music tapes.

On Boxing Day 1988, Hiki Brown, who was in C block, had set his mattress on fire and killed himself. A couple of other guys were overcome by the smoke and had to be carried out. C block was shut down and everyone, including Mike, moved to D block. While they were waiting to go back to C block, Corrections seized Mike's desk. They told him they'd found 400 grams of dope in his cell; and many months later they also claimed they'd found a further 450 grams, 750 joints and $800 in cash.

Because Mike was doing life, this was going to impact his chance of parole. I'd promised him that he wasn't going under for it. There was a chain of command regarding the collection of evidence, involving about eight or nine screws, and they'd made a mistake. Mike's belongings had been searched so many times, and put into storage and other spots in the prison, that the chain was tainted. And how could it be that cannabis had been found so long after he'd been evicted from his cell? That didn't make sense to me.

We went to court, and we won. The charge was dismissed, and was upheld on appeal after appeal. I never sent Mike a bill, but he tells me I've been a thorn in his side because of the obligation for many, many years. (Another time, I helped Mike make an ACC claim when he was attacked by screws and his wedding-ring finger was damaged in the melee. His coffers were increased by about $1500.)

In 2004, Mike and I were both out and fancy-free. After celebrating his birthday one night at a steakhouse in the Hutt, I was dropping him home when — almost as an afterthought — he said, 'I'm going to Wainuiomata to meet this chick Carolyn, she's dying to meet you.'

He told me she had a gang-member boyfriend, and I said 'Oh for Christ's sake, if she's hanging around with some Black Power prick I don't want to know her. Who knows what she could get up to?'

But Mike was adamant that I had to meet her. He showed me some modelling photos she'd had taken, and I thought 'Jeez, she looks alright, doesn't she?' She had poured pints in pubs in the UK, and had done nursing as well. Carolyn was 29, while I was nearing 50. I was flattered that someone as young and beautiful as her had taken an interest, but I said, 'Don't give her my phone number because I've got enough women harassing me on the phone already.' Which I did, actually. But none of them were as beautiful as Carolyn. With her long blonde hair, she looked like Daryl Hannah.

Idling in my driveway that day, she said she was en route to Auckland, for a date with a mate of mine from the Head Hunters; Choc, we called him. 'I thought I would stop and have a coffee.'

I didn't need asking twice.

'Yeah, alright, love. I'll come down and lock the dogs up and let you in.'

First thing I said to her was 'You don't want to have a fucking date with Choc, he'll drive you mad. He's a hard-out gangster.'

She showed me how to download music to my computer while we listened to Rodney Rude. Eventually, I said: 'Carolyn, I've got to go to bed; it's getting a bit late, love. Where are you staying tonight? Because you shouldn't be on the road to Auckland, driving all that way.'

'I could stay here.'

It was a three-bedroom house and there was a spare bed, so I showed her in there, but to cut a long story short she ended up coming and jumping into my bed.

W e married not long afterwards, at Mike's mansion in Upper Hutt, in December 2004.

Carolyn had moved in with me a couple of months after we met. One Tuesday morning we were in bed and she said, 'Why don't we get married?' I said I wasn't the marrying type: I could end up back in jail at any time.

She said she didn't care, so the next day I proposed on the beach in Wellington with a ring. Once I make up my mind I get straight on the ball, so we were married just days later. The day before the wedding, I had rushed to The Terrace in Wellington to get a marriage licence, and Mike and I then went to the Upper Hutt police station because I knew what the cops would have been thinking: 'What the fuck? This is a *massive* gathering of criminals.'

Mike went in and said, 'Look, we'll make sure there's no trouble, but we don't want you coppers up there harassing us and interfering with Arthur's wedding.' So they agreed to that — and they kept their word, too.

Hundreds of people came. It was a who's who of the criminal community. There were hoodlums from all over the place who'd driven down from Auckland and Hamilton; we had to take over a couple of sections for them all to park their cars. They brought heaps of presents.

Even the *Sunday Star-Times* was there, taking photos. Carolyn, in a traditional white lace dress and heels, pulled up in a purple Cadillac with a skull on the bonnet. I was in a suit. We had two bands and the party went all weekend, but that's when the trouble started.

Someone obviously wanted me up all weekend, so they put P in my drink. Well, I don't need P. It might surprise people, but I don't touch drugs. I don't need them — I can stay up all weekend if I want to — but they thought they were doing me a favour. The P spun me right out, sent me into overdrive, and that's when all the trouble happened and I got arrested. I didn't know it at the time, but my wedding day was going to be one of my last tastes of freedom for many, many years.

They had put P in Carolyn's drink, too, and that spun her out as well. After the wedding, she and I were driving over the Paekakariki Hill Road and she was trying to open the door and jump out of the car. We could have been killed. I had to knock her back to avoid causing a massive car crash.

When we got home, she tried to jump out the window of the two-storey house. She threatened to commit suicide. It was a nightmare; I wasn't used to that sort of carry-on. I rang a guy I knew, and he said, 'You'll have to give her Valium, Arthur.'

I said, 'Where am I going to get that from?' So he came over, with a bottle with 120 tablets in it.

Next thing, I get a call from my police liaison officer, Andrew Fabish. He's a good cop. Andrew used to come around to my house regularly. He was a detective sergeant in Paraparaumu and Kāpiti and Porirua, and a well-known commander of the CIB. I had a lot of respect for him, because he respected me in turn.

'Arthur, listen, I have just had a call-out from Comms — they are mobilising the Armed Offenders Squad. Apparently Carolyn has rung them from your house claiming she's a prisoner.'

He said he was coming up, and that I should just escort her to the door and he'd take her away. So that's what we did. Andrew wanted to take her to hospital to get her checked out — but the other cops wanted to take the opportunity to question her about what I was up to, so she was taken to the police station in Porirua.

Still high on the P, Carolyn told them that I had a massive drug warehouse. That she didn't know its location but she knew approximately where it was. On 16 December they came to my house with a search warrant and found a pound of pot, so they arrested me; then they found Carolyn in a hair salon and she pointed them in the direction of my storage unit in Paraparaumu.

They found Class B and C drugs, 276 grams of cannabis, 78 grams of cannabis oil, some weighing scales and morphine. And all sorts of other shit: a cut-down semi-automatic pistol, a semi-automatic shotgun, home-made firework pipe-bombs, substances to make bombs, a robbery kit with tape, handcuffs and a balaclava, and $60,000 in cash. Most of it was mine.

The next day I ended up facing a whole lot of charges. Kidnapping, assaulting Carolyn (those charges were dropped because she refused to give evidence), possession of a rifle, explosives, a pistol and morphine, and possession of cannabis for supply. I was taken to Rimutaka Prison.

The story in the *Star-Times* about our wedding had a sequel: a story about how I'd bashed Carolyn. Carolyn tried to put things straight: she told journalist Tony Wall I was innocent. 'He did not kidnap me; he gave me a black eye, that was about it. I took an overdose of Valium on Sunday night and I've only just come right now . . . I'm not going to court, I'm not going to testify. I've sent him some photos of our wedding, I love him, and please, I'm on his side.'

Unusually, the police said, 'Listen, Arthur, plead guilty and we'll drop the possession for supply charges. We'll charge you with simple possession and you'll just go under for the firearms.' But I didn't want to go under for the firearms, because one of those guns was a submachine gun and that would look fucking terrible on my record. It had a laser sight, a silencer and a big magazine, and if you looked at the photo of it you would think it was a terrorist weapon. That, coupled with explosives, made me think: 'No, that's going to be bad enough. I might get four years out of this.'

By no means was that the end of my relationship with Carolyn. If she had been in her right mind, she would never have done it. The cops took full advantage of her — she was very sick. Sometimes you've got to be a bit bigger about these things.

The criminal fraternity wanted to take revenge on her, but Mike took her in, looked after her and kept her safe. Meanwhile, I sat on remand.

One day, police came to my cell at Rimutaka and said they had a warrant from a judge to take my blood. They said that if I didn't submit, they'd call in the riot squad. Believe it or not, I actually called a lawyer — who said, 'Look, Arthur, just give it to them and we'll sue them afterwards.'

They wanted to run it through their DNA databank because they had some idea there were hundreds of unsolved crimes around the place committed by me. I heard that when they got my DNA, they rushed it by courier to the airport to be taken out to the forensics testing centre at Mount Albert. They got nothing.

Sure enough, after I sued them they were ordered by Judge Ron Young — now chair of the Parole Board — to destroy the sample. But get this: they admitted that they had broken the law, but then argued 'We've got it now, your honour, we might as well hold on to it.' Judge Young was flabbergasted. He issued a declaration that they had taken my DNA unlawfully and then he ordered them to destroy it and that was that. They had to provide a certificate from the ESR, who maintains the databank, to say that it had been destroyed.

It wasn't just my own legal battles I had going on that year. In 2005 a long-running appeal that I'd helped Ian Douglas Johnson with finally came to fruition. Ian, who had been involved in our BNZ heist, was appealing his murder conviction. I liked Ian, but he was a bit too ostentatious with his spending for my liking. I'd organised a few other robberies for him to do and he'd gone on spending sprees all over the country. He bought a fucking hang-glider when he didn't even have a car.

I said, 'Look, Johnno, use that money to get your pot business growing — you'll actually do us a fucking favour.' He knew I wasn't going to organise any more robberies for him, so became an armed robber himself. He robbed some Credit Union place in Mount Eden; I was sitting in the back of my house in Paton Ave one day with Anne-Marie and it had flashed up on the news, this guy being dragged out from under a house with all this money falling out of his shirt.

In 1999 Johnno had been found guilty of killing his flatmate, Stavros Stavrianos, in the coastal West Auckland suburb of Green Bay. Stavros had disappeared that January; in February, a plumber who came to investigate a broken toilet found part of Stavros's skull in the U-bend. The Crown claimed that Stavros had been shot in the face, then dragged to a wardrobe, but where his body went after that, nobody knows.

Johnno ended up in Mount Eden Prison, where he met Peter Francis Atkinson, the 'Grandfather of Crime' — at the ripe old age of 70-something he was one of the country's top cooks for the Head Hunters. He'd blown up lawyer Christopher Harder's car by putting a stick of dynamite on the back wheel. Then he set fire to the late Peter Williams QC's house.

Atkinson wanted bail, and knew that the cops were desperate to get Stavros's body back, so he went to old Johnno and said, 'I'll give you $50,000 if you tell me where that body is. I'll sell that body to the cops so they drop the opposition to my bail.' The cops wouldn't go for it, so Atkinson rang up Stavros's family, to put pressure on the police — that's how devious he is. Johnno didn't trust him. I said, 'Tell him you want the 50 grand in cash. I wouldn't take a cheque or an IOU.'

Of course, Atkinson wouldn't come up with the $50k so it all fell through. Johnno got found guilty of murder and was sent to Pare for life. He's not liked by the other inmates because he's so paranoid, but he's a real entrepreneur. On Valentine's Day, he'd make heart-shaped cane baskets to sell to the other inmates to send to their girlfriends. I'd bought one years earlier and given it to Anne-Marie. If he turned his hand to legitimate business, he would probably make more money than he does at crime.

Ian had mostly argued that his trial lawyer had given him bad advice. On 3 May 2005, the appeal was lost.

The following year, at trial for the lockup charges from the end of 2004, I represented myself. I said that the lockup was mine but I'd given the keys to Shane Dalley, who had died in Rimutaka earlier in the year of natural causes. I said that he must have put the items in it, except for the precursor substances, which I'd taken from someone else to keep them out of trouble. I told the court how I used the shed for storage, particularly for legal files. Shane Dalley had keys, too, and to my knowledge it must have been him who'd left cash and drugs and guns, etc.

The prosecutor, Cameron Mander — he's a judge now, who many years later would sentence the Christchurch mosque shooter, Brenton Tarrant — suggested that it was convenient for me to blame a dead man. I replied that I would have loved to have put Dalley in the witness box, and that I could have if the trial hadn't been delayed for so long.

I should have taken the deal they'd initially offered me. The jury didn't buy my story, and found me guilty.

Unlike in other drugs and weapons cases that had come before the courts, Justice Forrie Miller heard from Probation that I was capable, energetic and intelligent and had been working as a trial consultant. Even the Crown prosecutor, Mark O'Donoghue, said I clearly had abilities, albeit in the same breath as calling me a career criminal. Despite my positive attributes, jail was inevitable. Justice Miller essentially said that I'd defended myself skilfully, but sentenced me to eight years' imprisonment.

Sitting in prison, I became very worried about Carolyn's health. Prior to our wedding she'd been taken to hospital with some heart problems, and she was continually getting sick.

At one stage she ended up in hospital, and I needed to visit her. The cops were nervous about me escaping; they came to me and said, 'Look, if we can secure the hospital we'll escort you in there.' But it was taking too long. At the time, Carolyn had been banned from visiting the prison because the screws thought she'd snuck a battery in.

When she was discharged from the hospital my plans were already in train, so I went ahead. On a Tuesday afternoon I reached up into the ceiling light of my cell and pulled down my phone to text *Sunday Star-Times* journalist Donna Chisholm.

'Carolyn had 2 go 2 Wgtn hospital by amblnc on Sat morning . . . it made me feel helpless I wasnt ther 2 lk aftr her,' I wrote. 'It was hell. I stil havnt bn abl 2 talk 2 her mch & find out xactly what hapnd.'

I was being let out to go to a family group conference regarding the custody of my infant son Kane, whom I'd had with my ex, Leighanne. Even though my relationship with Leighanne was difficult, I still wanted to be in Kane's life. When he was born, I quickly saw that he needed better care around him. They uplifted Kane from the hospital the day he was born. Leighanne went around Wellington that night with a team of helpers, putting banners up saying 'Child, Youth and Family have kidnapped my baby'. We fought like hell to get him back for her. Then I started getting reports that things were going wrong. Kane had been seen on a road without proper supervision, so CYF (now called Oranga Tamariki) took action.

The family group conference was to be held on level eight of the CYF offices on Manners Street in Wellington city and was to follow on from one held a month earlier in Paraparaumu. When the cops found out about that one, they'd freaked out and warned Corrections: keep an eye on him. The first conference had gone smoothly, however, and CYF had reported that I'd behaved in an exemplary manner, and that I was an active and encouraging participant.

Because of the complexities of the arrangements, and the number of people involved, it was decided that the Kāpiti Coast office space was too small and the next family conference would be in central Wellington. Corrections and police figured that the hour-long trip from Rimutaka Prison to Manners Street would be foolproof. Even though I was a high- to medium-security prisoner, because of my previous escapes I was escorted with maximum-security measures. They'd searched me before we left. They'd hand-picked senior, experienced and fully-briefed staff to accompany me. We drove in an unmarked car, on a pre-planned route. I was handcuffed to one of the three guards in the back of the wagon, joking and chatting with them the whole way.

As we neared the offices, a CYF worker smoking a cigarette in the basement noticed a man in a fluoro jacket loitering nearby. I was starting to get a bit nervous. I'd been in touch with Manu Royal; we'd known each for years by that stage. He was a tall guy, about six foot, and by this stage he was a grey-haired bastard. His help would ensure that I'd get to see Carolyn.

The van pulled in behind the Manners Street building, through a sort of back alleyway and up a ramp into level three of the car park building. The three guards and I jumped out, with me still attached to one of them, and then Manu appeared in a beanie, sunglasses and that fluoro green jacket and pointed an airgun at the officers.

'It's not your lucky day today,' he said, instructing one guard to unlock my handcuffs. Time was of the essence, so I hurried them along: 'Which one of you has got the key?'

'This isn't a game or a joke,' Manu said.

One prison officer later told the court that they thought they were going to die, and he'd been thinking about his family.

'Stay where you are. Don't follow us, and don't call anyone,' I told them as I unlocked the cuffs, then cuffed them to each other. I tried to get a cellphone off one of them but Manu was spooked and told me to forget it.

An office worker saw the whole thing unfold. She'd seen Manu but assumed that he was a maintenance worker. Then she saw him pull out the gun. While Manu issued instructions to the guards, she flew into a nearby lift with the office security guard to raise the alarm.

Manu and I took off down the stairwell and ran into Victoria Street, across the road and up Edward Street. I figured that the best thing to do first was get some cash from the local bank. The BNZ had these business deposit boxes which I knew weren't secure, so I thought I might as well go and get some money because the cops would be watching my bank accounts. I was in the roof space of an Edwards Street building when things became unstuck — literally. A shop worker had gone to the toilets, and as she walked in she could see some dust and debris and tiles on the floor, hand basin and toilet. Next thing she looked up and I was plummeting towards her as the ceiling collapsed. I saw this woman sitting on the toilet, and I thought 'Fuck.'

I steered to avoid her because otherwise I would have crashed right on top of her, and I managed to land on my feet. There was this fucking mass of dust and plaster everywhere. I helped her outside, and sat her down and asked if she needed a doctor. She later made a point of telling the court 'Mr Taylor was very nice to me.'

Most escaped prisoners would have incapacitated her immediately, but I figured that a story would be my best bet. 'I was up in the fucking roof fixing the fucking air conditioning.'

Then I took off at high speed towards a nearby Wilson car parking building.

Central Wellington was sealed off and there were cops everywhere, as you could imagine — at least 12 Armed Offenders Squad members with rifles and dogs out searching, shining torches to check under every parked car. Office workers weren't allowed to leave their buildings; the place was in complete lockdown. Some people were up on the roofs of buildings looking down, and I saw them right across the road from me — I was on the top of the car parking building, also looking down to see what was going on.

Meanwhile, the lady from the toilet reported what had happened to her manager, and he said, 'Jesus, what? We haven't got anyone fixing the air conditioning.' Seeing all these cops out on the road, he must have put two and two together and called the police. That gave them a head start. I suppose you could say that kindness was my undoing.

The dogs tracked up to the top of my building. I was hiding behind a car, and figured that I had a choice: surrender, or jump off the building. The police were armed, of course, so I surrendered. Constable Craig Pickering and Constable Sam Gilpin escorted me to the police station, which was a block or two away. I was sweating bullets at that point; I'd escaped for an hour.

Of course there was hell to pay. They hadn't seen anything like that happen in New Zealand for a long time, if ever — a gunman jumping guards to let somebody go. At Wellington Central police station they put on a hell of a performance all through the night, trying to find out who had helped me and where that person was. Of course I wouldn't tell them, but one of the officers later identified Manu.

J ust as I got back to Rimutaka Prison, I got a phone call from Carolyn: the police were looking for her. I had someone transfer her money so that she could head out of town fast, up north for a bit of a break before they caught up with her.

At Rimutaka they were now keeping me away from all the other prisoners, in segregation where the protective-custody prisoners were. My neighbours were Brad Shipton and Bob Schollum, who were in there charged with the rape of Louise Nicholas. They were later acquitted. A double murderer called Roberto Conchie Harris was also in segregation.

I was charged with kidnapping, presenting a firearm, and escaping. The law says that if you detain someone, even if only for a minute or 30 seconds, you've kidnapped them. (I'm surprised that cops aren't charged with this more often, considering that they do it on a regular basis.) Wellington prisons regional manager Dave East said that there would be an internal investigation into my escape, and congratulated the screws who'd kept calm during the whole thing, saying that they did the prison service proud. They'd been offered counselling. Detective Inspector Gary Knowles promised that they'd find Manu Royal.

Corrections was asked to explain why I'd been taken to a public place for a Child, Youth and Family meeting, especially given my history. They were also embarrassed to see the media reporting that I had a cellphone and that I'd been in touch with reporters again. At the time, Tony Ryall was National's justice spokesman, newly in Opposition, and he was effusive about how bizarre it was that prisons didn't have cellphone-blocking technology.

Obviously prisoners aren't allowed contraband, including phones. Just one month before the escape, Corrections had found one in my cell and confiscated it, but it's easy enough to get another in. The police even asked the *Sunday Star-Times* for my number.

I always have a phone in prison; was one of the first to get one as an inmate. There are always places to keep one. The prisons in New Zealand have these special lights that you open with a key, and I'd managed to obtain a copy of that key. That's where I kept my phones. Another handy place was the stainless-steel toilets because behind the bowl, once you get the water out, it's dry. I'd get a hook right down the bowl, then use a nylon line and a waterproof pouch. If the screws got near the door, I'd put the phone in the pouch, throw it in the toilet and flush it. They got onto this in the end, though, because they realised I was on the phone one night in D block and came raiding in. One of the smarties saw water on the floor around the edge of the toilet, so they got these plumber's cameras in to have a look.

Neil Beales, who is now the chief custodial officer, became so concerned at how many cellphones I was getting in that he sent a warning email to all staff, essentially saying 'You're toast once we work out who you are.' One of the screws showed it to me, saying, 'Hey Arthur, look at what this half-wit has just sent out.' A fucking laugh that was.

On 29 March 2005, Carolyn was arrested and charged with assisting an escape; she got bail. A few days later, on 4 April, Manu handed himself in at the Auckland Central police station some hundreds of kilometres away from where he was last seen. He was charged with possessing an airgun with intent to commit robbery, and rendering three men incapable of resistance while assisting an escape. He later pleaded guilty to kidnapping.

In February 2006, nearly a year after the failed prison escape and more than a year after our wedding, I was finally able to see Carolyn again. After that, though, Corrections declined three other applications for us to see each other, and it wasn't until May 2006 that a judge agreed she should be allowed to visit. Aside from the obvious thing of missing her and wanting to see her, it was important that Carolyn and I see each other so that we could prepare for the trial.

I defended myself at that trial in 2007. The jury again found me guilty. I had to have the sentencing moved to Auckland because they reckoned it was too dangerous to transport me to Wellington — I would escape, they thought. I was sentenced to four years in prison, on top of the sentence I was already serving for the lockup offences. With all my serving sentences combined, it added up to about twelve years.

Carolyn, who had never had a conviction in her life, was jailed for 20 months for helping me escape — she'd helped Manu get the airgun.

That wasn't the end of it, though. They again tried to get my DNA — this time through the courts, on the strength of the kidnapping charges — and I fought them tooth and nail right through the High Court for about two years. They won. The day they actually got it was quite funny. By law you're allowed a witness when you have a DNA sample taken, and I wanted my mate Bruce Andrews. Pare wouldn't let him in, so I said, 'Tell you what. The judge specified the day on which you can take my DNA at Auckland Prison. That day doesn't end until midnight. I'll just keep you waiting, if you don't let him in.' They let him in.

L ife goes on, of course. People think that life stops and starts when you're behind bars, but for me the windowless cells honed my concentration on the law. By this point I'd learned that my mind could open many doors for me. In 1641, Englishman Richard Lovelace was imprisoned for petitioning the House of Commons. While incarcerated Lovelace pondered his liberty, and in the final stanzas of 'To Althea, from Prison' Lovelace considers that so long as you have liberty of mind, you're a free man. I discovered this poem some time ago and my mind often turns to it.

Prison didn't stop my and Carolyn's world from turning, either. However, when your reality is controlled and cramped, your sunlight filtered and your adventures less spirited, your dreams take on new meaning. They're a chance to escape. In Pare one night I had a very vivid dream that Carolyn was holding a beautiful little baby and she was calling her Siobhan.

When I spoke to her the next day and told her about this dream, she said, 'We'll have to make it happen, babe, won't we?'

While some European countries allow conjugal visits, that had never been the case in New Zealand, and while the occasional expert would comment on its, perhaps, therapeutic and rehabilitative benefits, nobody had taken up the mantle of introducing it. So I said, 'How the fucking hell are we going to do that?'

Carolyn said, 'You've got your ways. You'll know how.'

Screws will do anything for a buck. I'll spare you the details, but the gold found its way to Carolyn. When she told me she was pregnant, I thought: 'Jesus, we've bloody made it happen. This will be a special miracle baby.'

I'd always loved kids. Kane had gone to live with a justice of the peace called Janice, then on to a private boarding school in Huntly. He's now in Wanganui Collegiate doing brilliantly, awesomely. My other son, Tyrone, became a foreman on a fishing trawler out of Nelson. I get on really well with both of them, and I was quite happy and excited about Carolyn having a baby.

Corrections, of course, denied my paternity — said there was no way I could be the father of Carolyn's baby. They didn't want to entertain the thought that I'd had help to make it happen.

C arolyn was in custody when Siobhan was born, I think in the early hours, at Middlemore Hospital on 12 June 2007. Having never been in prison before, Carolyn should have been a low-security prisoner. But because she was married to me she was treated like a maximum-security prisoner in the Auckland women's prison at Manukau. Within hours of Siobhan's birth they'd taken Carolyn back to prison — without her baby, which was very distressing for everybody. I posted a birth announcement in *The New Zealand Herald*.

I met Siobhan a few days later. Child, Youth and Family brought her in to see me at Pare, and we'd see each other regularly from then on, maybe for a couple of hours once or twice a month. She was like the Little Princess of the jail. The visits took place in an area called the glasshouse, which is where lawyers and their clients normally meet. Sometimes inmates walking past with officers on escort would stop and say hello, like she was a young star. Siobhan was, and still is, the image of her mum: blonde hair and big blue eyes.

I was allowed to talk to Carolyn at least a couple of times a month. Unsurprisingly, she wasn't doing well after the birth, and they put her in a suicide cell because they realised how distressed she was at being separated from our daughter. I immediately filed an action in the High Court.

I got orders to ensure that Siobhan saw Carolyn every single day. For over a year Siobhan was brought into that prison daily, but then they tried to reduce the visits to once a week. Corrections were making things unnecessarily difficult, saying that they didn't have the resources to facilitate the visits. We said we'd settle for every two days, but fortunately Judge Margaret Rogers, of the Manukau Family Court, stepped in.

Judge Rogers was very perceptive. She summoned the women's prison manager to court, and I had them pull out their whole prison schedule. That's the advantage of knowing how prisons operate. I know they have schedules, and they have to know exactly where everybody is at a certain time on a certain day. So there would be spaces there to accommodate visits between Siobhan and her mum. In the hearing room we had them combing through their days, and then Judge Rogers went through it herself, and said 'There, you can accommodate one there.'

Carolyn was coming to the court, too, which was a good chance for us to see each other. The women officers would bring Carolyn, and I'd be escorted in from Pare with our guards. It was quite funny because the women guards would bring chocolate cake for my guards. While they were off having lunch, we would be in the Manukau Court cells having a date of our own.

When Carolyn was released, we were faced with a choice: get Siobhan back to her mum full-time, or keep her with her caregiver family, in Auckland, whom she'd bonded with. We decided that we couldn't just take her off them, it would be too much of a wrench. You have to place the interests of the child first, over what you might want yourself.

CHAPTER TEN

SPIDER + WEB

Tuesday, 2 September 2008

At the North Shore police station they were assembling in their dozens. Detectives, senior sergeants and constables had been weaving an intricate web across the North Island, a snare that began because of a grisly death, and ended with investigators silently listening to late-night mutterings inside the cells of Pare. Now, they were about to catch their prey.

The disappearance of Grant Trevor Adams, known as Granite, had kicked off Operation Spider in March 2006. This was a police operation to figure out who had knocked him off and whether it had anything to do with drugs. There was a rumour going around that I had authorised his murder. If there's some serious crime going on, police think that I must know about it, or authorise it, or be involved somehow — which is a load of bullshit. I'd never heard of this Adams in my life.

At the time Granite disappeared, he was on the run because he had assaulted a pregnant woman. The police thought his disappearance was a drug deal gone wrong, that my brother-in-law, Brett Ashby, had knocked Granite off. They began bugging phone conversations. I'd met Brett in Pare decades earlier, and had introduced him to my baby sister, Joanne, who was then seventeen. When Brett got out they married, moved to the Bay of Plenty and had several kids.

In the process of the investigation, police got wind that something else was afoot out of Pare. At the time, Brett was facing methamphetamine manufacturing charges. They'd dug up his rural property and found waste from precursor substances. So they applied for multiple search warrants to bug prison cells and private homes to try to work out what was going on. Operation Spider began covertly listening to my and Brett's conversations.

D etective Sergeant Mike Paki of the Criminal Investigation Branch would become second in charge of this operation. He listened thoughtfully to the conversations and decided that a far larger investigation needed to be carried out. He proposed to his supervisors that they should apply to the court for more surveillance. The bosses agreed, and so did the court. Operation Spider was about to branch off into Operation Web.

The conversations were monitored at the Crime Monitoring Centre in Wellington. The intercepted lines were given code names: Birch, Cedar and Oak. Other police were able to access the CMC remotely if they wanted to listen to the calls, and they could even eavesdrop live, often straining to make out words and conversations over bad internet connections, the low throb of prison hubbub, and their targets talking over one another excitedly. It was common for prisoners to share phones, to all be on one call, and sorting the chaff from the wheat became quite a task. Detective Vanessa Cook listened to our lives. She learned that inmate Rocky Pulete was moved from his cell, and she heard inmates discussing a weird buzzing noise that infiltrated the prison one day. She heard me talking to Joanne, and to my other family and friends. Mostly, that's all she heard.

After they'd settled on what they needed, Operation Web reached a crescendo when the cops were all assembled and given specific instructions that would see them splitting off in various directions to search homes and prison cells.

I t was still early on that Tuesday when Detective Josh Meinsma and Detective Sergeant Murray Free, both of the Henderson CIB, wandered up the driveway of a home in Titirangi, West Auckland, and poked their heads through the door. The ten-year-old house perched on the brow of the hill had replaced an 1885 bach, one of the original buildings in the bush-clad suburb. Bruce Andrews had bought the house and the land for $85,000, and many years later the 51-year-old was completely astonished to see two cops, wearing stab-proof vests, clutching legal papers and asking to take a look inside. Well, *telling* him they would be, really.

'I can't believe you're here. You're making a big mistake,' Brucie told them as they confiscated the cellphone he'd been yakking on. Free and Meinsma told him that a police investigation had been under way for eight months and that he was suspected of importing and supplying drugs.

'Have you been speaking to any Asians by phone over the last eight to nine months?'

'Only concerning my work.'

'Do you know a person called Arthur Taylor?'

A light went on.

'*That's* why you're here — makes sense now,' Brucie replied.

Meanwhile, police were showing up at the Papatoetoe home of Karen Young (not her real name, as she was later granted name suppression) with a similar set of legal papers. Karen answered the door in a Holden racing jacket, while her sister looked on in her dressing gown. A child was asleep in the house, and the women were horrified. Karen was emotional, and cried as she told Detective Devlin and Sergeant Bartlett that she was terrified for her safety.

Some 'heavies' had been coming around and dropping off packages; she didn't dare look inside them. A man called Wanzhe Gui had also called her and asked her to buy five cellphones. She complied — her son was in prison and she was fearful about what could happen to him if she didn't. 'You don't know these people — my sons and grandkids will end up in a boot,' she told the officers.

At about 8 a.m., four police officers, including a senior detective, arrived at Pare and briefed Corrections before dividing into two teams. Constable Shawn Wanden marched off to East Wing, to the cell of Rocky Pulete. Rocky was removed by Corrections staff; two others remained nearby while Constable Wanden took grey tracksuit pants from his cell, along with a lined notebook with the name of a 'Bruce on Titirangi Rd' written in it, and other notebooks with names and bank account details.

S lowly, but surely, this wave of blue would end up at my cell door. I was sitting in my cell in C block because they hadn't unlocked us, which was extremely unusual for that time of day. The boys were surveying the landing with little plastic reflectors that they used like mirrors. 'Hey, the fucking police are here,' one of them yelled.

Whenever cops swept through the prison they'd be pelted with things through the bars. This happened so often that the screws had taken to using a large shield to protect the police as they walked past. The screws were walking down, carrying this shield, until they stopped outside my cell. The door cracked open.

'We've got to move you downstairs, and we're moving everyone else out of the yard.'

'Why? What the fuck is going on?'

'You'll find out.'

A warrant document decreeing a search on 'any prison cell occupied by Arthur Taylor' was produced. Sometime around 2007 I'd got my own office in Pare — an unused, windowless room about the size of three cells that I was allowed to spend a few hours a day in, in the morning and afternoon. I had a computer but no internet access, so relied on documents, books and old case law reports. (Of course, I didn't get this because they saw how well I was doing at applying myself to law, and came up to my cell and said, 'Oh, you want an office, Arthur?' I had to force it out of them. They made out that I took up half the prison's resources, but it was a room they weren't even using. I tidied it up, cleaned it, had my computer installed in there and away I went.)

When I saw the warrant, I just had to laugh. Evidence of drug paraphernalia, weapons, phones, cash, all sorts of shit. Okay, I might have a cellphone or two stashed away, but meth? Jesus Christ. If I'd had a hundredth of what they were looking for — that they claimed they had reasonable grounds to believe was in my possession — every screw in that jail would have been sacked for incompetence and dereliction of duty.

Detective Darren Attwood explained my rights and gave me a copy of the search warrant. He said they'd been investigating me and had been listening to my calls. They didn't arrest me on the spot — they didn't have enough evidence, as it turned out. Of course they thought they'd find some in my cell, but they didn't; so they had to re-consider matters and, I guess, re-strategise.

'Do you want to listen to any of the recorded conversations that we believe involve you?' Attwood asked.

'I don't know what you're talking about, mate.'

He explained the charges.

'You've got to be fucking joking. You're going to have egg on your face with this one.'

After evicting me from my cell, Constable Mitchell and the senior detective, Detective Sergeant Bothamley, began uplifting what they could from both my cell and my office. My computer and all my documents and files for my legal work were in them, and Bothamley's instructions were to take the lot, instead of just sitting and sifting through it like lame ducks. They took the TV and CD player out of my cell, and my ring-binders and files, hard drives and a six-page document entitled 'Extraction and separation of ephedrine and pseudoephedrine', dated 27 July 2006, from my office.

The cops spent several hours in my cell, and in the meantime the inmates had to remain locked up, having breakfast in their cells. By late morning the place was getting warm and people were getting impatient. Fires were lit in cells and corridors, and screws would have to come and douse them. When Bothamley and Mitchell left with all my documents they walked through corridors of shouting, heaving inmates. Smoke lay on the air.

I t became all about the numbers. It all sounded so impressive. Forty search warrants executed. Sixteen arrested and charged and put before the courts. A hundred and one text messages between Brucie and me over 32 hours. Twenty-five volumes of transcripts. Thousands of hours of phone calls.

And yet, a good eighteen months after the police first applied to listen to my conversations, charges weren't laid until seventeen days after my cell was searched. I was facing three counts of offering to supply, and one charge of conspiracy to supply, both for meth. It was such a bullshit carry-on. Rocky faced the same charges.

Detective Cook at the Takapuna CIB had also been given the tedious task of transcribing thousands of hours of conversations between others and me. The focus of the charges concerning me became a 32-hour period in early June 2007, during which I'd had several conversations with a guy serving a sentence in Rimutaka Prison. Rocky had rung me one day, greeting me by my nickname, Judge. He had drugs for sale, and I'd put him in touch with another prisoner, in Rimutaka. I'd contacted this guy — who'd eventually be given name suppression — and greeted him with: 'Get your wallet out.' Afterwards, I texted Rocky and let him know. 'That's good news, thanks,' he replied.

In the eyes of the law, that was a conspiracy. People don't properly understand this. If you and I are talking, and I say 'I would like to fucking rob that bank' and you say 'Yeah', that's the conspiracy complete — the moment we've agreed.

I'd first met a 22-year-old Rocky in 1992 in the Auckland District Court cells. We were both waiting to go up on charges, both for separate armed robberies. During my time listening to police scanners I'd heard Rocky's name more than once.

He was a Tongan bloke who'd come to New Zealand aged eleven and was expelled from school for smoking cannabis. He worked as a bouncer, and a labourer, then became a King Cobra. When we crossed paths, Rocky had been accused of robbing a Westpac bank in Albany, on Auckland's North Shore, and three BNZs of tens of thousands. Seeing him sitting in the cell on this particular day, being the friendly bloke I am, I ventured an introduction, of sorts.

'Fuck, are you Rocky Pulete? I've heard of you,' I said.

Later Rocky would tell me that he suspected me of being a cop, because I knew so much about him and his crimes from listening to police frequencies. If I'd known him before that meeting, I very well might have given him a ring and told him to get the hell out of the house that I knew the police were starting to surround.

We became good friends. We were on the same landing in Pare for several months, and at the time of our arrest I was helping him get compassionate leave to see his mother. When we couldn't talk in person, we called each other.

Fast forward to 2007. The deal didn't go through; the customer in Rimutaka couldn't pay. And that was it. A fucking innocuous conversation which could have been about anything. Pills. Cannabis. Pethidine. Cellphones. We could have been discussing anything, but it suited the Crown to invent some code words that they said I must have been using. They said I was coordinating, receiving orders, and organising payment and product — methamphetamine — for people outside prison by way of a smuggled cellphone and a phone diversion system so that I could call people who weren't on the approved Corrections list. But the proof — or, in fact, lack of it — was in the pudding. Despite their thousands of hours of transcripts and months of bugging and 40 search warrants, all they could come up with was a couple of brief conversations between Rocky, this other guy, and me.

By the end of the month of the arrests, investigative journalist David Fisher had published an article in the *Listener* magazine that alleged a massive conspiracy, positioning me in the middle as a sort of go-between for the gangs (the Mongrel Mob, the King Cobras, the Killer Beez and the Head Hunters), a contact in China, and some people who were pulling strings outside of prison. Fisher concluded that Brucie Andrews was my lieutenant, trusted to handle the mechanics and administration. The evidence on this just didn't stack up, though.

I'd met Brucie about a decade earlier, when he'd helped me with a car. It's true that we were in contact — he was a great help to me from outside prison. I'd transfer him money so that he could take care of my bills, and he kept in regular contact with my mum, who was unwell at the time. I routinely paid off her credit card and put money into our family trust, and I suppose to the outside eye it looked like I was spitting out cash left, right and centre. Brucie's only crime was being a helpful friend to me. A couple of years after he was arrested, he had the charge against him dismissed.

'The nemesis of my life,' Bruce Andrews had, understandably, told Detective Meinsma the day the police descended on his property. 'Arthur Taylor can't help himself — he always ends up in jail. If my wife found out that's the reason you're here, she'd be so disappointed. He's what you'd describe as a serious criminal. It would be better if Arthur Taylor stayed in jail, because that's where he belongs.'

By the time we got to depositions, I'd received a huge amount of police disclosure — boxes and boxes of documents outlining the whole Spider and Web operations — and it became clear what the fuck had happened.

A phone I'd got off a screw had been deliberately smuggled in to me. As I was reading these documents, I was thinking there was only one person who would pay a fucking screw to smuggle a phone in to me, and that was an associate of mine, a businesswoman, who did the odd job outside of prison for me, much like Brucie did. The whole thing was a jack-up.

You need people on the outside to help make your world inside go a bit more smoothly, and this businesswoman was a bit of a groupie. So one day she'd smuggled me in a phone — and lo and behold, the police could spy on my conversations. Crafty as. All that time, she'd been trading information with the police, and they'd authorised her to give a screw $600 to get that phone to me. The documents said she'd been assisting police for years, and had been giving valuable information on the Head Hunters, Hell's Angels — the only one missing was bloody Black Power, I think — which had led to many arrests and some people serving substantial prison time.

Normally the police work very hard to keep their informants' identities secret. You can see why, can't you? So long as an informant doesn't have to be accountable, you never know who you're dealing with or what their motivations are, though it's usually money. Police are more than happy to pay people for information. This time, they hadn't redacted some information in one of their disclosures prior to trial, and there was this businesswoman's name in plain ink — code-named 'Informant Oscar'.

While I was in the midst of preparing for trial one day, my computer inexplicably disappeared from my office. I was eventually told they'd wheeled it out — like a grand parade — as Neil Beales said it had to be examined by police. It didn't have to be examined by them — they could have had independent contractors do it. I was livid. Beales put on a big act when they returned it. He decided that instead of just having his staff return it, he would accompany them, along with fifteen of his officers. He marched down to my office and said, 'Taylor, I don't want to do this, but I've got to give your computer back to you.'

'Why didn't you get an independent examiner? I'm engaged in heavy legal proceedings with the police — they are alleging that I run a drug ring out of your prison. That's like we're playing France and the French put a fucking bug in the All Blacks' dressing room.'

All fifteen screws were standing around open-mouthed. One of them said, 'There's no need to get personal, Taylor.'

'Personal? That prick handed my computer over to my fucking enemies and my opposing party in this case. They'll probably know all the tactics and strategies I'm going to use now.'

After that, whenever he had my computer examined they had to pay $2500 to a private company to examine it. The police weren't allowed to do it anymore.

I was sitting in my office working away on my case one morning in December 2008 when I heard screams rattling through the windows of B block. It turned out that a one-legged Graeme Burton with newspapers stuffed down his grey prison clothes was chasing Dwayne 'Captain' Marsh down the landing with two shanks after confronting him in his cell. Captain, a senior Head Hunter, was screaming his head off while he tried to ward Burton off with the end of a mop. In the end, Burton got him in the chest.

The screws came back after lunch with blood on their shirts. One of them, a big fellow, said, 'That fucking mate of yours Arthur, Marsh, he's been stabbed.' I pretended I knew nothing, but I had a cellphone back in my possession and one of the boys had already called. I knew Marsh's family; he was a good mate of my brother-in-law, Brett. So I called the Head Hunters up and said, 'Get the fuck up to hospital, Dwayne's within an inch of dying.' Captain being who he was, I thought the doctors might just pull the plug without fighting properly for him. I figured that a clamouring family could be beneficial to his outcome. Plus, they deserved to know as quickly as possible.

Burton was charged, and then, much to my dismay, moved into D block near me. It annoyed me no end. So I said, 'Graeme, I will help you get out of D block, but I want your promise that you are not going to keep stabbing other inmates.' He promised. And Marsh survived.

Operation Web came to the High Court at Auckland at the beginning of 2011, after having been transferred from the North Shore District Court. The weekend before the jury was empanelled, *The Truth* published a story about the case, calling me a high-profile career criminal and a notorious prison escapee with an extensive criminal history that included drug and armed robbery convictions. It was unfortunate timing.

I had written to the paper complaining of the police's use of informants, still ticked off about 'Informant Oscar'. They ran the letter prominently, which was highly prejudicial to a jury. If a jury member read it, what do you think they're going to do? I raised this issue with Justice Edwin Wylie, who asked each potential juror if they had seen the story. One answered yes, and was dismissed. He was truthful — not every juror is. Overall, though, Justice Wylie wasn't concerned about the article. Some cases have been dismissed after prejudicial media reports, but Justice Wylie simply told me that I shouldn't have written to the paper.

By the time the trial got going, the warrants the police had used to listen to our conversations were four years old. Aside from that, it beggars belief that police would let me have a cellphone in a maximum-security prison. For years Corrections had, and would continue to, discipline me if I had a phone, their rationale being that if I had access to a phone I would organise an escape. And there they were, getting me one smuggled in. I'd battled to get my charges severed from everyone else's, which meant that the jury heard mine and Rocky's cases separately to the charges they'd laid against the manufacturing side of the syndicate.

High on my agenda was getting to the truth of the matter regarding 'Informant Oscar'. I believed that the police had launched into this surveillance nonsense based on the word of this woman, who had clearly been in it for the money. Both the court and the police tried very hard to prevent me questioning 'Informant Oscar' myself. If I used her name in court they'd plead ignorance, which was ridiculous. There shouldn't have been a problem with compromising her identity because everybody knew who it was. It was right there in the documents.

During the depositions hearings at North Shore, I had issued a summons requiring her to come to court. One day, Brucie was in court and whispered to me, 'Look who's behind us.' And sure enough, there she was, sitting among the cops and trying to make out like she had nothing to hide, as if we didn't know what she'd been up to.

Judge David McNaughton said, 'What's this summons all about, Taylor?'

'She's got information about this case and I want to cross-examine her under oath.'

He ordered her to stand, and she did, like a possum caught in the headlights. Everyone's eyes went to her.

'What do you know about this case?'

'Nothing, your honour.'

'Well, Mr Taylor wants you to attend as a witness, so you'll have to.'

Well, after that, I never saw her again. I reckon she got a massive payout from the police for not having that information redacted and having her name out there as a gang informant. Christ. I don't feel sorry for her, though. Most people would be terrified to have pissed off that many dangerous people but I reckon she'd only be disgruntled that she's not making money anymore for informing.

When my attempts to out Oscar failed, I applied for an order to have the judge simply discharge me on all the charges. I argued that the evidence obtained under the warrant should have been inadmissible, and that the prosecution should be stayed because the police took so long to charge me after the warrant was issued. That, too, was denied.

So in February 2011 we found ourselves at the High Court in Auckland watching a jury being sworn in — a laborious process that can take up to a day. The media bench was full. Radio New Zealand had applied to record the proceedings. TV3 and TVNZ both wanted to film. The programme *Sunday* wanted footage for a piece they were doing about me. (Interestingly enough, Mike Bush appeared on *Sunday*, basically saying that I was the worst of the worst and 'central' to the methamphetamine ring . . .)

Initially, security tried to lock me in the dock to stop me running off; all the other defendants were allowed to sit in the courtroom. I was handcuffed to a security officer, which I could see was going to be a fucking nightmare because I wouldn't be able to take notes. And when you're handcuffed for hours the metal chafes on your skin, causing rashes. It was also an affront to human dignity. Imagine a lawyer having to conduct their case while they're attached to a guard. Normally, prisoners aren't handcuffed during hearings.

Justice Edwin Wylie was presiding over the case, and he asked me what I made of the proposition that I was gearing up to flee at any moment.

'It's a load of rubbish, your honour. I'm not going to be running off anywhere — I'm here to clear my name. How am I even going to get anywhere? The place is surrounded all the time.'

Which was true. All the many defendants, plus their families, plus lawyers, plus the media. The depositions alone were a circus. The car park was overflowing. One day the driver of the escort van I was in backed out of the driveway of the North Shore District Court and right into the side of a police car. Another day Brucie put on a sausage sizzle out in the car park. The cops were spewing.

Justice Wylie ordered that my tether to the courtroom could be appropriately managed by having two uniformed police staff in the room throughout the hearings, and one security guard sitting on either side of me, so on the first day of trial I sat at a court desk listening to prosecutor Brett Tantrum open his case while the jurors listened intently. Part of me felt sorry for them. Despite the promise of a global meth ring orchestrated by yours truly, as the media were saying, it was going to be a boring-as-fuck trial that centred on a few messages strung together to form a not-very-coherent narrative.

The Crown's case was that the intricate web that had included Rocky and me led all the way to China. They claimed that Rocky was a supplier for a wider ring, and this person Karen in the suburbs, whose son was in prison and clearly owed a few favours, was acting as a go-between, taking instructions from Wanzhe Gui. She delivered or collected the meth, and had had the charges against her abandoned (along with being given name suppression) in exchange for telling the police what she knew.

The prosecution asked the police to school the jury on meth. Uniformed officers stood in the dock, explaining that sales in New Zealand at street level had grown dramatically since the late '90s. Uncut meth was called pure, or P, or speed, white, crack, smoke. Imported meth was ice, rock, crystal. You bought it in bags measured in 0.1 of a gram, called points, dots, dotties, dollar bags or hundy bags. Dealers making a buck might under-deliver on weight — buyers weren't often in a position to argue. Police often found that a point bag only weighed 0.075 or 0.085 grams, rather than 0.1.

A gram of meth was worth anywhere between $600 and $1000. A gram was a g, a g shock, a little one, a small one, or gangsters. You could buy an ounce for $12,000. An ounce, the police told the jury, were called O's, round ones, big ones, wholes, or holes. Meth could also come wet or dry. Wet upped the weight for no gain. Diluted or cut meth — mixed with other things — was called goey, goie, go fast, or speed.

The magic ingredient to make meth was pseudoephedrine,

and that ingredient is hard to find in New Zealand; the government even took cold and flu medicines containing pseudoephedrine off the shelves. Meth makers ship large amounts of ContacNT, Continuous Action Cold Medication, in from China where you can get capsules of 90 milligrams off the shelf.

I've never taken meth myself, aside from that time when someone snuck it in my drink at my wedding. That was awful enough.

I had only limited resources during the trial, so I had to concentrate on the most serious charges. I figured that if I could knock out the three charges of offering to supply methamphetamine, I'd save myself from looking down the barrel of a life sentence, and surely it would logically follow that I couldn't possibly be guilty of conspiracy.

Conspiracy sounds magnificent, doesn't it? But when you peer at the cobwebs, often all you see are holes. A conspiracy is simply a plan to commit a crime with two or more people — according to the Crown, these were the Rimutaka inmate and Rocky Pulete. But if there's no evidence of a crime committed, then where's the conspiracy?

Despite their months-long investigation, in which they'd combed through my bank records, TAB accounts, cellphones and the thousands of documents in my cell and on my computer, interviewed my friends and family and peered into the lives of several big-time crooks, the police 'evidence' amounted to three text messages and two seconds-long phone calls where not once do you so much as hear me whisper the words 'meth' or 'P'. No drugs were ever found, nor money; nothing of the usual attributes of drug dealing that you would expect to find.

The warrant to search my cells had been executed on the basis that police had reasonable grounds to believe I had scales, pipes, money, P, heroin, pot, etc. in my possession. I tell you what, though — nobody in their right mind would have thought that any of that would be in my cell or office, and sure enough they found none of it.

The document they became excited about was the one on how to extract ephedrine and pseudoephedrine. For me, finding out about this was an academic exercise. I'd learned of a technique years earlier whereby you could manufacture methamphetamine without pseudoephedrine. I found the original information in sources relating to World War 2 Germany, when the Germans made it for their soldiers before sending them into battle. It was called the Nazi method because the soldiers would be dead soon, so it didn't really matter that it was harmful to their health.

From this, coupled with a radio they'd found in my cell which they claimed I was using to charge my cellphone, they surmised that I was trying to supply three ounces of meth for $12,000.

Here's the kicker: after the police had obtained the 2007 warrant and listened in on my conversations, they'd decided not to charge me. They'd charged Brett with the murder of Granite and some drug offences, but left me alone. It wasn't until local police in the Bay of Plenty, where the murder was alleged to have happened, turned over the evidence to Auckland region that they started having another look. I guess they thought 'Well, maybe there's something in this?'

I wanted to be able to say to the jury: look, never mind this snapshot of our conversations in 2007; let's look at all the time they had my phone bugged when there was no criminal activity discussed whatsoever. But Justice Wylie wouldn't allow it, saying that we had to confine ourselves to looking at the conversations from 2007. Any evidence post-2007 was barred.

That could have been a dagger in the back for my defence, but I considered it just a piece of the jigsaw puzzle. Police had only identified the Rimutaka inmate's voice on a 2008 recording, not a 2007 one. With the 2008 evidence now ruled out, the court was bound by that. Because of this, he was able to argue for a discharge without conviction on the basis that there was effectively no evidence that he was the inmate I had corresponded with.

I had been charged with conspiring with this man — if he was deemed to be acquitted, where did this leave me?

Justice Wylie's reply was essentially that the inmate from Rimutaka didn't affect my case.

What you've been presented with by the Crown as the evidence in this case, is really a cut and paste job of edits placed together, so as to present the Crown case in the best possible light,' defence lawyer Peter Winter told the jury of twelve on Valentine's Day 2011.

Peter Winter had been representing Rocky throughout the trial. On this day he was summing up his defence, and it was quite good.

'The effect may be to distort the flavour of the particular conversation. This is particularly so in a prison setting where people are talking about drugs in the same way that ordinary people might talk about the weather, or what they did on the weekend. Because prisoners don't have a weekend and the only people they can talk to, except on visiting days, are other prisoners.'

Winter's closing remarks came hot on the heels of my own. I'd fought as hard as I could, and I hung my last words with the jury that morning.

'You're probably used to seeing on TV screens big tables piled up with methamphetamine and money and guns. Well, you haven't seen any of that here,' I said.

Carolyn was in court when the jurors trod quietly into the courtroom, one by one. The registrar asked the foreperson, 'How do you find Mr Taylor on count one, offering to supply?'

'Not guilty.'

'Count two, offering to supply?'

'Not guilty.'

'Count three, offering to supply?'

'Not guilty.'

And finally, the conspiracy charge: 'Guilty.'

Carolyn and I had thought I was coming home. We really did. I was gobsmacked when the verdict came out.

Believe it or not, though, the verdicts were a small win. Everyone in court was cheering because I'd got off the charges that carried a life sentence.

13 MAY 2011

Some months after the verdicts, I was squaring off against the Crown yet again, for sentencing. This time I had help, from an unlikely assistant I'd taken on in Pare.

Bushy-haired Jason Somerville was a lost soul. Around the time that cops were listening to me chatting to Rocky Pulete, Jason had murdered his neighbour, Tisha; a year later, he also murdered his wife, Rebecca. He'd strangled them, stuffed knickers in their mouths, had sex with their dead bodies and then buried them under the floorboards of his Christchurch home. Later he confessed to the police. Most of the boys in Pare didn't like him, but to me he was like a lost puppy that needed direction. I felt sorry for him. I figured out that he was basically honest — a lot of those guys in Pare you couldn't trust. Not only that, but they lacked the good work ethic I needed in a legal assistant.

Jason had never been in jail before, and had never had any criminal convictions before these killings. I got talking to him one day, and offered him a job. The Pare guards were pleased to get him off the landing, where the other prisoners were beating him up, and into my office, where he was under my wing.

He was a bloody good worker. He kept my office with its white-painted cinder-block walls and boxes under the table cleaned up, and organised my paperwork. I had heaps of files, and would say

'Jason, can you please put that in file such-and-such, that's to go with the such-and-such case', but he knew how to do it himself in the end. He would know what I was working on and he'd say 'Well, that goes there, Arthur', but you would be lucky to get ten words out of him throughout the day. A very quiet, reserved chap.

After someone leaked the story about Jason to the media and they went to Corrections head office, head office said '*What?*' They rang Pare, and Pare management were so embarrassed that they denied it all. A good thing was turned into a bad thing — they ordered Jason out of there.

At sentencing, the Crown argued that for the conspiracy to supply meth charge I should be jailed for five years, with an extra two to three years added on because the alleged offending had been committed in prison and Rocky and I both had criminal backgrounds.

Judges don't just pluck sentences out of thin air. They have to comply with the principles of sentencing, and take into account any mitigating and aggravating factors, whether or not a defendant is remorseful, what they've done to address their motivations, and what rehabilitation they've done. An offender who continues to deny their offending is seen in the court's eyes as showing a lack of remorse — but that's exactly what I continued to do: I kept telling them I wasn't guilty, because I wasn't. There was no evidence. It was a shit charge.

Wylie took Probation Services' word for it that my 'refusal to accept culpability for the offending was demonstrative of a lack of remorse'.

'Your long history of criminal offending is considered representative of your deeply ingrained way of behaving, and it was noted that breaking this pattern of behaviour might well prove challenging for you,' Wylie told me. 'You have failed to remain conviction-free for any significant length of time throughout your adult life, even while being held in custody.'

In the end, Wylie jailed me for seven years with a minimum

period of half that. It was a bolt out of the blue. Along with the other sentences I was serving — for the morphine and cash and explosives, and for escaping — I was already serving twelve years. It was ludicrous. Everybody had said I wouldn't get more than eighteen months. Sure, some of the most serious cases of conspiracy — massive multi-million-dollar conspiracies — were getting seven years, but they hadn't proved that my case was anything of the kind.

Looking down the barrel of another lengthy sentence, I was devastated, but by this time I'd learned that if I can't do anything about something, then I have to accept it. My philosophy is: if you can effect change, do it. If there's nothing you can do, don't be crying over it. Save your energy.

In this instance I opted to do something. The following year, in July 2012, I appealed the conviction and the sentence in front of Justices Harrison, Potter and MacKenzie at the Court of Appeal. I told them that the jury's verdict was unreasonable, that there had been a miscarriage of justice, and that the sentence was excessive. The jury was unreasonable to find me guilty of a charge that my co-accused, the Rimutaka inmate, was found not guilty of, and it was unreasonable to find me guilty of conspiracy when the supply charges weren't proven.

But in the end, the only plank I succeeded in changing was the sentence. I'd argued that the sentence of seven years breached the totality principle — meaning that the judge must have consideration for the overall total and balance it with the offending — the Court of Appeal instead decided that the sentence was excessive because Justice Wylie had considered the offending to be at the high end of the scale.

The Court of Appeal noted, 'Mr Taylor properly makes the point that the police found no drugs or money, and did not uncover any further evidence of offending under warrants issued in 2008 . . . we are mindful that he was convicted primarily on the evidence of a limited number of telephone calls and text messages on a charge of conspiracy to supply which did not proceed past the communications stage.' They reduced my sentence to five and a half years.

That meant that the final term I was serving for all the matters, including the events after my wedding to Carolyn, was seventeen years and six months, which wouldn't end until 2022. I'd served so much of my sentence already, though, that I'd be eligible for parole in just a few months' time, on 12 September 2012.

T he murder that had kicked off operations Spider and Web went nowhere. Although they'd charged my brother-in-law, Brett Ashby, with Granite's murder, Brett had liver cancer and died before the case got to trial. He never got the chance to clear his name.

Joanne cared for him right to the end. When Brett was arrested, in July 2007, the police had surrounded their home. Joanne got a phone call at 5 a.m. from a policewoman in Tauranga saying, 'Get your son and come outside: your house is surrounded by armed offenders.' Joanne replied 'I'm not leaving my house', and hung up. She opened the curtains and turned on all the lights, to show they weren't hiding anything. When police advanced on the house they found poor Brett lying ill on the sofa.

My mate Rocky was sentenced to six years and three months; a glowing Probation Service report had convinced Justice Wylie, at least in part, that Rocky had a crime-free life ahead of him. Kershaw Training Enterprises had taken a group of at-risk youths to his property and he'd talked to them about the realities of bad decision-making and prison. Rocky also wrote Justice Wylie a sincere letter, painting a picture of a rosier future, and I have no doubt that he meant it. He wanted to help others avoid making the same mistakes he had. He's kept to his word, too.

After he was paroled, Rocky suffered some health issues and now he's largely immobile. He's a battler, though, Rocky. A bit like myself.

CHAPTER ELEVEN

IN THE BELLY OF THE BEAST

I found solitary confinement the most forbidding
aspect of prison life. There is no end and no
beginning; there is only one's mind, which can
begin to play tricks. Was that a dream or did it really
happen? One begins to question everything.
Nelson Mandela, Long Walk to Freedom, *1995*

A t the end of 2011 I circled back to Graeme Burton and the
promise he'd made about not hurting anyone again, and I
challenged his continued isolation in D block. Burton was
being held 23 hours a day in directed segregation, and I reckon
he was going slightly crazy. He could talk to us through the grate,
but he couldn't mix with us. I thought 'This bugger is going to kill
somebody, maybe even a screw.' He seemed depressed.

I got Burton to apply under the Privacy Act 1993 for all the
paperwork related to his segregation. I went through it, and found
where they had fucked up a few times. Under the Corrections Act
2004, if they're going to hold you in segregation for more than three
months then they have to get a Visiting Justice to rubber-stamp it.
Corrections hadn't renewed Burton's management plan within the
prescribed statutory periods, so I went to Shelley Sage, the Visiting
Justice for the prison, who I'd got to know quite well. I told Shelley
I thought he was becoming mentally ill, which was news to her
because Corrections obviously hadn't mentioned it. So when the
next renewal came around, Shelley refused to sign it.

However, Corrections didn't move him straight out of D block
like they were legally required to. They had to have legal authority
to hold people in D block, over and above the normal prison units.
Obviously, they were trying to figure out a way to get around this,
but eventually they had to transfer him out to B block — where he
behaved himself.

Burton got himself down to the West Division and became a

medium-security prisoner, but then he got out of his head one day on pills and drugs and they had to call the riot squad down. He's a strange character, old Graeme.

There are some scumbags I'd never help — the likes of murderer George Baker, for example, because he was just a bad piece of work. George was serving a life sentence for murdering seventeen-year-old Liam Ashley in the back of a prison van in 2006. In 2009 he took a fellow Pare inmate hostage, and also tried to kidnap a prison guard in a separate incident. Later, in 2020, he was sentenced yet again for an attack on another Pare inmate, after he microwaved some jam for ten minutes until it was scalding hot and then threw it in his victim's face. There was no good in him that I could find.

The worst offender of all was Nick Reekie, who raped and traumatised women from the ages of eleven right through to 69. The first time I saw him, anger took over and I smacked him right in the head. I got him the name Sick Nick, which he's carried to this day. Sick Nick Reekie. Many years later, when I was being interviewed by broadcaster Duncan Garner, he asked, 'There's some people in jail that never should get out — name one.' Without hesitating I named Sick Nick Reekie, thinking 'Fuck, this cunt will be choking on his cornflakes hearing this.'

One thing I couldn't stomach was the lengths Reekie went to to harm other prisoners: smearing faeces over their windows, or threatening to rape their sisters and mothers. He was never unlocked with other prisoners, because if the boys could have got their hands on him he would have been strung up from the nearest shower-head. Those kinds of scumbags can't live with the normal prisoners, because we wouldn't tolerate them. I've seen them get their heads rammed down toilets.

The possible exception to this is Steve Williams, who killed little Coral Burrows while high on meth. Steve really regrets what he did to Coral. He puts on a front to most people, but it has been the death of him. I was so worried that he was going to kill himself that I pulled a few strings and got him a job in the laundry in D block. Lots of people would say 'Good job if he did', but I'm not one of those people. I think the worst thing in the world is a young life bleeding out on a concrete prison cell away from their whānau.

When I was talking to Steve one day, and sort of giving him the heads up that he might not be that popular with the boys, he said: 'I know. If I could only turn the clock back. I would give up my life if I could bring her back.' I really think he meant it. However, he's continued to be violent in prison. In 2019 he was sentenced to preventive detention after throwing boiling water on an inmate and then stabbing him with a sharpened plastic knife. Steve's convictions are nearing a hundred, and at one court sentencing he threatened a photographer.

I knew Steve's mother. She was a working girl, a prostitute, who used to own the Tauherenikau pub in Featherston. His sister was convicted of manslaughter for killing her boyfriend. I tend to know everyone's parents, because they contact me to see how their children are going in jail. I tell them the facts and how they can help them. That's how I became friendly with Scott Watson's family, I know his dad and I knew his mum, and his nana, too.

All murders are different. Some are planned; others, well, something happens and someone loses their power of self-control in a situation. Anybody is capable of killing; I think of those American conscripts in Vietnam, eighteen- and nineteen-year-olds put there to kill people who've done nothing to them, trained to dehumanise the enemy. Most of the lifers in prison had never committed a crime before in their lives, but something happened and they were driven to it. Planned killings are very few and far between.

T he Department of Corrections will tell you that there is no solitary confinement in New Zealand, and they will say this because experts in humanitarian causes will tell you it's a form of torture and punishment. In 2011 the UN's expert on torture, Juan Méndez, told the General Assembly's Third Committee, tasked with dealing with humanitarian issues, that in most cases solitary confinement should be banned and that it was contrary to rehabilitation. Using various words — including cruel, inhumane, degrading and torture — Méndez said it should only be used in exceptional circumstances and for as short a time as possible.

In 2000, another UN committee had reviewed the regime in Denmark and declared it a harsh penalty with serious psychological effects. New Zealand human rights lawyer Tony Ellis has described the system of solitary confinement in New Zealand prisons as one of disguise, because, instead of 'solitary', Corrections employs a regime called segregation — which is close enough to the same thing. There are two kinds of segregation. Protective segregation for prisoners who might be a target in prison, and directive segregation for the purpose of security or good order of the prison.

Segregation is dealt with by way of sections 58 to 60 of the Corrections Act 2004. In essence, they are the legal powers to keep prisoners apart from other prisoners. Of course, solitary confinement — being isolated from other prisoners — is a consequence of segregation. Under the law, segregation should only be imposed when absolutely necessary. Prisoners must be told in writing using a standard document that also outlines their conditions and the regulations, and must sign the paperwork. They cannot be held arbitrarily.

On 15 June 2011, soon after I'd been sentenced for the alleged conspiracy, screws found a cellphone in my cell. They panicked, and ordered that I be 'kept apart from others to avoid disruption or a possible security breach'. They put me in a detention unit. A segregation document was hastily prepared and waved under my nose for signing. It said that my initial segregation would be for fourteen days. In the end, I'd be held for ten months.

My new cell was spartan, steel fittings on off-white walls, a single bed and a metal toilet. The front of the cell was completely covered with a steel plate, so darkness was the default. Light occasionally filtered in through a tiny inspection panel on the door. The water and light were controlled from the outside and often shut off. Inside, I was allowed a television, a radio and books — though it's important to note that not all prisoners can get hold of these, just the lucky ones who can afford it or whose friends and families can.

The European Committee for the Prevention of Torture and Inhuman or Degrading Treatment or Punishment has said that a reasonable size for a single cell is 7 square metres. Six square metres is acceptable if the prisoner spends a significant amount of the day outside the cell and has extra space for a toilet. All of the cells at Pare were around 3 metres by 1.8 metres, making them about 5.4 square metres.

However, the problematic nature of segregation doesn't just lie in the size of the accommodation — it's also the restrictions on your liberties that not even the maximum-security prisoners are subjected to on a daily basis. In segregation I had no contact visits, no exercise in the open air, and no direct access to sunlight. I was allowed out into an indoor pen for exercise, but there was no sports or exercise equipment. Other prisoners had taken to making balls out of their own clothing. Likewise there was no access to facilities to make good use of my time, or to rehabilitation programmes or counselling.

In conditions like these, a cup of water becomes an oasis in the desert. The basic ingredients for a rudimentary life become precious, and you quickly notice when you're being denied them.

Less than a fortnight after I was directed into my shoebox, shortly before 1 p.m. on 22 June, Auckland's regional prison manager Neil Beales emailed all staff, asking them to print out a paper notice and tape it to all the landings.

A Liverpudlian father-of-two who'd grown up in South Africa,

Beales — a blue-eyed, rough-bearded sort — had been an actor, then had joined the United Kingdom's prison service in the early '90s. In an earnest profile written by a Wellington blogger, Beales had poured his heart out about his difficult teenage years. 'I made a promise to myself never to forget what it felt like to be sixteen and feel isolated and ostracised.'

The paper Beales wanted staff to put up in the prison had the title in bold and underlined: The Truth Newspaper. The *New Zealand Truth* was one of New Zealand's oldest weekly tabloids, first off the presses in 1905, and was considered a unique outlier on the fringe of the media. Its journalists were muck-rakers, its editors firebrand figures the likes of Cameron Slater, who later became a central figure in the *Dirty Politics* scandal of the 2014 election and who'd received a media award after exposing Auckland mayor Len Brown's affair with a council staffer.

The *Truth* prided itself on reporting what other media might consider off-limits or controversial, and it took a special interest in prisoners' rights. In 2011 it had featured several prominent stories that were negative about the management of Auckland Prison at Paremoremo and the safe and humane custody of the prisoners. This specifically included the conditions in D block.

'Effective immediately,' Beales wrote to all prisoners, 'The Truth Newspaper is prohibited and will no longer be permitted within the East Division of Auckland Prison.'

The next day, the *Truth*'s journalist, Stephen Cook, wrote to Corrections' senior communications adviser Rebecca Powell. 'We're planning on running a story next week about Corrections' refusal to allow our esteemed publication into Auckland Prison at Paremoremo,' he wrote. 'I would have assumed *Truth Weekender* would have been compulsory reading for all inmates, not to mention staff, but there you go. Could you get Neil Beales to explain why Corrections has introduced such draconian censorship into the prison system?'

Four days later Powell replied, confirming the ban and stressing that other media weren't banned. 'This is due to the negative effect that the sensationalised, and often inaccurate, reporting has on the good order of the prison.'

I'd had a weekly subscription, and the ban breached my right to seek and receive information and opinions of any kind, under any form, under section 14 of the Bill of Rights Act 1990. From that day on, my paper was sent straight to the Auckland Prison receiving officer where it was put into storage. Years later, when I was ordered to move prisons, I had to remove a year's worth of yellowing newspapers.

I continued to be confined 20-plus hours a day to a windowless concrete box. My days became numbers logged on a spreadsheet under sections like 'shower and clean', 'computer room' (which was the size of my cell), 'workshop' (the size of three cells), and 'total out of cell'. A micromanagement of my endless days. I was allowed to spend some of my unlock time working in my office, but had no access to fresh air or natural light. Working wasn't exactly a break from the monotony.

My one hot meal arrived about 3.45 p.m.; breakfast was served at 8.15 a.m. There was nothing in between. Milk — trim by default and given to you at breakfast — spoiled quickly because there was no fridge. Meals were served on paper plates, and eaten with rickety plastic cutlery prone to breaking. If you broke your fork, it wasn't replaced and you'd have to eat by hand. You had to reclean your cutlery, but as the water in the cell wasn't particularly hot, this was unhygienic.

I used the time to read. I could retreat into books, shutting the outside world out of my mind, because focusing on what I was missing made things much harder. I tried to focus on the moment, to live day-by-day, not thinking about tomorrow, or the day after.

Of course I complained. Repeatedly. I wasn't given my legal requirements outside my cell — those numbers that tracked my activities would later show this — and the paperwork they continued to wave under my nose every time my time in the pound was increased wasn't correctly filled out. Those documents said that I was a risk to the prison, but never stipulated in much, or any, detail how — particularly when I continued to be isolated from others.

Before a segregation order is extended, approval must be given by the assistant regional manager; for extensions beyond three months, this must be given by a Visiting Justice. But I'd be given paperwork saying that my stay in segregation was being extended before any approval was obtained.

When directed to segregation, a management plan must be completed within one working day. The management plan I'd signed on 15 June stipulated one hour per day of exercise and a five-minute phone call each week, excluding legal calls. Meals were to be had in my cell, and there could be one 30-minute visit per week in a booth. The management plan stated that the one hour of rec time included a shower, cleaning, phone calls and yard time, which breached Corrections' rule that rec time is separate to cleaning and calls. One document proposed that they would look at all my outgoing mail, but the general prison rules are that you can only look at it if it appears to contain an unauthorised item — not as a matter of course.

Every time I signed those pieces of paper I would say, 'I understand but I do not agree. I have not been provided with the reasons for segregation, copies of misconduct reports, or other relevant documentation.' I also repeatedly requested a review by the regional manager or inspector.

On 24 June, the prison extended the initial segregation to one month. They said they'd searched my office two days earlier and found a piece of a hacksaw. It certainly wasn't mine. It was routine for screws to turn up things that had been hiding in cells for a long time. They didn't even charge me over it, I believe, which meant that they must have realised it couldn't have been mine.

Nonetheless, in using this as an excuse to extend my stay, residential manager Tony Queree wrote of the discovery: 'It's clearly evident that prisoner Taylor has taken excessive advantage of the unit staff's efforts to support him . . . No matter where we place him he has continually shown that he presents a significant ongoing threat to the security and good order of this institution.' Again there was no supporting evidence attached to the shambolic paperwork. The 'supporting reasons' for the extension were things that had happened before the initial segregation order, rather than being an ongoing risk. Queree railed against the fact that I had an office in the first place, which the Ombudsman would eventually give short shrift to — it wasn't at all a valid reason.

The *pièce de résistance* when it came to my detainment in isolation was a trio of fires within the prison that saw smoke creep under my door. Late on the evenings of 27 June and 5 July, and 16 January the following year, inmate Tony Adamson sparked fires in his nearby cell. The fires were so big that they activated the smoke detector — but not the sprinkler system — and on at least one of those occasions the guards couldn't deal with it themselves and the fire service was called out. Adamson was a known fire-starter and they should have recognised the risk. He threatened to start fires all the time. In the second two fires, the thick smoke filled my cell quickly and I became unconscious. To my knowledge, nobody ever checked on me.

My solitary confinement for the alleged good order of the prison went on, and Queree continued to moan that I was a pain in the backside. 'Staff have taken a "step back" in managing him to avoid the stream of prolific formal complaints he generates and to avoid accusations of preventing him from making adequate preparations,' he wrote.

Every few weeks they'd give me more paperwork that extended my stay. June turned into July, which became August, and August stretched into November with a three-month extension. On and on it went. Between October 2011 and May 2012 I was given an hour a day outside my cell, often in internal rooms with little to no light. There were a number of days when that hour did not come. In

March and April 2012 I was entitled to 28 and 30 hours of exercise respectively, and received 15.3 and 24.5.

One excuse they used was that I'd called an unapproved person by using another prisoner's telephone PIN. Another time, instead of making a legal phone call, I'd rung my sister, Joanne. This incensed them. 'He has shown that he will go to great lengths to circumvent the system and to bypass our security measures for all forms of communications including the mail system — hence the strict measures in place to monitor his telephone calls and mail,' Queree fumed. 'While he behaves in this manner he will continue to present a very high risk to the good order, security and safety of the institution.' No substantive reasons for the continued segregation were provided.

On 13 December 2011, approval was given to extend yet again. This time they shuffled me to the high-care unit for a few weeks. By this time I'd been sitting in segregation for six months and, according to the latest document, my release into the main prison wouldn't be until nine months after I'd first walked away from my usual cell. I was returned to D block on 24 February, where I was held under restrictive conditions, and then moved back to the high-care unit until March. That unit was the worst, because a light shone into the cell through a window 24 hours a day. There were no hand-washing facilities, running water, power outlets or storage, and I was monitored 24/7 by CCTV.

Again I signed a management plan, which was a direct copy and paste of the plans they'd served me with in the detention unit — and I knew this because it referred to the detention unit rather than the high-care unit. Again, I signed with 'I do not agree that the contents of these instructions are lawful — I request that they be reviewed by the Inspectorate and Ombudsman and that I be assessed by a psychologist.'

When, in April 2012, I emerged from the belly of the beast and was finally able to breathe under sunlight again, for the first time in ten months, I complained to the Ombudsman about my treatment. Ever since that bashing by the screws in Waikeria in the '70s, when my parents had instigated a complaint through the local MP and I'd written to the Ombudsman, I'd begun registering complaints myself. I've lodged hundreds upon hundreds since the 1990s, with the Office of the Ombudsman diligently tracking them and coding them.

The Ombudsman is usually my first port of call. It doesn't cost anything to complain, and a decision or a letter from the Ombudsman's office is good enough to wave right back at the screws. This time the Ombudsman launched a special investigation. He found that the initial decision to put me into segregation was reasonable, but after that the wheels had fallen off. The paperwork wasn't in accordance with either policy or practice. Nor were the types of restrictions on my minimum entitlements, the decision to house me specifically in high-care units, or the length of time that my opportunity to associate with other prisoners was denied.

The final report castigated the half-wits at Corrections. Queree's moaning about my legal work and my office wasn't a valid supporting reason to keep me cooped up in the pound, the Ombudsman said, 'as approval had been given by the Department for Mr Taylor to have an office area, and there is a legal obligation for the Department to provide assistance to prisoners for the preparation of legal proceedings.'

He continued: 'The investigation has found that in many cases most, if not all, Mr Taylor's rights and entitlements listed on the management plan were restricted despite no risk being identified in relation to those areas.'

My period of segregation was nine years ago at the time of writing, but I haven't forgotten it and my treatment during that time still burns. It's like being taken hostage — your senses deprived, your control gone, your life reduced to tiny, forgettable increments, while officials tell you that you don't have any right to what you're owed.

I decided to sue Corrections through the High Court for this treatment, and for many other incidents in which I considered that my rights had been violated. This action is set to be heard in 2022.

I was able to use a lot of my knowledge about segregation to eventually help a Ngāpuhi bloke called Paki Toia. He's dead now, but in Pare he was a tormented soul. Paki, a Head Hunter serving time for serious sexual offences, including rape, was living out his years in D block. You might wonder why I'd help someone like Paki, who by most accounts was a bit of a bad bastard. But for me, it all came back to the rights of the prisoner.

Paki had very staunch Māori cultural views, and that conflicted head-on with the way a prison was run. One D-block manager had the gall to tell Paki that he was in his house now; Paki simply replied 'Your house is on my land.' For some reason they would refuse to give him toothpaste, and I had to give him mine or he'd swap his fruit ration with others for some. Screws rolled apples on the floor, meaning that he'd have to pick his food up off the floor.

I arbitrated between him and the screws to try to make life liveable for all sides, but Paki was a man of very little compromise. He took to covering his cell door with his blanket most of the time, not just when he was on the toilet. Prisoners did this all the time, to secure a bit of privacy, and the screws turned a blind eye — until Paki started doing it more frequently. The more Corrections tried to stop him, the more he'd resist.

They put him in the at-risk unit, a small pound designed for prisoners who might harm themselves. Paki wasn't suicidal, and he saw the move as a punishment. They'd watch him at all times through cameras. In the high-risk unit he wore a single jumpsuit, was observed every fifteen minutes, and allowed out only for an hour a day.

Even a perfectly sane person would suffer in those conditions, as I had, but an unwell person would sink quickly. It's often astounded me how 'at-risk' rooms are generally worse than even the worst D-block cell. If you weren't already going mad, then in there you would be. I could see that Corrections wasn't complying with its own regulations, and this infuriated Paki further. A war began to rage. A beleaguered Paki took to tipping his own shit on to a pan, which he'd send through the slot in the door designed for food delivery. In response, the screws directed him to segregation.

In 2013 I helped Paki take a lawsuit against Corrections. In the High Court he said that the way Corrections had treated him in prison breached the Human Rights Act. The hearing took ten days, and I gave evidence for Paki by audio-visual link. The prison said that it was too dangerous to have us in the same courtroom, even though we were both at Pare at one stage and used to exercise together in D block.

Paki told Justice Timothy Brewer that he had no faith in lawyers and wanted me to be his McKenzie friend. Given Paki's limited knowledge of the law and how to conduct the proceedings, Justice Brewer was fine with this but left the decision up to Corrections.

The Pare prison manager at the time, Tom Sherlock, told the court that they wouldn't let Paki and me see each other to discuss the case, and would only permit us to exchange documentation. Sherlock's built like a brick shelf, all legs and thighs — the sort of guy who would be alright on the doors as a bouncer, but the moment you put him in an office running the show it's either going to go bankrupt or the place will burn down. The only reason that Pare didn't go bankrupt was because unlimited taxpayer dollars were pouring in. We had run-ins all the time. Sherlock didn't like me anywhere near the other prisoners because he didn't like me educating them. Sherlock's thinking was of an old slave master.

Even though I was making the prisoners better people, Corrections was consequently enduring more complaints and more people challenging them. Sherlock couldn't handle that.

'Mr Taylor has a real negative influence over a number of prisoners,' Sherlock told the court. 'I believe he is the driving force behind this particular case and sees this as an opportunity to present his views of the world to the High Court and in front of the media.'

I gave Paki advice in writing, telling him how to conduct his case because he hadn't a clue. In this way I got some semblance of order into the bloody proceedings.

Justice Brewer ended up upholding three of the issues Paki had brought to him, including that putting Paki in the at-risk unit, in segregation, breached sections of the Corrections Act. Although Corrections was at pains to say that they weren't segregating Paki, per se, it was easy to see this was a de facto consequence of putting someone in the at-risk unit for 23 hours a day.

Justice Brewer said that D block sounded primitive and he doubted that minimum standards were being observed. Although Corrections said that Paki refused his option to get out of the cell for an hour, I raised the point that he was only allowed to travel from the cell to another, slightly bigger, room. This shouldn't be mistaken for an hour of meaningful recreation. Paki used the time to shower instead, or to come and talk to me.

The $1.7 million we had asked for wasn't awarded, or indeed any money, but Paki got something that meant more to him: a declaration from the High Court that vindicated his rights as a prisoner, and a reminder to Corrections that they had to comply.

CHAPTER TWELVE

NO SMOKE WITHOUT FIRE

> Prisoners will be forced to go cold-turkey on
> July 1 next year after a government decree to ban
> smoking.
> Stuff, *2 July 2010*

When then Corrections Minister Judith Collins announced that prisoners would no longer be able to smoke, she cited the safety of Corrections as the reason. Corrections jumped on board, saying that inmates used lighters to set fires. Two-thirds of the prison population, about 5700 inmates, were smokers, and I could see from a mile away that this wasn't going to go down well. Prison's atmosphere is barren, and smoking is one of the few things that prisoners have to brighten their day. It's a de facto medication.

Smoking played a very, very important part in the prison world. The prisons even used to subsidise tobacco in the 1970s. You could get 1 ounce, called a fig, for 14 cents, and virtually all prisoners smoked; I was one of the very few who never did. In special cases officers would hand out free tobacco to prisoners to calm them, and up until 2010 you could smoke in your cell.

When they proposed the ban on smoking, I realised immediately what the consequences would be. A massive increase in violence, for one, because prisoners have very little else to do. A ban would just make the life of people who have already got a hard life even harder. I have known people who have suicided, and who would still be alive today if they had just had a smoke, a bit of tobacco to calm them down. I would sooner take the risk of them dying of lung cancer in 40 years' time, than risk them bleeding out in a cell.

There was another important aspect as well. If you breached a prison rule, you could be charged with a prison offence. The consequences for people who'd defy a ban on smoking wasn't just that they could be put in the pound, or suffer loss of privileges. Internal charges had a big impact on people's prospects of parole.

I was determined to fight the ban. I looked at the law under which they were proposing to act, section 33 of the Corrections Act 2004. This gives prison managers — not Judith Collins, but prison managers — the power to make rules governing how their prisons operate (within the law, of course). The prison managers couldn't make a rule that was in conflict with other law, and a prison manager couldn't overrule parliament.

In this case, a direction had been issued from Corrections' head office to all prison managers that they were to change the rules and ban smoking. That infringes an area of law, which says that if a power is vested in somebody by law, that person can't be told how to exercise that power — which means that Corrections can't tell prison managers how to make the rules for their prisons.

Having determined this, I made some Official Information Act requests and found that the general prison rules were identical throughout every prison in the country. This was important, because it showed that the rules came from a single source rather than from individual prison managers, and were all to the same effect. Under administrative law principles this was illegal; an infringement against the principles against dictation which say that a decision has to be made by the person who has the power vested in them.

We all know that it's beneficial not to smoke, but I was prepared to tolerate any personal risk of passive smoking for the greater good. In a closed world like a prison you have to tolerate things and make compromises. A lot of the prison officers smoked, too, so the reasons advanced to justify the ban clearly came from people who weren't familiar with the prison world.

I looked at the cost, and thought 'It's got to be done.'

True to Collins' word, on 1 July 2011 smoking was banned in prisons, and two days later tobacco and smoking items were classified as contraband. Two months later, in September, I filed proceedings in the High Court at Auckland against Auckland Prison seeking a declaration from the court that the ban was unlawful, invalid, and to no effect.

Auckland Prison brought in the big guns — the Crown Law Office — to throw the punches, while for much of the ensuing legal battle I'd find myself fighting with one hand behind my back after being put in segregation. But that handicap just made me more determined to carry on. I'll use the analogy of the America's Cup: I was never going to beat the opposition on money or resources — I had to do it on ability. And I knew that I could win with ability.

December 2012

The smoking ban argument landed at the High Court at Auckland before Justice Murray Gilbert about half a year after I was released back into my usual D block cell.

On the first day of the hearing I had Corrections trundle boxes of documents into the austere courtroom, after a long, early-morning trip in the van from Pare. The screws would do everything to try to make sure that files didn't make it to Auckland, like searching through beforehand and leaving some behind, by 'accident'.

Corrections had planned the trip out beforehand, memories of Manners Street haunting them. When I arrived, they took me down to the cells under the courtroom. I got on pretty well with First Security, which ran the cell area. After being screened through metal detectors I was taken up to the courtroom, where I laid out my paperwork. I was given the same desk as counsel — this time I was not there as a prisoner to be sentenced in criminal proceedings, but as a party to a civil court case, so for once I wouldn't be standing in the dock (although Corrections would have loved that).

The Crown could see that they were going to lose, so they threw a final sucker punch. They had quietly prepared regulations to replace the rules we were arguing about, so that when they lost they could still maintain the ban, despite what the court might say. Before we'd even come to court, the Corrections Amendment Regulations 2012 came into force, which said that tobacco and any device used for smoking were unauthorised. In another regulation they deleted the word 'tobacco' from a list of exempted privileges, which meant that this regulation was no longer in conflict with the rule that was the subject of the proceedings.

Nonetheless, right before Christmas, in a reserved decision, Justice Gilbert declared in very clear words that the smoking ban was unlawful, invalid and of no effect. He said that at the time the rule was made, it was inconsistent with the Corrections Regulations 2005 — but, of course, by that time smoking implements were banned. Corrections was saying, 'Okay, you might be allowed to drive the car but you're not going to get any gas to run it.' While Corrections had given up trying to ban smoking per se, tobacco was now essentially illegal and so it was a disciplinary offence to smoke it.

I looked closely at these new regulations and thought 'These are illegal as well.' They infringed the Smokefree Environments and Regulated Products Act 1990, which (as Justice Timothy Brewer would later rule) more or less stated that a prisoner's cell is their home and therefore what goes on in there — as long as it's within the law — is no one else's business. So after New Year, in January 2013, I filed a new set of proceedings, effectively saying that the Crown had no power to make these regulations.

I gave Justice Brewer the allegory of tormenting a dog. If you whip it, starve it, what's it going to be like? It will bite the hell out of you the first chance it gets. It's the same with people. They react to how they are treated. If you explain to them that they've got some rights, then they might be far more inclined to respect the rights of other people. If you don't respect any rights they've got and treat them like shit, then they're just not going to care.

Justice Brewer unequivocally ruled that the 2012 regulations were unlawful, invalid and of no effect. He suggested that prisoners who had been caught smoking during the ban could seek remedy. In his ruling, he referred to the Latin phrase *Vox populi, vox Dei*, meaning 'the voice of the people is the voice of God'.

'In New Zealand, that voice is made law by Parliament,' he said.

I n the midst of all this litigation, Labour's justice spokesperson, Andrew Little, came and saw me at Pare along with Kris Faafoi and Darien Fenton, all MPs in Opposition at the time. Judith Collins called them all ninnies for coming; she reckoned that they were basking in my celebrity status.

The way I looked at it, these MPs wanted to be making decisions on behalf of the community, so they wanted to have lots of input from all sources so they could make the right decisions. Judith's criticism undervalued her in my eyes, because she didn't really care about getting the decision right; it was just whatever was politically prudent. I reckon she underestimates Kiwis, because I find that when they get the right information they will actually listen.

The meeting with Andrew et al. took place in the prison visiting room, with no prisoners there except me. For about an hour we talked about voting and prisoners' interests, and they seemed genuinely interested. I tried to get the idea across that, actually, if we wanted to have fewer victims, unless we could have a policeman at the bottom of every street, we had to try to rehabilitate prisoners, and the best opportunity to do this is while they are doing their prison service.

I've got a lot of respect for Andrew. During the Labour–Greens–NZ First coalition I understood the battle he was up against with certain hold-outs in Parliament, or in trying to get anything done, especially the business of that three strikes law, which is frankly ridiculous, counterproductive.

Those three weren't the only ones to visit. Another time, Labour MP Kelvin Davis came. He said at the time, 'Jesus, Arthur, I had the *Herald* ring before I even got to the gate.' Green MP David Clendon — nice bloke — also visited. Garth McVicar of the Sensible Sentencing Trust tried to visit. Tom Sherlock refused to let him in, saying that there was no lawful reason for him to be there. That was incredible. Garth has got his bailiwick and I've got mine, but we are both in the same business — we want there to be fewer victims of crime.

In the meantime, the Crown pulled a final bow and arrow from its armoury, amending the legislation so that the smoking ban was actually legislated with a National–Act majority. I see it as they had to go to parliament to rescue them from their folly — and there was quite a debate in parliament about it at the time. The Corrections Act now made tobacco an unauthorised item, and smoking was made a disciplinary offence under section 129. Under the Smokefree Environments etc. Act, the exemption of a prison cell was removed from the smoking in the workplace rules. The rules were no longer in contradiction to other laws.

I might have lost the battle, but these actions brought home to the government the significance of the rule of law — that they can't just do whatever they like. Judith Collins (and Anne Tolley who became Corrections minister during this fight) *had* to comply with the law, even if they were a Minister of the Crown. It also reinforced the notion that prisoners actually mattered in the world, that their rights could be fought for and upheld. This should have triggered a flurry of actions by other lawyers on behalf of their clients, saying, 'Well hey, okay, parliament's acted now and passed the law, but all through that period you stopped prisoners from smoking — and that was illegal and they were being treated inhumanely and therefore they should be compensated.'

But nothing happened, because the lawyers weren't up to it. Many probably didn't realise the significance of the action because they tended to concentrate on the things that lawyers win and not what other people win, so they tried to downplay it. In their eyes, much of what I did devalued the LLB that they'd spent four years getting. I took personal pride in that — with all of these expensive lawyers trying to stamp out my court action, it reinforced to me the fact that I could actually beat them.

In June 2013, Carolyn won first-division Lotto. She and I had maintained our relationship, but weren't seeing much of each other as she was living in Christchurch, where she met this half-wit boyfriend, Shaun Reinke. Although I'd always loved and cared about Carolyn, it was common sense to me that she moved on with her life. When you are in a relationship, you need to support each other and make each other's life more rich, and this was something I couldn't do. When she called to tell me that she'd met someone and wanted to dissolve our marriage, I was disappointed, perhaps hurt, but I knew she had to move on — I wasn't about to be released anytime soon. I didn't want to stand in her way. It was just a shame that it had to be with that guy, though. Carolyn and I spoke regularly, despite her new relationship, and her entanglement unfurled before me.

Reinke got in Carolyn's head, and said 'Arthur will want half that Lotto money', because we were still married at that point. I couldn't have given two stuffs about the money. Reinke stepped forward like a knight in shining armour, and said, 'You can pay it to my bank account.'

Of course, after she paid it into Reinke's account she couldn't get the money back off the fleabag. So she stayed with him. We divorced at the end of 2013, and she married him.

A round the time that I was preparing to fight the smoking ban, the UK's coalition government had produced a draft Bill that gave three options for allowing prisoners to vote in elections — there was a blanket ban in place at the time, which the European Court of Human Rights had ruled unacceptable. A committee scrutinised the Bill and said that prisoners serving twelve months or less should be allowed to vote. Investigative journalist David Fisher sent me a note saying, 'Arthur, this might be one you might like to look at.'

The UK debate was a case in point of how contentious the right of prisoners to vote was, and remains. Six months, or twelve months? A total ban? I'd always considered myself politically engaged. The last time I'd voted, on the outside, was in 2005, when I'd gone for

Labour in the Ōtaki electorate (the way I look at it, Labour is the lesser of two evils). At the time I was on remand at Rimutaka. Time has fogged my memory, but I think the first time I voted was for Margaret Shields. I've always voted Labour. I liked Norman Kirk — a genuine man of the people who gave a stuff about the worker. I was eighteen when he died. Dad always supported Social Credit; he was rapt when its first MP was elected.

I've always thought that it's very important for prisoners to be as engaged with the community as possible, because that's where they return when they finish their sentences. It's important for them to retain every link with the community that they can. The obvious way to encourage an interest in the outside world is to give prisoners a say in who governs their country. Prison is an artificial world; everything in there is upside down. What's good in the outside world is bad in there, and vice versa. That's how the prisons operate, so inmates need to be exposed to the good. They need to understand that their right prevails.

It's also particularly important because prisoners pay tax and GST on what they buy in the canteen. Consider the rallying cry of the American Revolution: 'No taxation without representation.' Why should prisoners be paying taxes towards something they have no say in?

There's no legitimate reason to keep arguing against prisoners having the right to vote — apart from as some sort of punishment and to make their life as hard as possible. Preventing prisoners from voting is counterproductive because the more interest they have in what's going on in the world, the better. Rather than sitting around in prison wings talking about committing crimes and robberies and drug dealing, imagine if they were talking about politics and what was going on in the real world. They've got children on the outside, they've got whānau, and having even a tiny say in it is very important.

I also saw this as a good opportunity to explain to the public that prisoners are people, that they have rights.

The history of prisoner voting in New Zealand is a lesson in attrition. In ancient Greece and Rome, the disenfranchisement of serving prisoners was thought of as civil death. Those who committed terrible crimes became infamous, and forfeited their civil rights. This was one of the planks that led to the earliest rules around prisoner voting in this country — in 1852, the New Zealand Constitution Act ruled that anyone in custody for a crime couldn't vote. If they had finished their sentence, they could. Then, in 1879 the Qualification of Electors Act said that criminals couldn't register to vote for a year after they'd finished their sentence.

In 1905, the Electoral Act removed the twelve-month disqualification period but also changed the definition of who couldn't vote. This now depended on what sentence they were serving — if you were sentenced to death or to more than one year in prison, you couldn't vote. In 1956, the year I was born, the law changed again, removing the one-year threshold. Again, no convicted prisoner could vote. However, remand prisoners could vote, because they were still presumed innocent, and so could prisoners on parole.

The law would change again, repeatedly, but come 1993 the Electoral Act allowed some prisoners to vote — those who weren't serving a minimum of three years, or life, or preventive detention. Then, in February 2010, the Electoral (Disqualification of Sentenced Prisoners) Amendment Bill was introduced by National's Paul Quinn. Quinn was into social contract theory. Under his Bill, which took effect in the form of legislation in December 2010, no prisoner detained on voting day could register to vote. It passed with a majority.

I've always believed that it doesn't matter how insurmountable a hurdle might look — if you put your heart into it, you can do anything. The first step in challenging this legislation was to get women prisoners on board. I wanted a cross section of the population involved in the action, including those who'd be affected by the law change. As it were, because I wasn't allowed to vote anyway, I hadn't technically been affected, though of course being a prisoner, it was about my rights too. I asked a lady I knew in Christchurch Women's Prison, Hinemanu Ngaronoa, to find some female prisoners who wanted to join the action, and she quickly found three others: Sandra Wilde, Kirsty Fensom and Claire Thrupp. Initially, we applied for a judicial review seeking a declaration that the amendment was inconsistent with section 12 of the New Zealand Bill of Rights Act 1990. But as the election loomed, I applied to the High Court under urgency on 6 September 2013 for an injunction, essentially asking that prisoners' right to vote be preserved.

During 2013, journalist Lisa Owen wanted to interview me about the litigation I had been involved in. Corrections was trying to present me to the public as a troublemaker, so she applied to the department to interview me about prisoner voting and smoking. I like Lisa. She's a terrier, and she goes after people. I like her interviewing style. Corrections, of course, as it was doing routinely for all prisoners, denied her request.

The media has a very important role in explaining things to the public, and when it doesn't have access to prisons or prisoners, it's constrained in what information it can report concerning them. I see it in these terms: if my neighbour came along to me and said that our other neighbour was an arsehole, I would start thinking the same — but he might not be. The public needed to hear from both sides to make informed decisions about what they thought about prisons and politics. I believe that you have to cooperate with the media because their job is getting to the truth of matters.

The law says that the media should have access to prisoners, in certain circumstances, and that consideration must be given to the protection of other people. When Lisa applied, they hadn't taken the situation fully into account, so they hadn't complied with the law — so, of course, I took legal action.

First, I lost in the High Court after I got Richard Francois, a Harvard graduate, to do the case for me because I was tied up with the other actions. When I heard we'd lost, I thought 'Oh well, it was Justice Paul Heath, he's a really fair judge', but when I read his judgment I'd wished I'd argued the case myself. Richard, as good as he is, wasn't aware Corrections was arguing based on things that never happened. The person who knows the facts best is the client themselves.

Well, I knew the law. So I appealed to the Court of Appeal because the decision had armed Corrections with a precedent. Even though denying me an interview wasn't a bad decision, Corrections had put incorrect information before the court — claiming I had flooded the landing and jammed the locks in the cells, making out I was a dangerous prisoner. They could now use the decision to deny other prisoner interviews. I had to persevere.

Corrections tried to knock me out of action by saying that I needed to pay thousands of dollars in costs for security. Then they tried every procedural device they could to knock the case out of court because they didn't want to deal with it on its merits.

We won at the Court of Appeal. The court made a point of saying that 'Mr Taylor is not taking this legal action for his own interests, he's a genuine advocate on behalf of prisoners and to reinforce the value of freedom of expression for all people.' By acting on behalf of others in this way, I was, essentially, protecting the rights of other people.

Corrections had spent $86,000 fighting this. If I'd been a lawyer, I would have been entitled to full costs. So that saved the taxpayer another $90,000 in costs because Corrections didn't have to pay properly for its obstructive attitude. The case seems to have had little effect, however. Corrections still routinely denies prisoner interviews. You can ask an inmate today; it's as if this case never happened although I understand some journalists have used the reference when trying to seek access to prisoners.

Lisa ended up interviewing me twice over the years, (once in Pare and once in person at Waikeria). She had to do the first interview, at Pare, by email. They reckoned that she wouldn't be safe at the prison — effectively saying, 'Arthur Taylor might kidnap her, take her hostage, or he might grab the micro-fucking-phone.' What the fuck would I want to do that for? It would've been counterproductive to the message I was trying to get across. They are crazy, honestly.

It was a funny case. It had transpired that when Corrections was considering Lisa's application to interview me, an official received an anonymous text saying, 'Arthur Taylor has just flooded the landings in Paremoremo Prison, and is a dangerous threat to security.' He didn't even know where it came from; it just came from within Pare. As a result of this, he decided that I couldn't have an interview.

He struggled to explain *that* in court. What senior civil servant acts on an anonymous text that he thinks has come from within a prison? Who sent it? The cleaner, the prison manager? No one knows. They've never worked it out. They had the number, but they weren't interested in finding out.

Carolyn spoke to me two days before she died, wanting to get her marriage to Reinke dissolved. I wish she had just told me what was up; I would have got the money out of him one way or another. But she probably didn't want to admit that she had made such a monumental cock-up.

Carolyn was working as a nurse aide when she died, sometime during the night of 23 and 24 July 2014, at her home in Phillipstown, Christchurch. Her friends and family were worried that she'd been murdered, or that her death had been 'helped along', so the police investigated.

Carolyn was 38. By that time she and Reinke had been together about two years, but she certainly wasn't happy. She had three children, including Siobhan, but none of them were living with her. Carolyn had a history of opiate use, along with hepatitis C and long-standing depression. She'd abused alcohol, and had amphetamine and sedative dependences. She'd sort of alluded to previous attempts at suicide but my read on it was more that they were cries for help.

Complicating her life were various investigations the Ministry of Social Development took against her in relation to her entitlement of the DPB. Carolyn was terrified that she was going back to prison.

A few months earlier, the Ministry of Social Development told her she was being investigated in relation to her entitlement of the DPB, and that she had been overpaid by $116,000. Carolyn was terrified that she was going back to prison.

The day she was last seen, someone staying at their house heard Reinke say 'Kill yourself, bitch' — which Reinke denied. Carolyn said she was leaving him, and left the house. She went to work at 8 a.m. but left two hours later. When Reinke came home, she wasn't there and he thought nothing of it. He didn't find her body until the next day.

I got the call in prison from Melissa Wepa, a hard-out girl who'd served time for stabbing somebody about 50 times. I was fucking devastated, obviously. For me, and for Siobhan. Melissa started gathering intelligence for me about what was going on. Carolyn always told me that if she ever died she didn't want to be cremated, she wanted to be buried, and have Prince Tui Teka's songs played at her graveside. So this prick Reinke cremates her, and wouldn't hand her ashes over until I forced them out of him later.

Thinking of Siobhan, I had the High Court freeze all his assets, including the properties. After that, Reinke started suffering a lot of bad luck. Within three months he had been in hospital three times, and I'd heard his lawyer got knocked off his bike. Carolyn was probably getting them from the grave.

In the end, though, I had to compromise. I had to let Reinke have some money, but I got a lot back for Siobhan to go into a trust. I insisted that Carolyn's ashes be returned immediately to her mother, so that they could be buried with her sister. They were officially handed over in the lawyer's office one day, along with a certificate, because I thought Reinke might have swapped them.

People move on in their lives, but Carolyn and I had a lot of common interests. We used to have lots of fun. We never said a cross word to each other. I think about her every day, and still wear my wedding ring. I manage her Facebook page, too.

There's a photo of us that I love. Carolyn's wearing a pink top, and she's tanned and glowing and has her arms around me. She's looking at the camera with a cheeky glint in her eyes, and I'm looking off in the other direction, not appreciating that our time together would be finite.

On 3 August 2017, police told the coroner that in the absence of any further information, and based on the information in the investigation file, they were satisfied that nobody was criminally liable for Carolyn's death. The coroner ruled it a suicide.

My campaign for the prisoners' vote was launched from my office in Pare, in September 2014, beamed through a small television monitor into the courtroom at Auckland's High Court. The Crown lawyer was in a blue and white pin-striped collared shirt and tie, a suit and robes. Justice Rebecca Ellis was presiding over the hearing in her robes. I was wearing a dark T-shirt with a bright-orange jacket.

My prison room was empty, the desk an anomaly. At the High Court they'd picked one of the smaller rooms for my hearing, and it was stacked with members of the press. Most of that first day centred on arguments around whether the 2010 law change was legal, because it needed a 75 per cent majority to pass. I submitted that every other party in parliament voted against the legislation: 'Even Peter Dunne did. The only people that supported it were National and ACT, by a two-seat majority, I understand.'

In the back of my mind I thought that if Justice Ellis was on our side we might be able to vote in the September 2014 election, but we also needed to exhaust all our avenues of redress before we could complain to the United Nations Human Rights Committee. And sure enough, we had to go the long way around. Justice Ellis rejected my application, saying that however constitutionally objectionable the Act might be, parliament had made its decision. 'Although the Bill of Rights expresses the right to vote in unequivocal terms, Parliament has an undoubted power to make a policy decision to modify, or even nullify, its effect,' her judgment said. 'The court is unable to intervene.'

She continued: 'It is, perhaps, notable that the Amendment Act did not originate as a Government measure but had its genesis in a Private Member's Bill. Also notable is that the Bill was not referred to the Justice and Electoral Select Committee but, rather, to the Law and Order Select Committee which received official advice in relation to the Bill from the Department of Corrections.'

Justice Ellis had laid some Easter eggs that suggested to me I was on the right track. Legal experts called her ruling 'scathing'. Essentially, she was saying, 'Mr Taylor is not a lone voice in the wilderness.' Otago law professor Andrew Geddis made much of this paragraph. He wrote, on the website Pundit, 'Just to translate "notable" for you non-judgment readers out there, in judge talk it means "completely f*&%ng outrageous".'

Justice Ellis also noted that my participation in the proceedings from prison was less than satisfactory. The sound was glitchy, and I often had to turn my microphone off while others were speaking to avoid interference. She commented that self-represented prisoners should be given careful consideration when it came to letting them argue their case in court, 'unless and until the court's AVL system can be upgraded'.

Around this time, Corrections started making life difficult for me in other ways.

> A prison manager tries to slow down prisoner voting campaign again. Yesterday, he issued a directive to staff that I am to have only 3 boxes of documents at

> a time in my cell. As I am working on several cases,
> this could slow me down.
> However, he seems to be meeting some staff
> resistance now, because this directive patently has
> NO legal authority.
> *Arthur Taylor's Facebook page, 24 October 2014*

Despite the difficulties, the women also tried the Waitangi Tribunal route, given that Māori were disproportionately affected by the voting ban, but the tribunal said while the issues were important, they couldn't be considered in time for the election. This took place in September 2014, and National was elected to governance, again. Prime Minister John Key would remain at the top of the Beehive.

> Last week, the Electoral Office was instructed by
> the Judge to provide us by Monday night with
> information on numbers of remand prisoners
> who voted in 2014. We believe most were given no
> information at all, even though they were legally
> entitled to vote. We also believe disenfranchisement
> occurred in 2011. In 2011, there were prisoners
> serving sentences of 3 years and under at the time
> the new law came in who would have been entitled
> to vote. I'm not aware of any electoral activity
> among my fellow inmates then. We will ask about
> them next. The rot in the system keeps getting
> bigger the more we explore.
> *Arthur Taylor's Facebook page, November 2014*

There's more than one way to skin a cat, and I wasn't giving up. The action was a very important way of educating the public, and officialdom, and bureaucracy. I saw the 2010 law change as a dangerous precedent, because they weren't taking the vote away from individuals — they were taking it away from a group. It didn't matter what any individual prisoner had done: if they were a prisoner, then they lost their right to vote.

In a democracy, the people are meant to be the masters of parliament, and parliament is meant to act in the interests of the people. They're our servants, and here they were saying that they were now the masters. They were saying, 'We will decide who can vote for us.' Okay, prisoners today — but who's it going to be tomorrow?

In the interests of all Kiwis and of democracy, I had to fight it, and win it. An attack on one person's right to vote is an attack on everyone's right to vote. It's the thin end of the wedge. Whatever the cost, the battle had to be fought and won.

In January 2015 I asked the High Court for a ruling that the Helensville electorate votes were unlawful because they didn't include prisoners at Paremoremo. This just happened to be John Key's rural electorate. I also sought a declaration of inconsistency, that the statute preventing prisoners from voting — i.e. the Electoral Act and its amendments — contravened the Bill of Rights. On the Helensville tilt, law professor Andrew Geddis wrote, 'Let me go on the record as saying that it has zero chance of success . . . As clever and as well-argued as Taylor's claims are — and believe me, they are clever and well-argued — there is just no way . . .'

The case went to a hearing in April, where I faced off against the Attorney-General, represented by the very experienced, curly-haired Crown lawyer Aaron Perkins, who opposed the application on jurisdictional and discretionary grounds. Justice Paul Heath heard the arguments.

Lo and behold, come July, Justice Heath — while not agreeing to null and void the electorate's votes — did make a very important ruling: he formally declared that the Electoral Act was inconsistent with the Bill of Rights. His judgment started by saying: 'A democracy is built around the idea that a state is governed by elected members of a legislative body. For that reason, the right to vote is arguably the most important civic right in a free and democratic society.'

It was the first time that the High Court had made such a declaration. National's then Justice Minister Amy Adams said that the Key Government was considering the judgment but noted that it didn't automatically invalidate the Act. Jacinda Ardern, then justice spokesperson for Labour, said that the law should never have been passed. Andrew Geddis commented that parliament and the government had a decision to make: 'In the end, Parliament is sovereign and it can do what it wants . . . but I really think it ought to re-examine this issue. They've essentially been told they've made law that good nations like New Zealand shouldn't make — but do they care?'

In May 2017, the Crown sought to overturn Justice Heath's declaration through the Court of Appeal, which rejected the application. They then took it to the Supreme Court — and in November 2018 the Supreme Court also upheld the declaration. The following year, the Waitangi Tribunal found that the law breached the Treaty of Waitangi.

I pondered Edmund Hillary's triumphant climb of Mount Everest and wondered — aside from knocking the bastard off — whether he'd enjoyed a moment of the public adulation he received. Because I sure did.

CHAPTER THIRTEEN

THE PERJURER

Saturday, 19 September 2015

On this Saturday, I spied an unusual classified ad in the *Weekend Herald*. A man called Mike Kalaugher wanted to speak to jurors in the trials of David Tamihere, Scott Watson, Teina Pora, Christopher Ngarino, Stephen Hudson or Mark Lundy. All were trials where controversial verdicts had been reached. 'I am conducting research on the role of secret witnesses or in-custody informers in New Zealand criminal trials,' the ad said.

Within a few weeks, Mike was sitting directly across from me in the visiting room at Paremoremo. Mike noted that all the Plexiglas that had previously separated inmates from their visitors had been ripped out, and I told him I'd complained after seeing another inmate unable to hug or kiss his newborn child through the barrier. The prison had taken them out shortly afterwards.

Mike was in his sixties, a retiree living in Tauranga who'd grown up sailing. He'd taken an interest in double murderer Scott Watson's case after hearing of the curious ever-changing details about the mysterious ketch that Ben Smart and Olivia Hope were last seen boarding. The original description of the wooden ketch said that it was a 40-foot boat with ornate ropework, two masts and portholes. Scott Watson had been convicted, but his boat, *Blade*, was a 26-foot steel sloop with one mast. When Mike learned that jailhouse informants had alleged that Watson had confessed to them, his interest was piqued.

I told him about my experience with the informant who'd told police I'd confessed to robbing the Te Kauwhata TAB. This had given me a lifelong disgust of these fleabags. Mike was particularly interested in the David Tamihere case. Dave had been convicted of the murders of Urban Höglin and Heidi Paakkonen, two Swedish tourists who'd disappeared in the Coromandel in April 1989. Dave had stolen their car, so when the pair vanished he was the prime suspect. Already a convicted killer and holding a conviction for sexual assault, he was the ideal suspect for police. However, there was no physical evidence linking Dave to the pair's deaths. The police didn't even have any bodies, but detectives eventually had an arrow for their bow: double murderer Roberto Conchie Harris.

Harris had gunned down two people in Northland some years before the Swedes disappeared, in 1983. He'd lived with his victims, a couple, and then shot them to death after an argument, later grotesquely remarking that his murders felt just like 'eating ice cream'. This metaphor would later become shorthand for a threat, but I'll get to that.

Harris and Tamihere would eventually cross paths at Pare in 1989 when they were both in custody for murder. Dave was awaiting trial, while Harris had already been convicted. Harris would later say that the pair struck up a conversation and Dave allegedly told him about the Swedes' murders. He claimed that Dave had confessed to coming across them picnicking, and had brutally sexually assaulted them; that'd he'd killed and disposed of them both, saying that he'd beaten Höglin to death and then thrown him into the sea, having taken Höglin's watch as a memento and later given it to his son.

The detail was compelling, and Harris would become the Crown's star witness. Two other jailhouse witnesses gave evidence against Dave, and the three individually became known as witnesses A, B and C (Conchie Harris). They all received name suppression.

Less than a year after the trial in which Tamihere was convicted, Conchie's yarn started to unravel. In a major breakthrough, Urban Höglin's body was found by pig hunters in the Parakiwai Valley, about 75 kilometres from where the couple was last seen and where the cops claimed they'd been murdered. He was wearing his watch, and slices through his clothing and cuts on his skeleton suggested that he'd been stabbed. The evidence was such as to obliterate Harris's story and the Crown's case.

Some years after Dave's trial, Harris recanted his evidence. He claimed he'd been promised money and bail by late Detective Inspector John 'The Gardener' Hughes. While he got the bail, he didn't get the money; Harris was obviously incensed, so he signed an affidavit taking back everything he'd said. A year later he told the *Holmes* show that he regretted playing a part in locking an innocent man up.

'What can I say? No words can make up for it. I am terribly sorry the whole thing took place and I hope this whole thing will rectify his innocence,' he told Holmes. A year afterwards, in 1997, he even wrote to Dave expressing his regret. It turned out to be critical that Dave kept that letter. Still in the envelope and everything.

Now, in 2015, Harris was the jailhouse snitch Mike and I were interested in the most. Conchie was the only informant from that case who was still alive and traceable after all these years. I knew enough about Harris to know that if he tried to sell me a fucking used car I'd have a mechanic go over it and check it out 100 per cent. He is an inveterate liar.

Mike told me that he'd tried to get lawyers to look at a perjury case against Harris. He didn't believe that the police would be interested in a charge.

'I've been told, Arthur, that we haven't got a hope in hell.'

'Well don't you believe it,' I said. 'I'm going to look into this'.

It was time. I had looked into plenty of miscarriages of justice and mistaken identification cases, and the most significant cause was jailhouse informants.

I thought we had enough evidence to prosecute this bastard in the criminal courts. There had been an investigation into Harris by what used to be called the Police Complaints Authority. At one point Harris had said that the police put him up to it and he had lied, and then when the shit hit the fan he said that the police were only absolutely appropriate and professional. I believe the PCA rubber-stamped the matter instead of looking into the truth, and accepted Harris's word yet again. The police were obviously not going to do anything about it — and the PCA didn't have jurisdiction to look into a matter of perjury, anyway. Later the police would say that nobody had asked them to, as if the onus were on someone else to bring it to their attention.

I've often observed a tendency to protect the establishment at all costs, particularly within our judiciary. There are a few instances where the court has overturned a significant high-profile case. Arthur Allan Thomas's convictions were never overturned by the courts; they upheld the convictions all the way. It was only when he was pardoned by the Governor-General that his convictions were quashed. David Bain had a re-trial and was cleared by a jury. Teina Pora, convicted of the murder of Susan Burdett in a grave miscarriage of justice (Malcolm Rewa was finally convicted of her murder, decades later), had to go all the way to the Privy Council to gain a reprieve.

With poor Dave Tamihere, there were massive holes in his first appeal. They'd found Urban's body by then, and learned that Harris was lying, because the watch was on Urban's wrist, he hadn't been beaten to death or thrown into the sea. That significantly undermined the Crown case, but the Court of Appeal just let it stand.

Jurors are not equipped to deal with people like Harris, and they don't know all the facts about what's going on. They make decisions based on what's in front of them. That's why, as well as a trial, we also had to get Harris's name suppression revoked. Because we were bound by the suppression orders, I was struggling to get information and the public wasn't being told the full story of the sort of people the police were putting forward as witnesses.

If, say, Harris was giving evidence for the defence, he would have been attacked by the Crown and undermined — the prosecution would say 'You can't believe a word this liar tells you' because of his whole life of dishonesty. But when he's giving evidence for the Crown, with name suppression, he suddenly becomes a truthful witness. It's no good the Crown saying 'it's up to the jury', because they put these people forward as witnesses of truth. They are saying, 'We believe him.'

You just can't convict anyone on the word of these informants. They are not in the same position as an eye-witness. If a private citizen saw a crime going on and gave a witness statement, they'd have nothing to gain apart from wanting to see justice done. In contrast, jailhouse informants have absolutely everything to gain by putting forward a version of events that suits the prosecution. There are all sorts of rewards, like better prison conditions, or letters in support to the parole board.

If I trotted into court with a witness who I was paying, the judge would tell me to get the hell out of there because the prick was bought and paid for. But a guy like Harris gets all sorts of inducements.

It was an absolute blight on the justice system. The more I delved, the more I thought: 'We can't have a fair system when all the protections that are in place are abused.'

We used to have a lot of trouble with police verballing defendants (i.e. putting words into their mouths), like saying 'he confessed' when he hadn't at all, so all sorts of protections were brought in. For example, if you're interviewed by police it'll probably be taped, and you'll be asked to sign a transcript or a statement to say that everything they've noted down is correct. And yet a guy like Harris can come forward and say that someone else confessed, and there are no checks or balances whatsoever. Such informants are given more credence than a police officer, because in those circumstances the police officer's evidence would be excluded as unfair.

Mike Kalaugher put it very well. He said, 'Whenever one of these secret witnesses walks in the front door of court, Lady Justice marches out the back.'

Mike and I joined forces. His first port of call was Dave Tamihere's door, to introduce himself and tell Dave what we wanted to do. We needed him to be on board, to give evidence — and, crucially, he was able to produce the written apology from Harris. Meanwhile,

I conducted all my research from prison, including getting hold of Dave's trial transcripts and analysing Harris's 'evidence'.

The transcript from the original trial showed how Harris's graphic testimony had affected the jurors. One of them was visibly sick. Harris hadn't been challenged. I would have ripped him to shreds in court, because I knew every little trick and turn he could pull. I'd have nailed every door shut before he'd even opened them.

We filed an application in 2016 with the Auckland District Court, to lay eight charges of perjury and one of perverting the course of justice against secret Witness C. The public didn't yet know that it was Roberto Conchie Harris. Judge Brooke Gibson approved the application in June after hearing that there was a letter from Harris that could be produced in which he admitted that he'd lied. The matter was transferred to the High Court at Auckland on account of its seriousness.

Simultaneously, we also filed an application with the High Court to lift Harris's name suppression. It had been granted to him in 1989. On 10 August 2016 I argued that application for the first time by video-link from the prison, while Harris's lawyer, Chris Wilkinson-Smith, opposed it from within the court. The suppression application was declined, so I took it to the Court of Appeal and it was eventually overturned.

I met Dave and his lovely wife, Christine, for the first time before the trial when I was trying to get Harris's name suppression lifted. He shook my hand and said, 'Thanks for what you are doing, Arthur.' The poor bugger, in my opinion anyway, was so demoralised. He had been rebuffed at every turn; he knew he was innocent, and his wife knew he was innocent, and they were just over it. I think they thought they had nowhere to go.

In August 2017, at the High Court of Auckland, the trial of Roberto Conchie Harris began. I'd enlisted the expertise of lawyer Murray Gibson to prosecute for me — I wasn't allowed to do it myself because I didn't have a practising certificate. Murray had encouraged me not to even attend the trial. He was worried that I'd be a bit of a sideshow.

To a panel of twelve jurors, and Conchie who was in the dock, Gibson launched our case: 'We've got a murder trial, no bodies . . . you can imagine that a witness such as Roberto Conchie Harris would be persuasive and very significant. But it was all a lie, and he's admitted as much.'

Harris's defence lawyer, Adam Simperingham, said that while the evidence Harris gave at trial in 1990 was obviously incorrect — Urban Höglin's body proved that — he was only relaying what Dave had allegedly told him. Dave's brother, the ex Cabinet minister and former broadcaster John Tamihere, was one of the first to give evidence, recounting a 1995 telephone call with Harris in which Harris told him he wanted to recant his evidence. John had told him that there would be serious consequences for doing so, but he thought Harris understood and wanted to forge on anyway. His evidence reinforced everyone's opinion that, at one point, Harris had been ostensibly sincere in his efforts to recant.

The following day, Dave gave evidence. I heard later that he was pretty upset, actually, when he gave evidence of what he'd learned Harris had said about him, and the things he'd purportedly done to the couple. He told the jurors that he'd kept to himself while he was in custody, but had devised a scheme to learn who he could trust in prison, at the time.

'I would tell people different things, nothing major. The idea being you sit back and see if it comes back to you, then I would know who was talking to the police. As for lying about killing the Swedes, or not killing the Swedes, it is a different matter altogether. I never went there.'

Mike Kalaugher sat at the back of the court and looked on.

Somebody told Harris he was going to get acquitted. He told someone at court that 'Arthur is just bringing a show-pony case against me, I'm getting acquitted, I've been told I'm getting acquitted — I am getting off, don't worry about that, there's no way I'm going down for this.'

He was so cocky that when the jury came back with a couple of questions during their deliberations, Harris turned to his lawyer and said, 'Don't they know how to spell "not guilty"?' But the jury didn't have 'stupid' tattooed on their foreheads. Back they came on 1 September: 'Count one, guilty'— oh, Jesus, see his face — 'Count two, guilty.' Right up to 'Count eight, guilty.' That was a victory for justice that day.

Just an hour after the jury began their deliberations at 3 p.m. on a Thursday afternoon, Roberto Conchie Harris was found guilty of all the perjury charges, but not the perverting the course of justice charge. I found out over the phone in Pare. Shouts resounded around the prison: 'The bastard has been found guilty!' All the boys were rapt.

I was proud that I'd brought the case to public attention and got this mongrel convicted, but there was still work to be done: sentencing. I knew how to deal with sentencing, having been through enough of it myself, so I knew exactly what to look for; I also knew that Justice Christian Whata, who'd overseen the trial, was an extremely fair judge. He'd bent over backwards to ensure that Harris got a fair trial. From the point of view of a defendant, he's the judge you want.

I enlisted Richard Francois to make submissions for sentencing. Harris got eight years and seven months, the longest sentence for perjury ever handed out in a New Zealand court.

Together, if we'd been working for the Crown, Mike and I could have earnt the best part of half a million dollars. That's what it would have cost us to prosecute, and it annoys me to this day that there was no offer from the Crown to reimburse us. Murray Gibson took the case pro bono. They could have said: 'What did you spend out of pocket in bringing this prosecution? We're going to reimburse you for it because it's our job; taxpayers pay us to do it.' At the very least, I could have been sent a letter of thanks from the Police Commissioner, Mike Bush — who'd hunted me in the bush in Tairua all those years ago — for doing his job for him.

It's the Crown that is supposed to uphold criminal law in New Zealand. The police have a duty to prosecute someone for a crime, at their expense. But in this case the police did nothing — despite having known for years that their key witness was a liar — and instead a civilian had to bring an action. In any other country there would be an outcry; they'd say, 'How come Arthur Taylor can sit in his cell and convict this prick — what were you doing? You've got search warrants, what's he got?'

Of course, neither Mike nor I had heard the end of Harris. On 18 September 2018, more than a year after the trial had ended, Mike received a five-page letter written by Harris in cursive script.

> To Mike, I have been waiting to express some
> ineradicable imperfections of my own based on
> diamond-hard beliefs. The grandiosity and lack
> of judgement pertaining to AT are the hallmark of
> someone with the intelligence and I.Q. of a banana.
> He will probably suffer the ultimate indignity of
> dying while stupid. His pitiful moment of fame
> on the Nation programme once again showed
> thousands of viewers and inmates he's lower than a
> sewer, a dirtbag, lard-arse, motor-mouth, snitching
> motherfucker . . . A hypocrite, masquerading as a
> wanna-be lawyer, like a fox guarding the hen-house
> and could fool a polygraph if he had to.

Eventually he got to his point:

> I often get engrossed in some topic and forget to
> extract myself, anyway, I can assure those involved
> over the past twelve months, yourself, AT, Murray
> Gibson, and the idiot Francois we will meet in the
> near future . . . I'll bring the ice cream to the party,
> yous can count on that as sure as night follows day
> . . . Sometimes the only thing more dangerous than
> a man with nothing to lose is a man with everything
> to lose. A sport I have missed dearly is hunting, I
> loved it from a young age, a hunter gatherer believe
> me, I have the instincts of a hunter and love the
> chase, but its [sic] the kill that gave me a deep
> visceral satisfaction.

He suggested that Mike give me a copy of the letter.

I was livid and complained to the police, essentially on behalf of Mike. I thought they should charge Harris for threatening to kill. They interviewed Mike but declined to prosecute Harris, saying that the letter didn't meet the Solicitor-General's guidelines and that any risk was mitigated by Harris being in prison.

In 2020, Mike and I both made submissions to the Parole Board in opposition to Harris's release on parole, attaching copies of the letter.

I'm not scared of Harris. The only thing I feel nervous about is the possibility that Harris might come into possession of money, so that he could pay somebody else to do his dirty work. He's in Ngawha prison in Northland. During the trial he was in Pare, but in the protection section. Sometimes he would be coming down when I got to go to court, and they would have to lock him away before I went through.

CHAPTER FOURTEEN

STRIPPING DOWN

Take your shirt off and hand it to a guard for them to inspect the cotton. Lift both arms up, overhead. Turn, like a ballerina. Open your mouth, poke out your tongue. Move it up and down. Put your shirt back on. Take off your shorts and underwear. The three guards will inspect these, too.

Lift your penis, your testicles, let their eyes wander over your body. Turn. Squat. You're bending at the knees until your arse is close to the ground. You're exposed. They will leer.

It's not over yet. Shorts back on as the three guards exit the cell. At the entrance to the landing a group of officers, more than ten of them, will watch as I'm ordered to spread-eagle against a wall while a portable metal-detector wand is run over my weaponless body. I lift my feet to let the detector be run over the soles of my footwear. Humiliating. Intimidating. Illegal.

Back in October 2016 while my fight for the vote was going on, three prison officers at Paremoremo were badly assaulted by four inmates in C block, which housed maximum-security prisoners. By this time I'd been moved to the lower-security unit, A block.

The assault should never have happened. One of the inmates had requested something, and when the officer opened the door to pass the item through, three other prisoners appeared and pushed the door open. Two of them had home-made shanks, and stabbed two of the guards with them. Other screws joined the melee; one officer was carted off to hospital and the other three treated on-site. The inmates had three weapons on them in all, one of which had been made out of a supposedly tamper-proof metal bracket for a television.

When dealing with maximum-security prisoners, there's a basic rule to follow: whenever they are out of their cells, you have three officers present for each inmate. You can't open the door without strict instructions. Sure, these guards had fucked up, but they didn't deserve to get hurt. Most of the other prisoners didn't agree with, or condone, the violence.

The guards thought that two of the inmates responsible seemed drunk. A plastic bag of fruit and liquid was recovered. The guards figured that they'd been drinking homebrew, though that was never proven because they never bothered testing the bag for alcohol. (Homebrew, alcohol made from fruit and sugar, is easily made in prisons, though the banning of the yeast-based Marmite stymied this enterprise somewhat. Inmates can have up to nine pieces of fruit in their cell, though, and have a daily ration of sugar.)

Typically, prison manager Tom Sherlock's instinct was to lock the prison down, which meant that every prisoner was confined to their cell. A few days later, Sherlock decided that every prisoner, including those in the special needs unit but not those in the management and at-risk units, should be searched for evidence of weapons or homebrew. It wasn't long before three officers marched up to my cell in A block and told me I was to be strip-searched. It was ludicrous. The assailants had nothing to do with us in A block, and it made no sense that I'd be hiding fruit or modified TV brackets between my butt cheeks. I could understand them strip-searching the prisoners that were involved, or even the other ones on their block. But our wing was the farthest you could get from them.

No matter how much a prisoner argues, front-line staff still carry out their orders. It's useless trying to deter them. The Corrections Regulations 2005 provide that if a prisoner is aggrieved by a lawful order, then he/she must obey it and complain later. If you refuse to obey an order, it will likely result in you being physically overpowered, and put in painful wrist locks and choke holds.

So now, these screws were in my cell saying, 'We've got to do it.'

'No. Listen, you've got metal detectors, you've got hand-held scanners, you've got X-ray machines, you've got everything. Why do you need to do a strip-search, and what are you looking for anyway?'

'We can't tell you, Arthur, we've just been ordered to strip you. That's all we know. We've got to do what we are told.'

'That defence isn't going to wash. When Nazis tried to claim they were only obeying orders for chucking people in the gas chamber, they still got tried at Nuremberg.'

But it was all above their heads. They were just following orders.

'd been strip-searched dozens of times over the years, but this time there was no rhyme or reason to it and I felt dehumanised and vulnerable. It was akin to someone wandering into your home and ordering you to take all your clothes off. Prisoners have got so few rights and dignities. I try to reinforce their sense of self-worth in the hope that they will respect others. They have to feel good about themselves, to feel that they've got some worth and value — but prisons operate to undermine, to tell them they've got no rights, to tell them they've got no dignity, and it's extremely counterproductive.

Strip-searching is a quick way to degrade a prisoner. Prison officers don't like doing it (although some nasty ones do), and I find it particularly offensive in relation to women. The Canadian courts have likened strip-searching to visual rape. Not too long ago we had a case where fifteen women prisoners were paid $25,000 each in compensation for unlawful internal searches. This time, it needed to be reinforced to Corrections: *You can't do this*. Sometimes you've got to draw a line in the sand and whatever the cost you've got to fight, even though it's going to be extremely disadvantageous for you.

More than 200 prisoners had been searched, and none of those searches produced anything from their persons, although some cell searches did — two shanks, a blade, and a container of homebrew. I wrote to the chief executive of the Department of Corrections pointing out what had happened and explaining to him the relevant law, the relevant section in the Corrections Act. I asked him to take legal advice and said that I was holding him liable, that the prisoners who had been strip-searched wanted an apology and they wanted some monetary compensation. That letter was sent about December.

T he strip-search case came before Justice Mary Peters at the High Court at Auckland in March 2018, eighteen months after the search. Tui Hartman was my McKenzie friend.

Tui Hartman was a 32-year-old paralegal living in Ontario, Canada, whose father was a Kiwi. Canada has similar laws to ours, so Canadian law students study a lot of my cases. New Zealand law professors teach them in law school, too. One day she rolled a dice and sent me a Facebook message to ask some questions about the law. She was shocked when I answered her.

We struck up a conversation, and then we got her telephone number put on my list so we could talk to each other. (As a prisoner, you can only call certain phone numbers that have been approved by Corrections.) We continued to correspond and in January 2018 she moved to New Zealand.

Tui visited me regularly in prison, driving hours each way. She loved the outdoors. We were briefly engaged, but we didn't marry. The police called her regularly, warning her off, so I said, 'You can't be subjected to this sort of nonsense — we'd better split up and have a bit of distance for a while.' She ended up working for the police in a data-entry job. We're still in touch.

It was a rather unusual relationship, but these things happen. There's no accounting for matters of the heart.

Even though it was short-lived, my romance with Tui attracted a lot of attention. I didn't mind, because I like to be an open book. I'm on Facebook all the time, which people think is unusual. I say, if I was in the underworld — and that's why it's called the underworld, because you fucking keep everything secret — I wouldn't want you knowing where I am and what I'm doing. Instead, I'm open all the time. But that still doesn't change the way the police or Corrections behave. They've got certain things lodged in their heads and they're determined to prove them right no matter what.

In this case, Phillip John Smith and I had joined action to complain that the search was unlawful, unreasonable, in breach of the New Zealand Bill of Rights Act 1990, and inhumane and undignified. We wanted a declaration that the search was unreasonable and sought compensation of $10,000 each.

I love cross-examining Corrections staff because they're not used to having to justify themselves. Once you get them on the stand and are asking 'Well, why did this happen — what's your statutory justification for this?' they can't answer. Here's a snippet of my cross-examination with old Sherlock.

'At the time you ordered the search of both Mr Smith and myself, the strip-search, not the search of ourselves, the strip-search of our person, you had no information whatsoever that suggested we were in possession of any weapons or items that could be used to make weapons?'

'No.'

'At the time you ordered the strip-search of myself and Mr Smith, did you have any information whatsoever that Mr Smith or myself were in possession of any unauthorised items?'

'No.'

'Did you give any consideration, whatsoever . . . as to myself and Mr Smith's individual circumstances before you ordered that strip search of us?'

'As individuals, no.'

This was significant. We argued that the search was unlawful because there was no belief that either Smith or I had an unauthorised item in our possession, let alone a belief held on reasonable grounds.

It took two years from the event itself, but in September

2018 Justice Peters ruled that the strip-searches were unlawful, unreasonable and a breach of the Human Rights Act. Those who had joined me in the action, including Phillip John Smith, were paid $1000 each.

I'll tell you a story about Phillip John Smith, convicted of molesting a child, then murdering the child's father, before escaping to Brazil while on temporary release. When he came back from his little stint in South America, the word went around prison that you could virtually kill him with impunity and the authorities wouldn't care. To me it looked like they had transferred him to where someone could get at him.

I had to put a stop to this chatter about knocking him off, because he was a very smart cookie. I had received 100 per cent assurances from him that he would never re-offend in that manner again. My choice was either to go along with the screws' propaganda, or identify Phillip's good points that could be used for the common good of all prisoners. When they saw that he was working with me on the strip-search case, all the heat came off him. Those strip-searches might well have saved his life.

'Has he got any money, Arthur?'

Lawyer Barry Hart had his eye on the prize, but who could blame him with the type of people he had had to represent. At one time, Barry — tanned, with white hair and expensive suits — had been one of Auckland's premier lawyers, but around 2012 he had a fall from grace after he over-charged clients, obstructed a Law Society investigation and failed to fully pay an investigator. So he was struck off. But not long before this, I'd given him a call.

Convicted rapist and murderer Liam Reid had been in contact with me, claiming that he was innocent. I'd heard this before, of course, but he'd sent some paperwork to show that there had been some sort of fuck-up with the DNA. 'Can you get me a lawyer?' he asked. 'No one will help me.'

Everyone is entitled to a defence, or an appeal, even someone like Liam Reid. This tattooed, bald-headed scumbag had raped and murdered deaf woman Emma Agnew in 2007. She was just twenty. He was also jailed for the rape and attempted murder of another woman, and was serving a life sentence with the possibility of parole in 2031. I regret helping him now, but at that stage I still thought he needed a fair hearing.

I rang Barry Hart.

'Barry, we've got this Liam Reid here, and he needs a lawyer.'

The first question: the money.

'No, he hasn't, but you must have somebody around the place who's not doing anything. Just do it for me, will you Barry?'

Believe me, I didn't believe that Reid was innocent, but it did need checking out, to cross the t's and dot the i's. So Barry sent a lawyer, a woman called Davina Murray.

Soon afterwards, Reid was transferred to Mount Eden Prison, at Davina's request, so that they could work on his appeal together. It can be difficult for lawyers to get into Pare sometimes — it's a bit far away — but really she was getting him transferred there so that they could have a little affair.

I was in D block when a screw called Rhino came down the passageway bearing news: 'Arthur, guess what's happened? We're getting fucking Reid back here.'

I'd thought he was doing quite well down at Mount Eden and expressed surprise.

'Yeah, doing too well he was — the little prick has been found with fucking cellphones, cigarettes and all sorts of shit.'

And, of course, Davina Murray was the culprit.

When Reid returned to Pare he spun a sad story about the screws setting him up, because he wanted me to help Davina. It was plausible; if you know how screws operate, then there was a possibility that they'd had a gutsful of Reid and wanted him out of

Mount Eden, and that this was a good way to do it.

But when I looked into the matter, I learned the truth of it. I spoke to someone at Mount Eden who told me that the affair had been going on for months, and some of the boys were pissed off because it brought attention to the place. It had been well known that Liam had a smartphone and he didn't know how to work it properly, so he sent it out with Davina to get fixed.

I thought, 'You poor silly woman, getting involved with him.' For some reason, she was besotted with Reid; there's no accounting for taste. For her sins she was struck off and convicted of bringing contraband into a prison. Tom Sherlock ordered a review, and introduced restrictions around how and if prisoners met with their lawyers — which was the real horror, in my opinion. Sherlock's evidence to the court made him sound like a wounded bird. 'I personally no longer feel like I can rely on the integrity of the legal profession when making decisions in the best interests of Auckland Prison,' he said.

In 2017, six years after Davina had smuggled the contraband to Liam, they married at Pare, much to the disgust of most of the country. I couldn't believe that. No one had been allowed to get married in Pare Max since Scott Watson had married Coral in 2004. After that they banned weddings in Pare Max, and you had to wait till you got to medium security. Well, they transferred that little shit, Reid, down to medium security for the day, costing the taxpayer a fucking heap of money. The screws don't do that for anyone, unless they are doing some sort of deal. Since then, Reid has been on protection, segregated, because other inmates don't like the little shit.

I wasn't invited to the wedding. By that time I had made it clear to Reid what I thought of him, and I'd told Davina that she was the craziest woman in the world. She'd convinced herself that he was getting out; that was never going to happen, but she was deluded. If he ever did get out, he'd probably end up killing her.

CHAPTER FIFTEEN

THE TRANSFER

High profile inmate Arthur Taylor kicked up a fuss while being transferred from his long-term home at Auckland Prison to a residential unit at Waikeria Prison.

'Mr Taylor was non-compliant with the instructions of staff, and actively resisted being moved,' the [Corrections] spokesperson said. 'In line with section 83 of the Corrections Act 2004 staff were required to physically move him to the escort vehicle due to his resistance. He was moved in a dedicated prisoner escort vehicle and accompanied by custodial staff and a nurse. The journey went without incident and Mr Taylor is now residing in a residential unit at Waikeria Prison.'

The New Zealand Herald, *20 December 2017*

I was ageing — in 2017, I'd turned 61. My security levels had been reduced and my repeatedly declined parole applications were only inching me closer to the day when I could be released. Each time you go before the Parole Board, it's like a dry run at the real thing. Those hearings gave me a blueprint for what I needed to do in the intervening period to have a successful bid the next time.

My road to freedom started with a bump and a hiss. In October that year I was reclassified as low security, which was good news to me — it meant that I could be in a self-managed care unit, which would give me a better chance of preparing for parole. I'd applied to be transferred to the Auckland South Corrections Facility at Wiri, which had self-care units and was the next closest prison to Pare. Brian McDonald, the chair of the Bond Trust, had written to Auckland Regional Prisons director Andy Langley in support of my transfer there. There was no reply.

In the meantime, Corrections had been threatening to take me quite a distance away to Waikeria for some time, but I knew that a transfer there would significantly disadvantage me. I had no family down there and it was out in the middle of nowhere, out in the sticks and away from civilisation. My take on their reasons? Well, the new maximum-security section at Pare was about to open, and I was the only one who would make them comply with their rules. They were sick of me taking effective action against them, and they wanted to have free rein to run things their way, regardless of the law. Waikeria is a lot further from the High Court at Auckland than Wiri, put it that way. I was also in the middle of the strip search case, and it felt like Corrections was keen to disrupt it by moving me.

Prisoners were supposed to be informed a minimum of seven working days before a transfer. I wasn't given so much as a date. You *could* conclude that they were trying to avoid me being able to organise an escape en route, but there was no logic to that: they were transferring me from a maximum-security prison to a minimum-security prison in anticipation of my eventual release, to prepare me for life outside the wire. If they thought I was an escape risk, why bother?

The operational plan for transferring me to Waikeria, one of the country's oldest prisons, built in 1911 and sitting on 1200 hectares near Te Awamutu in the Waikato, numbered seven pages. Bold lettering gave the master plan a code name: Operation Swift. There was even a 'mission', for clarity: 'To transfer prisoner Taylor to Waikeria'. From my first prison sentence, served at the prison's borstal, I was about to come full circle.

Around 9 a.m. on 20 December, all prisoners were to be cleared from my landing and put in the yards. Staff would switch on their body cameras. I was to be kept in my cell, and the screws involved would have a meeting before bringing me to the receiving office.

The staff to escort me were hand-picked. The water would be turned off so that prisoners couldn't flood the landings, and the power would be turned off, too. Corrections staff would lay out my property for me to look at, record it, box up my files in meticulously labelled boxes (Box 1 of 4, etc.), and would film themselves documenting the boxes. They would give me a choice of clothes to wear for the trip, and I'd be given time to change into them. Then I'd be put in a transfer vehicle and the guards would stay with me until I reached my new unit.

Clearly, Corrections anticipated a fight from me. 'Auckland Staff will assist Waikeria in responses to any OIA, Privacy Act, Reviews etc. that is generated by Taylor in regards to the transfer.' With regard to my anticipated refusal to leave, Corrections documented the law as it then stood. Staff were reminded of section 83 of the Corrections Act 2004, which said that screws and staff could use physical force, but not more than reasonably necessary in the circumstances. 'No more physical force than necessary and limited to minimum degree reasonable to resolve the situation and that all staffs are responsible for the force used.'

In charge of the escort was a man called Phil Shead. In charge of the entire operation was Solomon Nui.

On D-Day I was called into the office of A block's Principal Corrections Officer; initially, I was told, for an 'interview'. There, I was told that I was being transferred to Waikeria Prison right then. Of course, they hadn't given me the required advance notice — seven days — and I considered the move to be illegal. As much as I wanted to leave prison, Pare had become my home and I was due my appropriate notice, my time to say goodbye.

I told them I wasn't going anywhere.

Within three minutes, the Special Event Response Team had come up behind me. I kept my hands at my sides, and told the staff in general that what they were doing was illegal, that I would not comply with an unlawful order, and that any use of force would be assault. I said there would be legal action. I could feel a group of them behind me, could practically feel them breathing down my neck.

At that point, a group of officers grabbed my hands from behind me and threw me to the floor. The last thing I remember is someone kneeling on my back; then everything went black.

I woke up in a small, brightly lit room, dressed in nothing but a basic gown. Sun was drenching the space, and I was hot. Nearly an entire day had gone by. I hadn't eaten. I had no idea what had happened, or where I was. I could only presume that I was in Waikeria Prison. I knew I'd been unconscious.

On 22 December, I posted about the experience on Facebook. I'd had an account for some years, which I updated by phoning a friend, who'd write posts for me. It was my own way of making sure that the public knew what was going on inside prisons, given the difficulties of speaking with journalists. 'The Corrections spokesperson obviously forgot to tell [the *Herald*] that I was rendered unconscious,' the post said. 'It's an unheard-of level of drama to transfer a low security inmate to a low security prison.'

Very far south, in the cold climes of Dunedin, Otago University law student Hazel Heal read the post with disgust, and vowed to help.

Sensing an injustice, Hazel, despite having never met me, enlisted the help of law professor Mark Henaghan and consulted with Andrew Geddis. Together with my lawyer who'd helped me with my parole hearings, Sue Earl, we fought tooth and nail to retrieve the footage of what had happened after I'd fallen unconscious.

On 26 December, Richard Francois put Corrections on notice that I needed to be seen by a doctor promptly. I wouldn't be seen for six weeks.

azel is a no-nonsense woman with a pragmatic soul. She'd worked for Heritage New Zealand for eight years before one day, almost inexplicably, looking around the room and realising that she didn't want to be the shrinking wallflower, the lowly, low-paid administrator at the back of the room. She looked across the road at the university's Gothic spire and thought 'I'll study law.'

Like me, she felt the burden of recognising wrongs and needing to do something about it. In 1992 she'd been diagnosed with hepatitis C, which became terminal when her liver started failing right before her first law exam. By chance, she came across a way to import a generic drug that would give her life again. It cured her.

Not content to hold her precious life in her hands and feel grateful with that, she set about making sure that all hepatitis C sufferers knew a cure was available to them, at a low cost. She couldn't believe that New Zealand's drug-buying agency didn't already fund it, or advertise it. Unable to sit still, she started a campaign to cure the world of hepatitis C, through her health organisation Global Health New Zealand, and all from the office of her Dunedin home.

n my own fight, Hazel took up the mantle. Hazel was a blessing, because I can't look at the footage. I don't even like to read about it. It annoys the hell out of me; makes me furious. I am horrified that they would go to those lengths.

We filed a statement of claim at the Wellington High Court against the Attorney-General, alleging a breach of New Zealand's obligation to uphold its international responsibilities along with breaches of the New Zealand Bill of Rights and common law.

People have the right not to be subjected to torture or to cruel, inhuman or degrading or disproportionately severe treatment or punishment. We have the right to be treated with humanity, and to respect for the inherent dignity of the person. Prisoners, under the Corrections Act, are entitled to be treated fairly, humanely and in accordance with applicable law. All decisions concerning us are to be made fairly and reasonably, and we are to be detained in the least restrictive conditions consistent with the safety of the community. We're entitled to the right to health, including mental health. We're entitled to receive medical treatment that is reasonably necessary, and reasonably equivalent to the standard of health care available to the public.

My segregation, the conditions in D block, the blocking of my access to the *Truth*, and my transfer to Waikeria had breached all of these rights. I said that the Attorney-General was vicariously liable for the acts and omissions of Corrections staff.

I f Paremoremo was a concrete jungle, Waikeria was a hole. From a bird's-eye view, Waikeria looked like a mouse maze, and the rations fit the bill. By the time I was moved there they'd announced plans for a new prison, a 500-bed jail with 100 beds specifically for mental health and addiction patients. (It was just as well they'd started, because in the summer of 2020/2021 a group of inmates, who were protesting at the conditions, essentially burned the maximum-security wing at Waikeria down.)

One afternoon in 2018 the fire alarm went off, and while the Te Awamutu fire department dealt to it we were all moved to the upper sports field for an hour. The guards handed out sunscreen, which was sensible. The heat scorched. When you're inside all day, your skin becomes white silk. That sports field would hold our Christmas barbecue in just over a month's time. Only those who could afford the $6.80 for two meat patties, lettuce, tomato, sausage and egg would attend.

The easiest way for Corrections to save money is on food. That year, 2017 was the first time I'd ever seen prisoners scrounging around in bin liners for food that other prisoners had chucked out, because they were hungry. All prisoners are fed the same, and it's meagre rations. Anyone who says it's not should sample it. The menus put out by Corrections bear little resemblance to the food that ends up on the wings. It's nearly always cold, and it's prepared by prisoners who by and large couldn't care less, creaming stuff off the top for their mates. The staff aren't that interested in supervising them.

Some years earlier, celebrity psychologist Nigel Latta had been ranting and raving about prisoners, but then he spent a night in Rimutaka. He didn't even go into a unit with other prisoners, who would have given him shit all night. Instead, he went into a unit all on his own, and the prison guards would have been treating him with kid gloves. He still said it was one of the worst experiences of his life. I notice that since then he's not been so critical of prisoners.

For the majority of my sentence in maximum security, I ate in my cell. Cold comforts delivered on a plastic tray from a central kitchen where it had sat for half an hour, maybe an hour, beforehand. Milk was trim; they said it was for health reasons. I said that can't be so: my health requirements are totally different to some 19-year-old who needs that extra fat, but they stuck with it.

As a result of my and others' complaints, the prison menu was substantially altered on 20 October 2019. The horrible carbohydrate white shit bread was replaced by wholemeal bread. It was important, because you get eleven pieces of bread a day. The sandwich fillings improved, too.

Most prisoners are fed their evening meal about 4 p.m. and they don't get another one till 8.30 a.m. That's a long stretch of nothing. Unless they've got money to buy some snacks, they've got nothing to eat all night — and some of them are young prisoners. So now they get a muffin that they can save and eat during the evening, and yoghurt, too. There's been a marked improvement; little things like that make a big difference.

The current rations still sound a lot better written down than what they actually are. Breakfast: WeetBix, toast, margarine, jam. Weak tea, not coffee, and sugar. Lunch: mixed-grain-bread sandwiches with a choice of chicken luncheon, roast beef, corned beef, shredded chicken or meatloaf for the carnivores (veges get lentils, falafel or Vegemite). Dinner is a stagnant mixture of fish, beef or chicken with vegetables. The Department's budget is about $5 a day per person — and think what you can get for $5, even at bulk-order prices.

I never went hungry because I've always had money in jail, leftovers from my enterprises, so I've always had plenty of snacks, like chippies and chocolate, but other prisoners didn't. I'd usually hand them out treats. If one of the prisoners had a birthday, I would give them a packet of biscuits. Their faces would beam.

W aikeria had all single bunks, because the cells had been designed and built with one occupant in mind. The United Nations says that where there are two in a cell, it should be at least 9 square metres. These cells at Waikeria were about 5.5 square metres, 50 per cent less than the requirement for two. But by this time, prisons were bursting at the seams. About a year after I arrived at Waikeria, they suddenly decided that they were going to double-bunk some of the units (I should point out that mine wasn't one of those). They spent millions of dollars putting in the bunks. I warned them that this was not going to be acceptable. I said 'You are wasting your money, taxpayers' money', but they wouldn't listen.

I warned them again in writing. I made several complaints, because it substantially intrudes into a prisoner's quality of life if they've got to share the little space they have with someone else. The lack of space is an affront to human rights as well.

In the end I had to file action in the Hamilton High Court, but they heeded the warning, and one day, without warning, everybody went back to single-bunking.

However, after I got out of prison they waited a few months and then double-bunked that prison again. I couldn't take legal action this time, because by then I'd been released. I'd exchanged my standing for freedom.

CHAPTER SIXTEEN

OUTSIDE
THE WIRE

> The Board recognised Mr Taylor's future prospects
> and Mr Taylor's enthusiasm for what lay ahead of him.
> *New Zealand Parole Board, January 2019*

They sat, quietly, listening. I had a stage. I had an audience. There were no suits and ties, no robes, no arguments, no formalities. No security, no police. They had come to hear me talk.

The University of Otago is New Zealand's oldest educational institution, its Gothic registry perhaps the most photographed building in Dunedin. Its cherry trees and the Water of Leith are a gift for studious learners, and a bolt of beauty for someone used to concrete walls and dull floors. I'd never been to a tertiary institution; I hadn't even finished school.

In August 2019 the Otago Laws 204 public law class piled into seminar room 5 on the tenth floor of the Richardson Building, named after Sir John Richardson, a nineteenth-century New Zealand Cabinet minister who was Superintendent of the Otago Province during the gold rush years. He was integral to getting women admitted to the university. Behind me, a wall of black and white staff photos conferred esteem on the room.

Otago law professor Andrew Geddis — who'd written so eloquently about my prisoner voting case — had invited me to speak to the students. In an interview-style Q&A session he led me through my life of crimes, before getting into law. I spoke of my amusement at beating QCs and Crown lawyers without so much as an internet connection. The students asked questions, and I felt heard. A millennial in the room live-streamed part of the talk. Later, the students themselves invited me back to talk to their peers.

24 JANUARY 2019

Eight months earlier, in the beating heart of the summer, Judge Louis Bidois, Sir Ron Young, and Dr Sally Davis and Mr Grant

Crowley from the Parole Board had met with me through an audio-visual link. I was sitting in Waikeria Prison. The board was at Auckland South Corrections Facility at Wiri. My long-time lawyer, Sue Earl, was there to talk to the board. Hazel Heal had written a letter in support of my parole, and Probation Service officers had been out to her semi-rural Dunedin home to assess its suitability.

Convincing a Parole Board that you are suitable for parole is like training for an unarmed campaign. You hold your hands up in peace and tell them all the wonderful things you've been doing behind bars that make you a rehabilitated person. I'd been eligible for parole for many years, but had waived my right to appear before the board for a couple of years while my conspiracy case was pending. Between 2011 and 2016, I'd sought various adjournments because of those drug charges and the subsequent appeals. The outcome of those matters was important for the board to consider. Being maximum security at various times meant I couldn't undertake any rehabilitation to convince the board that I wasn't a risk. Since 2011 I'd been declined parole seven times, even though I'd had offers of legal research work from the University of Auckland.

On parole, you're not technically free — your sentence expiry date is still your sentence expiry date. When that day arrives you're considered released, but before that (as long as you have a parole eligibility date), the Parole Board — a mix of lawyers, professional people, industry practitioners and Joe Public — can agree to parole you to a suitable address. You're still monitored by Probation Services with any number of devices that the board and Corrections think suitable. You might be subject to a curfew, have to live in a particular place or avoid a certain area, and might even have to wear an electronic monitoring bracelet. You might be ordered to continue completing rehabilitation in the community. So it's hard to say that you're free, as such. But compared with the alternative, life on the outside was still something I wanted very, very badly.

I'd brought forward this particular hearing. With Hazel in my corner, I was optimistic that the board would consider her and her partner Rob to be sound people for me to launch my life outside with. It wasn't as simple as that, however. Although Hazel and I had been talking for over a year by that point, and Hazel had taken on my Waikeria transfer case, we'd yet to meet. But she was about to graduate with a law degree, and this counted for something.

'They are all interested in social justice,' panel convenor Judge Bidois noted of my household-to-be. 'Given the professional status of his sponsors, there will be intellectual stimulation. Mr Taylor and [Hazel] obviously share a common interest in the law. The advantages in the placement seen by the board is that it is quiet and semi-rural which will give Mr Taylor the opportunity to wind down in a non-pressured situation, away from the pressures of urban living and out of the considerable public eye.'

Nearly 40 years after I'd left the Northland I'd loved, I was moving back to the country. The thing I was looking forward to most was seeing my family.

After fourteen years behind bars, none of the clothes I'd entered with, including various clothes I'd worn to court, fit me anymore. The Friday before my release saw a mini-excursion outside of Waikeria, with three officers and a GPS tracker, to find a uniform for my release. We visited three op-shops but their prices were a bit eye-watering. I shop at second-hand stores where I can, particularly ones that donate proceeds to the less-well-off in the community, but their prices are getting ridiculous. At The Warehouse I gravitated towards camouflage gear; a green and black hooded vest and cap, jeans, and heavy-duty black boots.

When you check into prison, Corrections used to let you keep several outfits for your eventual release, but now you can only keep one. Over the years I'd amassed dress trousers and shirts that Carolyn or Joanne had bought me for court. Over the weekend I packed up boxes and boxes of documents and court files, some prison-issued jam and butter packs (I planned to reveal publicly how unhealthy they were), and a stash of p119s — food bought from the prison canteen through my inside account: chips, noodles and the like. I wanted to give my nieces and nephews something.

I did the rounds, saying goodbye to the guys, spinning a few yarns, tidying up loose ends. The boys were nervous that in my absence things around the place would start to slide. If a fridge or a toasted sandwich maker or some other item in the common area blew a fuse, it wasn't uncommon for the appliance to disappear entirely, ostensibly whisked away for repairs but never returned. I noticed that kind of thing, and complained. I told the boys what to do and who to contact after my departure.

There was also the matter of who would re-tenant my cell. Considered the penthouse suite, my cell was one-and-a-half the size of other cells, because it was a cell for the disabled and the shower on my landing had better water pressure. The other inmates were clamouring for the space, but my friend Ryan, housed in the cell opposite mine, was the best choice in my opinion. An Auckland North Shore bloke in his mid-thirties doing a stint for drug dealing, Ryan worked in the gardens and often brought me tomatoes, cucumbers and lettuces. In a prison these were little treasures. I had some influence with the unit manager, a really nice bloke, who assured me that he'd take my opinion into consideration. He made good on his word. Ryan later told me that after my exit the screws very thoroughly inspected The Penthouse. They seemed to have some idea that I'd had a cellphone in there.

On the day itself, two screws came and woke me around 4 a.m. To avoid any fanfare from the other inmates, and a media scrum outside the prison, Corrections wanted me out nice and early. I didn't even have to go through the receiving office. However, despite the fact that they would have liked to barrel me out immediately, I did another lot of rounds, saying goodbye to Ryan and my neighbours. On the top floor of the prison you could see the incoming and departing prisoners, and the boys cheered as I walked out.

Prison officer Geoff Palacio had specially volunteered to drive me the short trip from the prison doors to the car park where my family, Mike Kalaugher, and Radio New Zealand were waiting for me. Geoff was a bit of a hero — in late 2007 he'd helped a police officer who was being chased by a chair-wielding offender down the streets of Ōtorohanga.

It was still early; the sky was vivid blue with the sun just starting to rise, gently washing out the black with light. Flowering toetoe flecked the cark park. As soon as the white van glided to a stop, I leaped out. My darling baby sister Joanne was waiting for me. 'Hey, hey; hey, hey,' she sang out, with a big grin. We embraced. 'Beautiful morning to be getting out of prison, isn't it?' I said as the sun rose.

For nine months I lived with Hazel and Rob. Initially I lived in a sleep-out next to the house, then after a while they put in another one down the slope from their main home, a blue-corrugated-iron tiny house complete with its own bathroom, kitchenette, lounge and bedroom. Plans were afoot to build a deck around my new pad.

Over the ensuing month I saw my family and got used to taking care of myself again. Because I had always kept in close touch with what was going on in the community, nothing was hard to get used to except freedom itself — making decisions for myself, and being responsible for doing everything, like arranging doctors and medical care; the minutiae of life. I relaunched my social life through the internet, finally able to access and control my own Facebook page. I used it as a podium, and took to social media like a duck to water. I've always been oriented towards new tech; back in 1996, I'd been the first one in prison to get a cellphone.

I didn't have a driver's licence, so had to catch public transport everywhere. Or Hazel would shuttle me around, which was a massive burden on her. My licence, first granted in March 1980, had expired while I was in prison. If your licence has expired for more than five years, you have to apply for it again. Fortunately I only had to sit a written test, to refresh my memory, and avoided the rigmarole of being a learner and then a restricted driver.

Some road rules had changed, so I set about studying, buying the AA's books and tests to challenge myself ahead of the test. But as it turned out, my knowledge of how to drive wasn't the biggest problem. When I went to sit my test, the AA refused to process the documents because they claimed that my legal name wasn't Arthur William Taylor. They seemed to think that I was called Paul Colin Richardson, from Dargaville.

I loved the people in Dunedin. Paroled or released inmates are paid a modest figure to get started, though I have no idea how people with no support are supposed to survive on this. I went to Westpac Bank and the teller said, 'You're Arthur Taylor, aren't you? Can I have your autograph?' As a convicted bank robber, I was staggered. He said, 'Welcome to Dunedin.'

I talked to the students at Otago. The law department had made my cases a feast for those students. They'd learned that my smoking ban case had created new limitations on how much the authorities could interfere with a prisoner's home (their cell), and clarified what would constitute trespassing on a prisoner's personal space.

People began sending me things. I still quite often receive courier boxes of food and so on from well-meaning members of the public. One day, a box full of Cadbury chocolate bars; another day some sweet syrups. They must have thought I was hungry.

Initially I survived on a Job Seeker's benefit; I don't make anything except the occasional koha from my legal advice business. This year I'm eligible for the pension. I do have some money put away. I hate getting into my finances — journalist Lisa Owen has pumped me about this, and I always say: 'I pay all my taxes, I pay all my child support, and I've got no one that I owe any money to. I won't be sleeping under a motorway bridge.'

I was making money before the Proceeds of Crime Act came

into force in 2008. Essentially, that Act gave police and the Crown authority to take away anything you've earned as a result of committing crime. Every now and again, you see Harley Davidsons and Corvettes and expensive jewellery and houses belonging to gangs and drug dealers being snapped up by the police. But back in my bank-robbing days, I could keep my stash without fear of it being taken away. The Act wasn't retrospective, either. What I'd taken, I kept, unlike the criminals of today. However, I was meticulous about paying my tax on my robberies. I declared them as illegal earnings, and also claimed for expenses on gear I'd bought. (I learned the other day that my tax is overseen by a special unit in Wellington.) I've always remembered Al Capone, who was jailed for not paying his taxes; I never wanted to be in the same boat. One year I forgot to do my return — I think I was in custody at the time — and the IRD stung me for $85,000. Never again, I thought.

I n November 2019 — in time for the 2020 election — the Labour government passed a law that allowed prisoners serving less than three years the right to vote. It was a complete reversal of National's 2010 ban on prisoner voting, and the change had been informed by Justice Heath's formal declaration that this law was inconsistent with the Bill of Rights. About 1900 prisoners were expected to be able to participate in the election.

I felt vindicated. I was rapt — not so much for me, but for democracy. The Opposition, in the person of National leader Simon Bridges, of course came out and said that the government was soft on crime and promised to reverse the new law if elected the following year (as it turned out, this was an empty threat).

Then Minister of Justice Andrew Little, who'd come to see me all those years ago, repeated what I'd long been saying: someone who was going to be released back into the community should have the right to say who leads them. (Of course, I'd go further and say that those serving sentences still have that right, as legislation affects how prisons are run, too.) New Zealand First's Winston Peters was sceptical: 'Why do you want to make the laws if you're breaking the laws?' But his voice as good as vanished amidst the tide of support.

When I'd first started the case, polls showed that 90 per cent of the public were saying that prisoners shouldn't have voting rights. By the time the government announced that it was going to change the law, 54 per cent were in favour of it. It was a great turn-around in public opinion, and cemented my earliest belief that if you give people all the information, the context, the shades of grey, they can make a proper and appropriate decision.

I thought three years was a good balance that the community would find acceptable. Obviously, I would prefer all prisoners to have the vote, but we live in a democracy so we have to have a consensus about what's acceptable and what's not. I'm not going to war over it. I will support anyone who wants to take up the cudgel, but I can't myself, I've got too many other battles.

'Hand over the money. I said: *hand over the money.*'

Facebook Marketplace is a wonderful thing. You find an item you'd like to purchase, and then you toddle over and get it. I was in the market for a colour printer for my office. I'd found navigating social media relatively easy, taking to it like a duck to water. Years of using the computer in my office at Pare had primed me for this.

But my attempt at buying a printer online had led me to this home in Moera, Lower Hutt, where I found myself the victim of a crime, I think for the first time. I'd gone inside only to be threatened with a knife by a tall man, maybe in his twenties, who flew down the stairs, blocked the exit and demanded the few hundred dollars in cash I had in my hand. This prick had messed with the wrong guy, however.

'I'm going to give you some free advice: put that down before you get hurt,' I warned him. We tussled while I tried to get hold of the knife, in a scene reminiscent of my tumble with Beaney Webber all those years earlier, while two women in the house screamed bloody murder. I kneed him in the balls, pushed him off, opened the door and fled onto the lawn. Then I called the cops.

Across the road some onlookers were staring, horrified, and I thought: 'Right, I better get this sorted right away, otherwise I'm going to look like the bad guy here.' I found out later from the police that this was a regular ruse played out at this home, but unfortunately for this character he'd bitten off more than he could chew this time. The police arrived pretty quickly, and fortunately they'd sent a CIB sergeant who recognised me. After they'd searched my car — looking for drugs, I presume — and come up empty-handed, the sergeant pulled me aside next to the bus-stop while the cops barrelled the guy out of the house, and said, 'We could charge him, Arthur. It's up to you.'

I cast my mind back to Waikeria, and Epuni, and figured that this bloke must have had a hard life if he was ready to rob an old man like me of a few hundred dollars. I looked at her and said, 'I've never known locking up to do any good. I've just retired from that shit.'

With permission from my probation officer, in December 2019 I'd moved to Whitby in Porirua to live with a friend. To protect her privacy, I'll call her Belinda. Hazel and Rob had enough on their plate without me adding to it — the move there wasn't supposed to be permanent, and Dunedin was so far away from everything. Wellington seemed like the best place to be to continue my prison advocacy work.

I considered Belinda a friend and was quite fond of her. She was a few years younger than me but I looked out for her because she didn't work, was quite sick actually, and was probably what you'd consider vulnerable. But she looked after me. The house didn't get a lot of light, but it was tidy and the street was mostly quiet. I had my own desk and paperwork in the corner of the lounge and she let me get on with things.

Back on my old stomping ground, I visited the home my family had lived in for a short time in Porirua, and the old school grounds. I went to parliament and stood on its green lawn. I drove the winding streets up to Mount Crawford prison on the Miramar Peninsula, long since abandoned. Police and probation officers knocked on the door regularly, outside scheduled visits, which Belinda and I initially found amusing.

I started taking on small cases for people; advising them, checking on their lawyers' work. This took me around the country, from a dope grower in the Waikato to even having old Willy Bell on the phone from prison. People would pay what they could, but the money didn't matter to me. I considered it as paying the community back.

Sometimes I'd give lawyers a ring on behalf of their client to give them a hurry-up, because many just don't give a stuff. They get the same money whether their clients are found guilty or not — and meanwhile their clients are sitting in jail on remand. Half the people in jail would be out of it if they had decent lawyers. Although the Department of Corrections claims that it advises prisoners of their rights and entitlements, they don't; it's complete bullshit. It's counterproductive to their interests. They would rather have prisoners kept in ignorance.

Women prisoners would often write to me for advice, or just to chat. My theory is that I treat them better than most other men, and they know I can fight for them.

One woman, called Raerae, had found herself in a spot of bother in 2019, in the small town of Woodville. She'd learned that her partner was cheating on her, and had tracked him and this other woman down and attacked her. The police laid an aggravated burglary charge against her. She'd come across my work and contacted me. Could I give her a hand?

Finally, I managed to sit the test for my driver's licence. There had been months of backwards and forwards with the AA, police and Corrections over my identity — the latter two, of course, could vouch for my it. It was ridiculous. Corrections was laughing its head off. Finally the AA conceded. It was weird as.

Raerae had introduced me to a friend of hers who would occasionally stay at the house. Mya was eighteen and a bit off the deep end, but Belinda and I looked after her. She was studying for her own licence, and we quizzed each other. When the day of the test came I only got one question wrong: how many metres is an object legally allowed to overhang the front of your vehicle? Tricky bastard. Even now, I can't recall the answer. Within the week I was driving — a white Toyota Mark X that Bruce had organised for me a year earlier and dropped at Joanne's. I now had a licence and a vehicle. I was really free.

In March 2020 I drove home to Whitby from Wellington city, with Radio New Zealand blaring only slightly over the scanner I use that detects when a speed camera or a cop car is nearby. The gadget is dashboard-mounted. On this occasion it seemed like it was broken — it indiscriminately shouted every few seconds while Prime Minister Jacinda Ardern announced that the whole country was being plunged into a state of crisis that would from that day forward mean that our movements would be tracked by an alert system called Levels 1 to 4. In prison we'd call this minimum to high security.

The coronavirus pandemic that had started circling the globe had finally reached New Zealand. There were about 100 cases of the mysterious flu-like virus in the country, and the government saw fit to keep everyone in their homes to break the chain of transmission. My freedom, it seemed, would be short-lived after all; we were heading into lockdown.

From then on, New Zealand became all about the numbers.

Officials tracked the number of Covid-19 cases; the level numbers entered the vernacular. For me, this period became marked by the number of affidavits and submissions I'd have to make to fight for my own home and freedom. These matters are before the courts, so to keep it simple, I'll recount to you exactly what I told the police.

The period between March and May saw a spiral of events at Belinda's, and a place that had been a quiet refuge for me became marked by increased numbers of police visits. Belinda started drinking heavily, and her mother visited often. Having never been a huge drinker, the environment was not optimal for me; but we coped.

Mid-way through lockdown we were asked to take in Tiana, a young woman with a troubled background who had nowhere else to go. She'd committed some offences, was in a motel, and her victims were threatening her. In Level 4 lockdown her options were limited: find a suitable home, or go into custody. At least, that's what the Masterton police officer told me over the phone when they asked if Belinda and I would take her in. Both of us spoke to Tiana directly before agreeing to house her, but it was the right thing to do. Police came around and scoped out our home, and checked both Belinda and me out. Then the court officially approved us as a suitable bail address. Tiana was coming to stay.

She arrived on a Saturday and I assumed that the police had brought Corrections up to speed with the new arrangements. I didn't think much about it. While lockdown was in effect I was reporting to my probation officer by phone, and there was nothing in my conditions that stipulated that I needed to inform them of the presence of a new flatmate. On the night of 8 May, I stayed the night at a friend's home; she needed help with her teenage son, who was having mental health issues. I returned to Whitby the next morning to a firestorm.

Belinda's mother was there. Things turned ugly; the primary cause seemed to be Belinda's jealousy of my relationships with other women. Concerned once again, I called the police and asked them to remove her. They did. All was peace and harmony until a few days later, when Belinda arrived home. Coming up the steps, she smashed the bottle of beer she was carrying onto the cold, hard grey cement. She then stalked into the house, pushed Tiana, and accused her of sleeping with me. Again, the police were called.

On Tuesday, 12 May, I received an email from probation officer Jayden Southon, essentially evicting me from Belinda's home. Part of my parole conditions were that Corrections had to approve my address, and they no longer approved of my staying with Belinda. I was to leave by 10 a.m. that Thursday. I replied that given that we were in a national state of emergency, a pandemic, a state-wide lockdown, it was impossible to comply with the order. Where was I going to go? They responded by extending my deadline by one day — to 10 a.m. Friday.

On Wednesday I met with Southon and his colleague, who drug-tested me for 27 different substances. Clean. I suggested a remedy to Southon: Belinda had agreed to stay at her mother's in the meantime, and Tiana had found a new bail address. I could continue living at the Whitby property alone. Given the circumstances — the difficulty of trying to find somewhere to stay in lockdown — it seemed like the most practical solution for the interim, until I could find somewhere else to stay. This was denied; Corrections had made up its mind.

I was shunted between some dive-y motels in Porirua while Corrections continued to press their thumb down on me. You've got to find somewhere to stay, they repeated. Despite the fact that we were now out of lockdown, the options were few and far between. My family were all based loosely around the Waikato and the Bay of Plenty, but this was no good for my work, which at that stage was keeping me mainly in Wellington. Living in motels, I was essentially homeless. Mya kindly offered to help me claw back my belongings from Belinda — I wasn't allowed on the property, so she went there and retrieved a lot of my clothes for me.

On 27 May I ended up at The Setup on Manners, a serviced

apartment lot looking directly across the road from the building I'd escaped from many years earlier in Wellington city. I carted my clothes and papers into the small room while some of the residents watched, nodding and raising their eyebrows. They seemed to know who I was, because over the ensuing days I'd be approached by desperate people looking for gear. I told them I couldn't help them.

Two security guards were stationed permanently outside the motel, although it was unclear whether they were trying to keep riff-raff out or keeping an eye on the drug-addled, drunken people who'd taken refuge there. The lower ground floor of the units was occupied by gang members, and as I walked to my room they'd offer me meth and cannabis.

I stepped up my campaign to get the hell out of there. The day after I checked in, I wrote to David Howse, the lead service manager at Probation Services, and essentially asked in what respect did they think that housing a rehabilitating criminal at what appeared to be Gang Central would be a good idea? Although I knew that I personally had the wherewithal to withstand some pressure to be involved in drug dealing and gangs, it galled me that someone else with less money, less support and less motivation could end up in this position. Corrections spends a huge amount of time creating safety plans, monitoring your movements, checking in, hovering. This situation that they had forced me into was catastrophic.

I was also writing to ministers Kelvin Davis and Kris Faafoi, and of course probation officer Jayden Southon, pleading my case, to little effect. I can only guess that my repeated calls to get me out of there made my caretakers, as it were, nervous.

On 3 June, Mya visited. Security tried to block her from entering the motel, saying that after-hours guests weren't allowed, but I told them to piss off — it wasn't up to them who visited me. Little did I know that this would spark off a series of events that would hang over my head for the ensuing two years. Inside Corrections' Wellington head office, the machinations began firing up.

> Morena . . . I understand that Kris is busy, but he has
> met me in prison before and he knows that I need to
> be housed away from active criminals.
> *Arthur Taylor writes to Kris Faafoi's office, 4 June 2020*

Behind the scenes, the Ministry of Social Development's property broker, Dean Brosnahan, was sharing emails with Corrections staff. A day after I'd emailed Kris Faafoi, Jayden Southon wrote to Dean Brosnahan at 8.28 a.m.: 'Kia ora Dean . . . We are working on next steps with Mr Taylor and hope to have an update soon. Please do not advise Mr Taylor of any plans to relocate him yet.'

Of course, I had no idea what these next steps were.

Fifteen minutes later, Dean Brosnahan wrote to The Setup's manager: 'Morning Dani, Mr Taylor will be removed at some stage today; for now, just keep this information to yourself.'

Later that night, around 10 p.m., Mya and I were inside watching TV when there was a knock on my door. On the other side were two male police officers. They were there to take me back to prison.

When you're on parole, you're liable to be recalled at any moment. Corrections can make a no-notice application to the Parole Board saying that they think you're an immediate risk, and — without you having any opportunity to defend yourself — the risk-averse Parole Board will usually grant it. You're then given another hearing down the track to sort it out, which is when you're given the opportunity to dispute it.

The day they came for me, the police were well prepared. They had fire orders — instructions under which they could shoot me if the shit really hit the fan. But I didn't resist. I invited them in — welcomed them, in fact. Come and take a look, I said. Hardly the actions of anyone wanting to hide anything.

While I was handcuffed and marched out the door, police remained. Detective Sara Kennedy of the Wellington Organised

Crime Unit had been at the back entrance of the property while I was arrested, no doubt ensuring that I couldn't leave. She came into my room, sat on my bed and started talking to Mya, asking whether she was okay and reassuring her that she wasn't in trouble. Reports of Mya entering the room a few days earlier by the security guards had raised their hackles. Mya said she was fine and left, but not before grabbing a sleeveless jacket of mine that she'd retrieved from Belinda's a few days earlier, and thrusting it into the arms of one of the male officers. 'Arthur will want this.'

The warrant produced by police for my arrest stipulated that I was to be taken directly to my old haunt, Rimutaka Prison, but I was shuttled a few streets away to the custody unit at Wellington Central police station, a dungeon-like area with no windows, reached through the underground car park. By this time it was getting late. They searched my person and my possessions that I had with me, and then — either because it gradually dawned or because of my protestations — they realised that they were supposed to have taken me to Rimutaka. Close to midnight we embarked on the dark drive through the Hutt.

Nestled in that jacket pocket was a small plastic point bag containing an infinitesimal amount of methamphetamine. Of course I didn't know this. After Mya had handed them the jacket, the officer holding it, Gary Mitchell, had allegedly checked inside the pocket and discovered it as I was sitting at Wellington police station. Mitchell allegedly passed the bag to Detective Clarke, who photographed it and then stored it in the Wellington police's exhibits store.

I say allegedly because there's no footage of this event, and subsequent police notebook entries of the find totally contradict one another. The following day, Detective Calland noted in a warrant to search my other belongings that 'a small bag of white crystals, consistent with methamphetamine, was located in his sock'.

The night I was arrested, police had measured the crystals and concluded there was 0.7 grams there. They emptied the crystals into a brown envelope and discarded the plastic snap-lock bag, destroying any chance of being able to fingerprint the bag. Three days later, Detective Sara Kennedy took the envelope out of the store and weighed the meth again, concluding that there was 0.57 grams. Her notes record the same weight both with and without the bag, so the true weight is unknown.

Regardless, I had calls from Head Hunters in Northland who were cracking up. 'Fucken .57 grams of P, Arthur! It should have been 50 kilos!' I am sure that certain police will be saying, 'This is not Arthur's drugs.' Others will be saying, 'It doesn't matter because he's probably doing other shit so we might as well use this to get him while we've got the chance.'

The discovery of the methamphetamine — and it's common ground that it was not on my person when they arrested me, and had only recently come from Belinda's — set off a criminal inquiry. Rubbing their hands together, the police seized on the opportunity and applied for warrants that enabled them to search the rest of my belongings.

I found it very curious that it was the Organised Crime squad who'd overseen my arrest in the first place — it had been a classic recall job that could have been handled by anyone else on duty. Their subsequent actions might go some way to explaining why. They found a fake pistol that I used as a paperweight, which they used as evidence to the Parole Board that I should be kept behind bars. After weeks of to-ing and fro-ing, and just hours before the hearing, police were forced to admit that it wasn't real. The whole thing was looking more and more like Keystone Cops.

Without my knowledge — much like in Pare in 2007 — police had also successfully applied for a surveillance warrant, where investigators were granted an application to monitor my text messages.

T he morning after my late-night arrival at Rimutaka I was given a short-lived hero's welcome by the boys, but was quickly farewelled again when deputy prison director Viv Whelan showed up outside my cell with an entourage and informed me that I'd need to be moved to Manawatū's prison at Linton. This was because I had a victim at Rimutaka — a guard who'd been briefly kidnapped more than a decade and a half earlier during my quest to see Carolyn.

I was driven north that day. To tell the truth, I was relieved. Linton had nicer facilities, which was particularly important because during the tail-end of the lockdown incoming prisoners were being held in isolation for fourteen days so I was on my own in a cell all day again. I could chat to the other blokes across the landing, though, and was given some time in the exercise yard.

Luckily I didn't have much time to contemplate my new, frightening reality. I was too busy making calls — to my long-time lawyer Sue Earl (I figured it was a better look to have someone else advocate for me in front of the board than do it myself), to Hazel and, most importantly, to the Parole Board. At that stage I still had no idea why I'd even been recalled, but my fight to be released heated up again when the police laid a charge of possession of methamphetamine. *That* wasn't going to look good in front of the board.

Common sense prevailed, however. A few weeks later, in July, the Parole Board gave short shrift to Corrections' attempts to keep me in to serve the rest of my sentence. The charge was clearly in dispute and the evidence was flimsy.

In February 1919 in Washington DC, two men — the Silverthorne father and son — who ran a lumber company, were arrested at their homes. While they were in custody, justice officials illegally went to the company's offices and pilfered books and paperwork. As a result of this, a doctrine was established in 1920 that evidence becomes inadmissible if it's illegally obtained. Decades later, in a 1939 wire-tapping case, Justice Frankfurter dubbed this the Fruit of the Poisonous Tree doctrine, and it has been widely accepted around the world. It follows that if the tree is poisonous (the search), then so is the fruit (the evidence). That would be my defence: that police didn't have the right to search my belongings because when they did, they'd transgressed the limitations of the warrant. The differences in the police statements regarding the chain of evidence and the weight of the methamphetamine also threw the charge into doubt.

Unbeknown to me, in March 2020, thae prison guard who was the victim in my Manners St mall escape (who'd been the reason I was moved to Linton) had officially registered as a victim of mine — something he hadn't tried to do in the fifteen intervening years since Manu Royal had pointed an airgun at him. He didn't want me anywhere near him; he didn't even want me in the region. Corrections applied, and the Parole Board granted, a ban on my being in Wellington without prior permission. As soon as I set foot outside prison, a heavy black bracelet was attached to my foot. I was told to get the hell out of dodge, back to Dunedin, back to Hazel's.

Raerae picked me up from Linton Prison in a beautiful red Mustang and we powered the whole way to the Interislander ferry, where I picked up my van, stacked with the remainder of my belongings that my kind sister Sandra had collected for me from Belinda's. Corrections watched us the whole way. We weren't allowed to detour, or stop for lunch, and we were given a set timeframe to reach the ferry by.

By the time we got to Wellington, I was starving. Forty-four years after I'd boarded a ferry to the South Island with an appetite for adventure and my whole life ahead of me, I drove onto the ferry again — an older man, a bigger man, maybe a slightly wearier man, with everything but the kitchen sink in the back of his van.

EPILOGUE

DUNEDIN, 2021

I came across a brown photo album among my belongings in my cabin the other day. The deck at Hazel's is finished, and my cherry tomatoes have taken off. I love sitting on the verandah having a cold drink, listening to the lambs cry for their mums. It's been raining quite heavily of late, and it's cloudy and overcast. I don't mind, because it's washed the pollen out of the air and for the first time in a week or so I have no symptoms of the hay fever that has knocked me around. It's great feeling normal again.

You'd think that with 38 years inside, there'd be few photographs to pore over — but there I am, smiling into the camera with a big grin and an arm around my mum. She's wearing glasses and her hair is curly. I must be in my twenties. I have a gap between my teeth, a full set of hair and a chain around my neck. I notice that in all of the photos of our family that I have — just a few precious ones — we're all grinning widely. Mum died on 29 September 2010, aged 75. She wasn't well. I was able to talk to her over the phone before she went, which was something, but it was still hard to take.

To this day I don't like to talk about her death. I'm a forward-looking sort; looking back is hard. Just like my dad's passing, I wasn't allowed out for Mum's funeral, but come 2020 I finally had my chance to say goodbye. The whole family had waited ten years for my release to be able to gather together in Paeroa, in the Waikato, to inter her ashes. It was a very moving and emotional, ceremony, there with all my siblings, and their partners, and my nieces and nephews.

My photo album mostly holds pictures of blonde-haired Siobhan, the spitting image of her mum. Her caregivers send me updates regularly. Kane and Tyrone are in there, too. There's a young me by a green river in the South Island, there I am in front of a geyser in Rotorua. To this day, restlessness fuels me and I can't resist driving somewhere for the weekend. The other day it was Aramoana — it's so hard to believe the atrocities that were committed there. Recently Tui came and visited me, and so did my son Kane. We explored Otago.

My ban on being in Wellington without prior permission became the bane of my life. To defend my methamphetamine case in court I needed permission to travel to Wellington. Corrections demanded minute detail of where I'd lunch, vetoing the pub next to the court; all that beer on tap spooked them. Frustrated, I explained to them that there was nothing in my parole conditions stipulating that I can't drink alcohol, and neither should they be able to stipulate where I ate on my break. I was wearing a GPS bracelet. I didn't even want to drink on my break — I was there to concentrate on my case — but again the extent of the over-reach disturbed me.

After flying to Wellington for a case in the very early hours of one cold morning in September, I spent an inordinate amount of time at Wellington Airport while security and Corrections failed to get the electronic monitoring bracelet going. As time ticked on, and I risked being late for my hearing, I asked them to follow me to court so that I could at least be on time. They agreed. When I got to court, the Crown wasn't ready to proceed and the case was adjourned within minutes. All that way for nothing. I flew home that night exhausted. Later, having seen me disappear off the grid, electronically speaking, Corrections considered charging me with breaching my parole conditions.

This is the kind of unfairness I find myself up against on a near-daily basis.

I haven't relaxed. Whether I'm in custody or not, there is no 'normal' life outside of prison and Corrections for me now. Someone recently asked me what my vices are. I laughed, and thought about it. I don't drink to excess. I don't take drugs — I haven't even smoked a joint. I like a coffee in the morning, and like so many others before me social media has become my constant, my megaphone. So I had to say, 'I don't think I've got any.' Instead, my energy is channelled into upholding the law and holding police and Corrections to account.

For a while I contemplated trying to become qualified, studying law at university, but I realised that I was never going to get approval from the Law Society to practise, and I've found so far that I can teach myself what I need to know. In 2016 they amended the District Courts Act so that a company or a corporation can be represented by a lawyer, an officer of the company, or an attorney appointed by the company — and that last one means anybody. That opened doors for me: I can represent a corporation, the same way as a lawyer, in the District Court. Now I get consulted by car dealers and all sorts. One had a lot of trouble with the Motor Vehicle Disputes Tribunal.

Currently I'm channelling energy into my own upcoming legal action. After I left Wellington for good, the police — who had been monitoring my texts under that warrant — laid more charges of offering to supply methamphetamine. I'm defending this much in the same way as I did for the Spider/Web operation, where there was little evidence of anything other than innocuous conversation that the police had misinterpreted.

I'm also suing Corrections for my Waikeria transfer, and other instances of maltreatment including six unlawful strip-searches between January and February 2018, prior to and after visits at Waikeria. A prison inspector found that they were unreasonable, but neither the inspector nor the Ombudsman could order compensation.

Also included in my statement of claim is details of a 21 March 2018 drive to Waikeria for the purpose of attending a three-day trial in relation to my Auckland Prison strip-search case. Travelling in the van, I was handcuffed in a very small steel-framed dog box in the back, being forced to sit on the floor. It was claustrophobic and totally unsuitable for travelling long distances. We left Auckland at 5 p.m. and because we had to wade through thickets of traffic, and got lost on the way, we didn't arrive at Waikeria until after 8 p.m. No toilet stops. No water. Unable to brace around the corners, thanks to my metal-cuffed wrists, I'd be thrown head-first into the back door. I was a low-security prisoner in a single-occupancy vehicle. The Inspector of Corrections investigated the matter and found that I should not have been handcuffed.

For all of these things I'm suing the Crown for $1.5 million. The trial is set for 2022.

T he common denominator in prison 'success' stories is that the programmes are run by former prisoners, by those who have been through it and have overcome the enormous barriers to successful re-integration, people who know what those barriers are and how best to overcome them. The earliest lesson for me was: do not take people away from their family. While I've developed an aptitude for the law, I also had an aptitude for other things. I could have been an engineer.

It's very disappointing to me, of course, but even more so for my family who have had to cope with losing me, with me not being with them. My life was blighted by my first contact with the state machine, but it's very unhealthy just to hate the police as a body, or any agency. So I channel my energy into productivity. I regret the shit I've done, and try to make up for it by bending over the other way, to try to right the scales.

I get calls from prisoners all the time because they need my help and they don't know how to get it, or who to talk to, or who to trust, and they've heard about me and what I can do. I can't think about their crimes; I have to deal with them like they're you or me, identify the good pieces and support and magnify that side of them. You have to never lose sight of the fact that no matter what they've done, they are human beings and there's always good with the bad; so identify the good and utilise that for the common good. You just can't write people off — they've got the same fears, hopes, wants and desires as you have.

S hortly after my release in 2019, word had got around Auckland that Les Green hadn't been seen for a few days. He'd been confused, telling people he'd been assaulted; I grew concerned enough to convince a friend of his to let me into his flat, only to discover him just barely alive. Les's frail frame had been subject to a battering from resident insects and he was essentially prone. He was a far cry from the man who'd hidden in my skunk warehouse all those years ago. Time gets away from you quickly.

He died a few days later in hospital, from various complications of serious illness. Police investigated whether he'd actually been assaulted — which wasn't outside the realm of possibility considering his background — but in the end the coroner determined that he'd died of natural causes and, from what I can gather, mostly alone. It was a sad end for Les who, while a bad egg in the eyes of most of the public, wasn't that different from me. Just someone who'd chosen a different path, for good or for bad.

I've considered life's frailties. I'm getting older, and I want to enjoy my last years. Occasionally when the sun's not out and Police have trawled up my street again in the dead of the night, I consider moving countries — travelling to somewhere progressive, somewhere that offers a clean slate.

What does the future contain for me? All I can say for sure is what I see right now. I see a valley with fertile ground, and I see my growing plants, and I see a flock of ducks. I see an afternoon posting on Facebook about the unrelenting heat, and my latest case, and I see myself trekking to the local bottle shop to stand in the walk-in fridge for a bit.

When we broke out of prison in 1998, we spent time reading the paper, having fish 'n' chips at the beach and driving around enjoying the scenery. The average criminal enjoys these pleasures as much as anyone else; it's just that they've gone down a different path in another part of their life. People might be surprised; I'm not that different from them after all.

ACKNOWLEDGEMENTS

I would like to thank Kelly Dennett (without whose invaluable assistance and enormous research this book could not have been written) and Hazel Heal for her unfailing support and outstanding assistance to my reintegrating in the community.

Arthur and Kelly would like to thank the following people for their help with the writing of the book: Mike White for his expertise, advice and eagle eyes; Boris Jančić — for all the reading and rereading; Stuff librarian Lesley Longstaff for her extensive compiling of old news stories; Auckland Library Research Centre and National Library staff; and Professor Andrew Geddis for his recall.

We are thankful to Arthur's sister Sandra, for helping with memories from the past, Mike Kalaugher for his extensive research on jailhouse witnesses and to Dr James Freeman for lending his expertise in Arthur's upcoming case against Corrections. Thanks to *The Sunday Star-Times*, especially Tracy Watkins, for their patience and support. Particular thanks to Teresa McIntyre for her meticulous editing and fact checking and Michelle Hurley and Leonie Freeman for their enthusiasm and commitment to bringing this project to life!